Breaking the Blockade

Running Era Fall 1861 - Spring 1865

Breaking the Blockade

The Bahamas during the Civil War

Charles D. Ross

University Press of Mississippi / Jackson

The University Press of Mississippi is the scholarly publishing agency of the Mississippi Institutions of Higher Learning: Alcorn State University, Delta State University, Jackson State University, Mississippi State University, Mississippi University for Women, Mississippi Valley State University, University of Mississippi, and University of Southern Mississippi.

www.upress.state.ms.us

The University Press of Mississippi is a member of the Association of University Presses.

Copyright © 2021
All rights reserved

First printing 2021
∞

Library of Congress Cataloging-in-Publication Data

Names: Ross, Charles D., 1958– author.
Title: Breaking the blockade: the bahamas during the civil war / Charles D. Ross.
Description: Jackson: University Press of Mississippi, 2021. | Includes bibliographical references and index.
Identifiers: LCCN 2020030948 (print) | LCCN 2020030949 (ebook) | ISBN 978-1-4968-3134-7 (hardback) | ISBN 978-1-4968-3135-4 (trade paperback) | ISBN 978-1-4968-3136-1 (epub) | ISBN 978-1-4968-3137-8 (epub) | ISBN 978-1-4968-3138-5 (pdf) | ISBN 978-1-4968-3133-0 (pdf)
Subjects: LCSH: United States—History—Civil War, 1861-1865—Blockades. | United States—History—Civil War, 1861-1865. | Nassau (Bahamas)—History.
Classification: LCC E480 .R67 2021 (print) | LCC E480 (ebook) | DDC 973.7/21—dc23
LC record available at https://lccn.loc.gov/2020030948
LC ebook record available at https://lccn.loc.gov/2020030949

British Library Cataloging-in-Publication Data available

Pages ii–iii Ports Important in the Civil War: The front endpaper contains a map of a portion of the United States and the Caribbean, including especially the Bahamas. In order to present the ports of the Atlantic Seaboard and the Gulf of Mexico without crowding, the map is not projected. That is, latitude and longitude lines are shown at right angles. This has the effect of stretching the upper portion of the map, compared to the lower portion. Do not use the map to scale distances from point to point. The projection and the datum are WGS 1984. The scale is 1:20 million.

Pages 236–237 Bahamas Overview: The back endpaper contains a map of the Bahamas. The projection is Universal Transverse Mercator (UTM) Zone 18 North and the datum is WGS 1984. The map scale is 1:4 million.

To Julie
Who Saved My Life

Contents

Acknowledgments ... xi
Dramatis Personae ... xiii
Maps ... xvii

1. Two Arrivals ... 3

The Stage Is Set
2. George Trenholm Sees the Future ... 9
3. Heyliger Arrives ... 19

Interlude: Why Nassau?
4. "This Remote Western Maritime Colony" ... 35
5. The Bay Street Boys ... 44

The Great Carnival
6. Putting the Pieces in Place ... 59
7. The Lions of the Royal Victoria ... 79
8. Yellow Jack ... 94
9. A New Consul ... 110
10. Living for the Hour ... 127
11. Trouble in New York ... 141

The Curtain Falls
12. "It is rather sickly here" ... 157
13. "Blockade-running from this port has ceased" ... 169
14. Like a Town Sacked and Burned by the Enemy ... 183

Notes ... 195
Sources ... 219
Index ... 229

Acknowledgments

Researching and writing this book has been one of the great joys of my life. The story of what happened in Nassau during the US Civil War is fascinating and complicated, and working to understand that story and convey it to readers was both exhilarating and exhausting. There are so many pieces to the tale that I sometimes felt I was taking the perceptions of the blind men about the elephant and melding them into a cohesive narrative. Much of the information in this book is new, while some of it was previously known but unconnected. The saga of the Great Carnival is worth telling, and I hope I have done it justice.

Two of the first people I contacted about the book were extremely generous in sharing what they knew and became friends of mine over time. Ann Morley Carmel, who probably knows more about Bahamian genealogy than anyone else, helped me with mountains of information and with key contacts in Nassau. She has blockade running in her blood. Her great-great-grandfather, Charles Robert Perpall, was directly involved in the game, and his sister Mary Ann Perpall married Henry Adderley, the king of them all. She is also related to two of the others most involved in Nassau, Robert Henry Sawyer and Henry Rowland Saunders. Carol Bass, great-great-granddaughter of John Lafitte, was equally generous with her time and materials that she had collected over the years. Carol passed away before she could see the final product, but I hope her husband Bill and family will enjoy the book.

I want to also thank two more relatives of people involved in blockade running for their time. I am indebted to Robert Lafitte Howells, another direct descendant of John Lafitte. I was honored to speak with the late Ethel Trenholm-Seabrook Nepveux before she passed away. She paved the way for many historians with two excellent books about her great-grandfather George Trenholm. My pathway to understanding the Great Carnival was aided by work done by a number of early researchers in addition to Mrs. Trenholm. I'd like to particularly acknowledge the work of Thelma Peters, the work of Frank Tousley Edwards, and the classic book *Lifeline of the Confederacy* by Stephen Wise.

The digitization of books, journals, and manuscripts by Google Books, HathiTrust, and the Internet Archive has made life so much easier for researchers than it was during the time period when I wrote my first three books. Services like ancestry.com and Fold3.com have also opened up information that would have been almost impossible to find before the internet. I have my mother-in-law Lila Reach and my sister-in-law Bev Perry to thank for their generosity in helping me learn to take advantage of the nuances of these sites.

Some of the images in the book are being seen on a wide scale for the first time. I'd like to thank Ron Lightbourn for his time and generosity in providing many of these images and my father-in-law Bill Reach for helping me get them ready for publication. Walter Witschey applied his expertise to the four maps that I hope will help readers put the actions of the various characters in the book in geographic context. I'd also like to thank my former research student Garrett Josemans for his excellence as a research assistant and travel companion and for his work in obtaining a number of images in the book.

I was assisted by many kind people at various repositories of information around the world. Thanks to Dana Owen and her colleagues at Greenwood Library at Longwood University for their work in securing my numerous interlibrary loan requests. Thanks also to the following people and organizations: Mrs. Strachan and the other kind folks at the Bahamas National Archives, Jim Lawlor at the Bahamas Historical Society, Karen Stokes at the South Carolina Historical Society, Kate Gregory and Ryan Semmes at the Ulysses S. Grant Presidential Library, Elizabeth Dunn at the David M. Rubenstein Rare Book & Manuscript Library at Duke University, Cate Brennan and others at the National Archives, Graham Duncan at the South Caroliniana Library at the University of South Carolina, Anna Bolch of the Diocese of Charleston, and those helpful folks at the University of Rochester Rare Books and Special Collections, the Mariners Museum, the Library of Congress, and the Louis Round Wilson Library at the University of North Carolina,

So many people have helped me along the way that I am sure I will forget someone, and I apologize to anyone missing from this list: Tony Stellato, Trish Kaufmann, William Crozier, Kathie Gutierrez, Lolita Taylor, Charles Rigg, and Trudy Hawley.

My greatest thanks go to my wife Julie, who makes every part of my life better. She accompanied me on many fact-finding trips, proofread my drafts, and graciously put up with my often-distant stares as my mind was back in 1860s Nassau. When we were married in Nassau in 2003, neither of us knew that we took our vows only steps from the site of the Royal Victoria Hotel.

Dramatis Personae

Nassau

Confederate

Lewis Heyliger	CSA agent/depositary for Bahamas
Mary Virginia Fourgeaud	Euphrosine Lafitte's niece
John Baptiste Lafitte	Agent for Fraser, Trenholm & Co.
Euphrosine Lafitte	John Lafitte's wife
John Maffitt	Blockade runner, commander of CSS *Florida*
Charles Sidney Passailaigue	Privateer, Adderley clerk, informant for Thomas Kirkpatrick
William Boyd Sterrett	Commission merchant
Richard P. Waller	Agent for CSA Quartermaster Department

Union

Seth Hawley	US Consul March–June, 1863
John Howell	Proprietor, Royal Victoria Hotel, Nassau Dry Dock
Charles Jackson	Agent for US Insurance Underwriters
Thomas Kirkpatrick	US Consul June, 1864–1869
Epes Sargent	Union supporter, Nassau Dry Dock
William C. Thompson	US Vice-Consul, acting Consul July, 1863–June, 1864
Samuel Whiting	US Consul July, 1861–March, 1863

British and Bahamian

Augustus John Adderley	Son/business partner of Henry Adderley
Henry Adderley	Commission merchant

George Campbell Anderson	Attorney General of the Bahamas
Charles John Bayley	Governor of Bahamas, 1857–1864
Timothy Darling	Merchant, Former US Consul
George David Harris	Business partner of Henry Adderley
Benjamin Woolley Hart	Commission Merchant
Ramon Antonio Menendez	Commission Merchant
Charles Rogers Nesbitt	Colonial Secretary
Rawson W. Rawson	Governor of Bahamas, 1864–1869
Henry Rowland Saunders	Commission Merchant
Robert Henry Sawyer	Commission Merchant
Aaron Wolf	Commission Merchant
Many other commission merchants	

Charleston

William C. Bee	Businessman, Importing and Exporting Company of South Carolina
Edward Lafitte	Commission merchant, John Lafitte's brother
George Alfred Trenhom	Businessman, CSA Treasury Secretary
Theodore Wagner	Partner of George Trenholm

New York

Joseph Eneas	Commission merchant
Moses Grinnell	Insurance executive
Christopher John Rahming	Commission merchant
Francis T. Montell	Commission merchant

Philadelphia

William S. Stockman	Commission merchant

Richmond

Judah P. Benjamin	CSA secretary of state
Jefferson Davis	CSA president

Stephen Mallory	CSA secretary of the navy
James Seddon	CSA secretary of war

Washington

Lord Richard Lyons	British envoy to United States
William Seward	US secretary of state

Bermuda

John Bourne	Acting CSA agent
Major Norman Walker	CSA Agent

Canada

Nehemiah Clements	Shipbuilder and merchant
Benjamin Wier	Shipbuilder and merchant
William Wright	Shipbuilder and merchant

Cuba

Charles Helm	CSA agent for Cuba

England

James Bulloch	CSA naval purchasing agent
Caleb Huse	CSA, War Deptartment purchasing agent
Lord John Russell	British foreign secretary
Charles Prioleau	Partner of George Trenholm

Maps

Maps by Dr. Walter Witschey

Ports Important in the Civil War Blockade-Running Era 1861–1865   *Front Endpaper*
Bahamas Overview and Key Passages Departing Nassau   *Back Endpaper*
New Providence Island   *Gallery 1*
Nassau   *Gallery 1*

✦ ✦ ✦

There are four maps in this volume, each with somewhat different characteristics. All modern data, coastlines, and city locations are from ESRI Datamaps 10.1, distributed with ESRI ARCGIS Desktop software. ARCGIS 10.4 was used to prepare the maps.

Ports Important in the Civil War

The front endpaper contains a map of a portion of the United States and the Caribbean, including especially the Bahamas. In order to present the ports of the Atlantic Seaboard and the Gulf of Mexico without crowding, the map is not projected. That is, latitude and longitude lines are shown at right angles. This has the effect of stretching the upper portion of the map, compared to the lower portion. Do not use the map to scale distances from point to point. The projection and the datum are WGS 1984. The scale is 1:20 million.

Bahamas Overview

The back endpaper contains a map of the Bahamas. The projection is Universal Transverse Mercator (UTM) Zone 18 North and the datum is WGS 1984. The map scale is 1:4 million.

New Providence Island

The map of New Providence Island, within the text, also uses UTM Zone 18N and WGS 1984 datum. The scale is 1:160,000.

Nassau

The map of Nassau in the 1860s uses UTM Zone 18N, WGS 1984 datum, and a scale of 1:4,500. Building locations are based on material from IMRAY(1884), po210, BAHAMAS, NASSAU, and other sources.

Breaking the Blockade

1

Two Arrivals

On the morning of December 3, 1861, a seventeen-year-old boy set foot on the public wharf in Nassau. As he stepped ashore he was greeted by thundering salutes from the guns of the 2nd West India Regiment and almost equally loud cheers from the crowds surrounding the wharf. Over the next four days he toured New Providence island by carriage and yacht and was fêted at dinners, balls, parades, and outdoor exhibitions. This often-forgotten outpost of the British Empire was being graced by its first royal visit. The arrival of His Royal Highness Prince Alfred Earnest Albert, second son of Queen Victoria and second in line to the throne, had been anticipated for almost a year.

Prince Alfred came to Nassau as a midshipmen in the Royal Navy on board HMS *St. George*. The stone steps upon which the prince made his way onto the wharf would for decades be known as Prince Alfred's Landing. In May 1863 the Bahamian legislature enacted a law that the third of December would be a public holiday to "mark and perpetuate the remembrance" of the royal visit. A local newspaper summed up that the visit would "be long commented upon not only by our children but by our children's children, even when many of us who have witnessed the event, shall be forgotten and laid low in the dust."

As the St. George left the harbor on its way to Jamaica later in the week, most on the island felt that the prince's departure meant a return to their normal monotonous existence. These people were unaware that the royal visit had by chance coincided with the beginning of one of the most action-packed eras in the history of the island. It is sometimes said that the history of the Bahamas parallels the weather: long periods of calm punctuated by short periods of frenzied activity. Nassau was about to experience a storm of events that would be remembered long after Prince Alfred was long forgotten.

A little over three years later another boat made a much less auspicious landing. On February 26, 1865, Captain John Maffitt lowered a small boat from the blockade runner Owl into the roaring surf off Shallotte Inlet, about forty miles south of Wilmington, North Carolina. With the capture of Fort Fisher on January 15, blockade running through the Cape Fear River to Wilmington had stopped. When the Owl left Nassau several days earlier, no one on board knew that Wilmington itself had finally fallen into the hands of Union forces on February 22. By heading to Shallotte Inlet, Maffitt did his best to get the several men in the small boat to a spot where they might enter the Confederacy before he took the Owl south in search of somewhere to bring his cargo ashore.

As the small boat made its way toward shore in a cold driving rain, a large breaker swamped the vessel and threw the men and their luggage into the surf. The men succeeded in righting the boat and collecting their bags and finally hit the sand on the beach off the Shallotte River. Exhausted, cold, and soaked by rain and salt water, they made their way through a deserted village laid bare by Union raids. They continued through swampland until they found an occupied house. After assuring the frightened occupants that they were not Yankees, they were treated to a hot meal and comforting fire.

One of the men making the landing was William Boyd Sterrett. A native Virginian, he made his way to Nassau in the second half of the Civil War as had so many others looking to get in on the lucrative business taking place on the island. Sterrett made thousands of dollars selling cloth and shoes to a Confederate agent in Nassau, but by early 1865 it had become obvious to all that the fun was over. Packing his wife onto a more conventional steamer heading to New York, he decided to take a less conspicuous route home. Given his connection with the blockade-running trade, he was not assured of a warm reception in New York.

Accompanying Sterrett was Irishman Thomas Connolly, a member of Parliament from County Donegal. Connolly had intended to take part in the blockade-running frenzy himself, but when the boat in which he had part ownership was damaged and turned back off of Portugal, he continued on alone. He boarded a ship in Madeira and made his way to Nassau in late January 1865. The middle-aged bachelor was determined to make an adventure of touring the dying Confederacy. In his month in Nassau, he made a number of friends including Mr. and Mrs. Sterrett. During early March 1865, Sterrett and Connolly made their way through North Carolina to Richmond.

In the Confederate capital, Sterrett greeted old chums and the two travelers managed to resume their high-living ways, meeting with President Jefferson Davis, washing down fried oysters with Champagne, and finishing their evenings with cocktails and cigars. Connolly brought with him some diplomatic dispatches from England for officials in Richmond. By the time they reconnected with Mrs. Sterrett in New York in April, the war was over. Sterrett and Connolly parted ways in early May as the Irishman headed back to his aristocratic life and Sterrett planned a future based on his lavish Nassau earnings.

✦ ✦ ✦

Men won and lost many fortunes in Nassau between late 1861 and early 1865. Some men like Sterrett made their way out of the city in 1865 richer than they could have imagined, while others lost everything. Nassau was witness to a transformation that in retrospect seemed to turn the city into a mixture of Sodom, Gomorrah, and the Dutch tulip craze of the 1600s. One observer commented that "it was the obscurest of colonial capitals. . . . Then the war broke out and gold began to pour into its astonished lap."

As boats worked their way back and forth between Nassau and the Confederacy and between Nassau and England, everyone from scoundrels to naval officers wanted a piece of the action. While men died by the thousands on the battlefield, other men spent their time adding columns on balance sheets and watching their profits grow. Poor men became rich from one transaction, and dances, drinking, and gambling were the order of the day from the posh Royal Victoria Hotel to the decrepit boarding houses lining the harbor. British, United States, and Confederate sailors intermingled in the streets, brawling and eyeing each other warily as boats snuck in and out of Nassau.

A small group of loyal United States citizens in Nassau tried their best to interfere with the trade that was keeping the Confederacy alive, but they were often thwarted by the Southern sympathies of the British ruling class on the island and by the almost comical incompetence of the series of consuls sent by Washington to Nassau to police the activity. As the government coffers filled, physical improvements to the city came to life in parallel with a crime rate unimaginable before the war. By 1864, the island government had to request more policemen from England.

A history of the Bahamas written a couple of decades after the war captured it well:

> Everyone was wild with excitement during these years of the war. The shops were packed to the ceilings, the streets were crowded with bales, boxes and barrels. Fortunes were made in a few weeks or months. Money was spent and scattered in the most extravagant and lavish manner. The town actually swarmed with Southern refugees, captains and crews of the blockade-runners. Every available space in or out-of-doors was occupied. Men lay on verandas, walls, docks and floors. Money was plenty, and sailors sometimes landed with $1,500 in specie. Wages were doubled, liquors flowed freely and the common laborer had his champagne

and rich food. Not since the days of the buccaneers and pirates had there been such times in the Bahamas.

Another commented, "The atmosphere of indolent acquiescence in its own obscurity was exchanged by Nassau for an air of importance and a financial intoxication which must seem like a strange, exciting dream to the survivors."

But it was all to come crashing down as the Union blockade tightened and the final Confederate ports were captured. In the spring of 1865, dozens of boats sat at the ready in the Nassau harbor, but there was nowhere to go. The men who had made millions began to pack up their shops and warehouses and move to England or elsewhere. They had made far too much money to ever be able to spend it in the islands.

On October 1, 1866, one of the most violent hurricanes of the nineteenth century devastated the Bahamas. In Nassau, more than six hundred homes were destroyed, and almost all of the more than two hundred boats in the harbor were lost. The storm packed winds now estimated at 140 miles per hour and produced waves reportedly in excess of sixty feet in height. On the modern Saffir-Simpson hurricane scale, the storm would have been a fairly strong Category 4 hurricane.

Despite the era of debauchery, the permanent residents of Nassau were largely devout Christians. Some observers seemed to see in this storm the work of God in punishing a people for years of misbehavior. In short order, the city found itself back in the state it was in before the riches flowed in or perhaps worse. As writer Charles Ives said a few years later, "Nassau awoke to find herself only weakened by the dissipations which the great carnival had caused."

The Stage is Set

2

George Trenholm Sees the Future

George Trenholm was one of the savviest businessmen in the United States and probably the richest man in the South when the Civil War began. He began work as a teenage clerk for John Fraser and Company, a commission and shipping firm in Charleston. By the time he was thirty-one he had become a partner in the firm, and when John Fraser died in 1854, he took over the company as senior partner and principal owner. Handsome, debonair, witty, and creative, Trenholm has been proposed as Margaret Mitchell's inspiration for Rhett Butler in *Gone with the Wind*. Trenholm's would show his genius over the next four years in his ability to balance being a patriot and a profit seeker.

By the time the Civil War began, Trenholm built the firm into an international powerhouse that was highly respected by the powerful in New York and Europe. In addition to their main office on the North Central Wharf at the foot of Cumberland Street in Charleston, the company had a branch office in New York and had recently opened another office in Liverpool. Trenholm's partners were Theodore Wagner, James Welsman, Charles Prioleau, and Trenholm's son William. Wagner managed the Charleston operation and Welsman the New York branch. When the war began William Trenholm joined the Confederate army, and while a major stockholder, he was not active in the firm's operations.

Decades of acrimony between the slaveholding Southern states and the more industrial Northern states boiled over with the election of Abraham Lincoln as president on November 6, 1860. Three days later George Trenholm introduced a measure in the South Carolina General Assembly denouncing the election and stating that South Carolina should preserve her sovereignty by securing supplies and weapons to arm the state. The city was wild with restless energy.

On December 6, a large palmetto flag representing the state was raised next to John Fraser and Company at the office of Edward Lafitte and Company, another shipping firm. A large crowd cheered as the flag was raised and joined the members of the Lafitte firm for a festive, wine-soaked cruise around Charleston harbor on the steamship *Cecile*. Edward Lafitte's brother John would play a key part in George Trenholm's upcoming blockade-running adventures.

Two weeks later South Carolina made her feelings official by seceding from the United States. As if tensions were not high enough in Charleston, two US Army companies under Major Robert Anderson were stationed at Fort Moultrie on Sullivan's Island just outside the city. To avoid being overrun by state militia, on December 26 Anderson moved his men over to the much more secure Fort Sumter on an island in the middle of the harbor.

An interesting event with ties to Nassau occurred three days later. The steamship *Marion* made regular trips with passengers and freight between Charleston and New York. As the *Marion* passed Fort Sumter on its way out of Charleston harbor to New York, Captain Sam Whiting paid the courtesy of dipping his US flag to the Union defenders of the fort. So high were the emotions of the time that a number of people on the shore were incensed that he had not instead dipped the Palmetto flag of South Carolina. Charleston merchant John Tuomey sent a message to Whiting demanding to know which flag he had dipped to the fort. Whiting's reply by telegraph as reported in the *New York Times* and then throughout the country made him a hero in the North: "He was born under the Stars and Stripes, and had always sailed under them, and with the blessing of God would die under them." Before long both Whiting and Tuomey would be in Nassau.

Trenholm had his eye on the company's bottom line as he looked at the coming war. Charles Prioleau was already in Liverpool managing that branch, which went by the name Fraser, Trenholm and Company. Liverpool had a long history of receiving cotton from the southern states, and with ten miles of waterfront it was the busiest port in the world. The South did not have the capacity to build the kind of steamships that would be needed in the coming conflict, so Liverpool would become the perfect place for the creation of the new breed of blockade runners. To ease the company's dealings in England, Prioleau applied for and gained British citizenship. At this time, the company had five sailing ships making transatlantic voyages.

In February 1861, as South Carolina joined Alabama, Mississippi, Louisiana, Georgia, and Florida in establishing the Confederate States of America, Trenholm started a trend that would be rapidly copied by others: he began to change the registry of his ships to British and obscuring the names of the true owners. For example, *Gondar* was registered in the names of two British employees of Fraser, Trenholm and Company. George Trenholm was far ahead of others in seeing what was to come. During the war, most of his ships were registered to the Liverpool firm of M. G. Klingender and Co. Melchior Klingender was a strong Confederate sympathizer, and in an amusing twist his company's offices were in the same building as the office of US Consul Thomas Dudley.

Charles Prioleau sent the first rifled cannon to be used in the war to Charleston on the *Gondar*. The inscription read, "Presented to the State of South Carolina by a citizen resident abroad, in commemoration of the 20th December, 1860." All the other blockade-running firms followed Trenholm's lead by switching their boats to British registry. For example, as early as November 1861 Nassau merchant Henry Sawyer was changing the registration of *Island Belle* from South Carolina to British.

On April 12, 1861, Confederate forces bombarded Fort Sumter, and the war was on. The accurate cannon sent by Prioleau had arrived on April 9 and was used in the shelling. By the next day, the gun had done its work, and Anderson surrendered. He and his men were ferried away on the steamer *Isabel* to ships waiting to take them north.

One week later President Abraham Lincoln proclaimed a blockade of ports in South Carolina, Georgia, Florida, Alabama, Mississippi, Louisiana, and Texas. After federal property was seized in Virginia and North Carolina, Lincoln extended the blockade to those two states on April 27, 1861. The South had little in the way of arms and munitions or the machinery, raw materials, and expertise with which to make them. If the rebellion lasted any length of time, Lincoln intended to make it difficult for the rebels to obtain what they needed to fight.

Almost exactly a month after Lincoln's proclamation, Queen Victoria issued a proclamation of her own declaring Britain's neutrality in the American conflict. The proclamation stunned and angered many in the North as it essentially gave validity to the national status of the Confederacy.

But the British were taking a reasonable position. The South had always been a consistent customer for British products, and with the industrial North out of the equation, profits were sure to rise. The British in turn were highly dependent on cotton from the South for the many textile mills of Lancashire, and the British hunger for cotton turned out to be the main source of funding for the Confederacy. And from a legal standpoint, maritime law stated that a blockade had to be enforceable or it did not exist. It seemed impossible for the relatively small US Navy to effectively blockade the 3,000-mile coast from Virginia to the Rio Grande.

Within a week the provisional Confederate Congress came up with a proclamation of their own. In order to force the hand of England and France in recognizing the Confederacy as a legitimate nation, the proclamation prohibited the export of any cotton without government approval beginning on June 1, 1861. Almost twenty-five thousand bales of cotton left Charleston for England in May, but not a single bale was exported in June. Starving the Lancashire mills would end up not working in favor of the Confederacy. The huge cotton crop of 1860 flooded the market, and by the time that was used up, England had found other sources in India and Egypt to help. By the end of 1861, the South realized that they needed England more than England needed them, and cotton began to flow again.

Trenholm decided to test the blockade by sending *Gondar* from Liverpool to the Confederacy in early July. In addition to the British registry, which should make the ship untouchable on the high seas, Trenholm began what would become a most common deception of the war by listing the intended destination as Nassau. By sending a British ship from one British port to another, he hoped to hide the vessel's true intent. The US consul in Liverpool was not fooled and alerted Secretary of the Navy Gideon Welles to the changed registry and what was most likely a bogus destination. US ambassador to England Charles Adams wanted to catch the ship and bring the case to court to test the ownership, but *Gondar* made it safely into Beaufort, North Carolina, on September 2.

The Battle of Bull Run on July 21, 1861, made everyone realize that this war might not be over quickly. Many in the North expected the battle to be an easy, war-ending victory, but the Confederate triumph meant both sides needed to prepare for extended conflict. The Confederacy, lacking in weapons and industry, was going to quickly need help from abroad. Even before Bull Run, the two-month-long transatlantic voyage of sailing ships like *Gondar* had Trenholm thinking. To speed things up, especially when penetrating the blockade, he needed ships powered by steam. To this end, in June he purchased *Isabel*, the steamship that ferried Robert Anderson and his men off of Fort Sumter. Renamed *Ella Warley* in honor of partner Theodore Wagner's wife, this ship became one of the earliest blockade-running success stories.

In early July, he also had Prioleau purchase a steamer named *Czar* in Liverpool. The great advantage of steamships over sail was their speed, but they came with a voracious appetite for coal. As more ships became steam-powered, maintaining a sufficient supply of coal would be a critical objective for both sides in the coming years. The steamers generally had sails so that coal could be saved for those times when speed was necessary. The saying of the day was "you need steam to catch steam," and this blockade would therefore be different from all those that preceded it.

✦ ✦ ✦

While Trenholm was considering his options, others were also testing the waters. As the Confederates began to consider how to get through the blockade, they also went on the offensive by recruiting privateers. A privateer was a private armed ship that had been fitted out at the owner's expense and granted government permission to attack enemy commerce. The permission, in the form of a government issued Letter of Marque and Reprisal, gave a privateer the same rights as a government warship and differentiated the vessel from pirate ships. The owners of the ship were allowed to keep some of the spoils of their conquests, while giving a cut to the government. On April 17, 1861, Confederate President Jefferson Davis invited applications by individuals to become Confederate privateers.

Privateering had been practiced for centuries, and the United States had engaged in it during the Revolutionary War and the War of 1812. But the Declaration of Paris that ended the Crimean War in 1856 essentially ended the practice. The only major country not to sign onto the declaration was the United States, and this came back to haunt them in 1861. When Abraham Lincoln proclaimed his blockade two days after Davis's announcement, he also wrote British Foreign Secretary Lord John Russell indicating that the United States would now abide by the Declaration of Paris. This would mean that the crews of any Confederate privateers caught by US or British ships could be tried (and probably executed) as pirates. Russell, not wanting to be bound to treat Confederates as pirates, declined the offer.

The early attempts at Confederate privateering were largely ineffective and became more difficult as the strengthening blockade closed off ports where captured ships and cargoes could be delivered. While privateers were later replaced by more powerful government commerce raiders like CSS *Alabama* and CSS *Florida*, one of the earliest privateers has a connection to events in Nassau. The ship *Savannah*, formerly a Charleston harbor pilot boat, but now outfitted with a cannon and a crew armed with muskets, pistols, and sabers, set sail on June 2, 1861. The next day the ship captured the brig *Joseph*, headed from Cardenas to Philadelphia with a cargo of sugar. The captain of *Savannah*, T. Harrison Baker, then put a group of his men, called a prize crew, onto *Joseph*, and they sailed the ship (with the original crew now as prisoners) to Georgetown, South Carolina, where the cargo was valued at $30,000. When a prize crew brought a captured ship to port, an admiralty court determined whether the prize was caught legally. The court joyously so proclaimed the *Joseph*, and the ship was condemned to have the proceeds from the ship and cargo distributed to the crew and to the government.

The crew still on *Savannah* was not lucky enough to enjoy the proceeds as she was captured the next day by the brig USS *Perry*. *Savannah* and her crew were brought to New York, where they were imprisoned in the notorious lower Manhattan prison called the Tombs. The Tombs was intended for criminals, while prisoners of war were incarcerated at Fort Lafayette in New York harbor. Because the US government considered the current events to be an insurrection within their own country and not a war against a foreign nation, the Letter of Marque held by the *Savannah* was deemed invalid. Their trial became something of a circus as they were marched through the streets in irons as the crowd shouted for the "pirates" to be executed.

This treatment prompted Jefferson Davis to send Abraham Lincoln a letter informing him that he had selected an equal number of prisoners now held in Richmond to suffer whatever fate awaited *Savannah's* crew. Federal officials finally backed down and moved the privateers to Fort Lafayette. Two of the crew died in captivity, but the others were exchanged for Union prisoners held in Richmond in the summer of 1862. One of the crew who survived the ordeal was nineteen-year-old Charles Sidney Passailaigue (pronounced pass-a-lay), who left his newspaper job at the *Charleston Mercury* to join the crew as purser. Undaunted by the experience and itching to get back into the action, Passailaigue made his way to Nassau, where he played a very interesting role in the blockade-running enterprise.

✦ ✦ ✦

Both the Union and Confederate governments scrambled to put people in the right places to win the war. Trenholm offered to make his Liverpool business a financial conduit for the Confederacy, an offer that was quickly accepted. Fraser, Trenholm and Company had European connections and a sterling reputation, so the firm could obtain deals and credit where the Confederacy could not. For a commission paid to Trenholm, the Confederate government could deposit funds with the Charleston branch, and letters of credit would then be sent to the Liverpool branch. Southern agents stationed in England could then use the letters of credit to obtain cash for purchases there.

The first agent to show up was Captain Caleb Huse, who arrived in Liverpool on May 10, 1861, to direct Confederate purchasing operations there. Huse took a tortuous route to Liverpool. He made his way from Charleston to New York, where he met James Welsman at the Trenholm office downtown. Welsman advanced Huse enough money to get to Liverpool but told him not to sail from New York, as anti-Southern feeling was so high that if caught he would be hanged. Welsman closed the New York office not long after this and made his way to Liverpool himself. Huse finally found transatlantic passage from Portland, Maine.

He was joined in Liverpool on June 4 by Commander James Bulloch, who would oversee the acquisition of shipping for the Confederacy. One observer described Bulloch as a broad-shouldered, blue-eyed giant. Huse and Bulloch would work closely with Charles Prioleau, and Bulloch set up shop in the Trenholm office at 10 Rumsford Place. For the next three years, the dealings of Trenholm's company and the Confederacy became so intertwined that it was sometimes hard to unravel them. Perhaps it was an acknowledgement of their inseparable linkage when Trenholm was named the Confederate secretary of the treasury in 1864. The Union was also sending purchasing agents to Europe, and Huse and Bulloch successfully outmaneuvered them for needed armaments and supplies much of the time.

Bulloch's charge was to quickly procure armed ships that could be used to harass Union merchant shipping. While the Tredegar Iron Works in Richmond and the Augusta Powder Works eventually provided the Confederates with some self-sufficiency in weapons and ammunition, there was no place in the South where the kinds of ships needed could be constructed. Because of the Queen's neutrality proclamation, Bulloch's work would be quite tricky. Britain's Foreign Enlistment Act prevented ships for either combatant from being fitted out anywhere in the empire.

So Bulloch needed to have his ships built by one manufacturer, the weapons and ammunition by others, and then work out the logistics for all these things to come together somewhere outside of British territory. With US spies prowling the docks, everything needed to be done in secret. Despite the complications, Bulloch got moving right away. Before June was out a wooden cruiser known as *Oreto* was under construction, and a second boat called the *290* was started. These became *Florida* and *Alabama*. While waiting for Bulloch's cruisers to be built, the Confederates made an early attempt to go on the offensive by converting the steamship *Habana* into CSS *Sumter*. The ship, under the command of Raphael Semmes, broke through the blockade at the mouth of the Mississippi River in late June and roamed the seas for the next six months before breaking down and laying up in Gibraltar. She took eighteen prizes during that time.

The Union also made another move that at the time appeared to have little connection to the war. The US consul in Nassau at the beginning of 1861 was sixty-two-year-old Isaac Merritt. Merritt was apparently awarded the consul position in 1857 because of his mercantile connections in New York and his strong support of then President James Buchanan.

Merritt's work did not seem to satisfy some important figures in the insurance world. The wrecking industry in the Bahamas was a constant headache for those who insured the ships and cargoes. With few lighthouses and no reliable charts, the treacherous Bahamian waters claimed a tremendous number of ships every year. As soon as a ship was stranded, native sailors descended on the vessel to salvage the cargo that would then be sold at auction in Nassau.

Exacerbating the situation were under-the-table deals made between wreckers and ship captains for salvaged goods and the possibility of intentional wrecks by nefarious captains. Merritt did not seem to have the skills or connections to halt this activity.

The New York Board of Underwriters included some very prominent men of that city, including Moses Hicks Grinnell, president of the Sun Mutual Insurance Company. Grinnell had been a successful merchant and shipper before going into the insurance industry, and as president of the New York Chamber of Commerce, he was very well connected. In February 1861, President-Elect Lincoln visited New York, and Grinnell hosted a breakfast for him where he met about a hundred of the city's merchants. Not long after that, Grinnell and Jeremiah P. Tappan, president of the Neptune Insurance Company, nominated someone they thought would be a better fit for handling the maritime issues in the Bahamas. Choosing someone with skills that fit the position was something of an anomaly at the time. While British consuls were professional diplomats, most US consuls like Isaac Merritt landed the job as the result of political favors.

The man they chose was Samuel Whiting, the same man who had defiantly dipped his Union flag to Fort Sumter back in December. He seemed a perfect match for the job. An experienced sailor, he was widely known as "Captain Sam." Born on Long Island in 1814, Whiting had gone to sea as a teenager and been on the water for most of his life. He served on clipper ships in the Atlantic and Pacific Oceans and as a master of boats operating on the Great Lakes. In addition to three trips around the globe, he found time to take part in the California Gold Rush and edit the first newspaper in Panama.

After marrying, Whiting tried to settle in Winona, Minnesota, finding work in 1854 as assistant editor of a local newspaper. But his restless nature could not resist an interesting call to go back to sea. Arctic explorer Elisha Kent Kane and his men were stranded in polar ice and volunteers were needed for a rescue mission. Kane was actually in search of traces from an earlier lost expedition under British explorer John Franklin, and while not succeeding in that task, he had explored much of Greenland and discovered the Arctic Ocean.

Whiting resigned his position with the paper and joined the rescue expedition in June 1855. They found Kane a couple of months later, and miraculously Kane's expedition had lost only three men after having been in the far north for over two years. The rescue boats and survivors made a grand entrance back into New York harbor in October 1855.

The Kane expedition had been financed by Henry Grinnell, Moses Grinnell's brother, and Kane named one of the regions they discovered on the voyage Grinnell Land. Certainly, the Grinnells were acquainted with Whiting's efforts in rescuing Kane. Whiting returned to Winona and took a job as an editor with a rival newspaper. As well as being an adventurer and a dreamer, he was a poet and often published his original verse in the paper. He channeled some of his energy into being in charge of the 1857 territorial census and as a member of the local fire department.

But the prairies could not hold him forever, and by 1860 he was back on the water as captain of the *Marion*, running passengers and freight between New York and Charleston. Having achieved some minor notoriety as part of the Kane rescue mission, Whiting achieved national fame in December 1860 with the publication of his defiant reply to John Tuomey about the flag incident. A fearless man, Whiting took the *Marion* back to Charleston in January 1861. In defense of the harbor, the Southerners had removed many of the marker buoys, and Whiting ran the ship aground. Thomas Lockwood, captain of the *Carolina* and soon to be a blockade-running legend, came to Whiting's assistance by taking his passengers ashore. Whiting was forced to make his way back north by rail.

Back in New York, he became a popular speaker, giving lectures on both his adventures on the sea and his recent run-ins with the Confederates. The *New York Tribune* described how well one of his speeches was received:

> The gallant Commander of the steamship *Marion*, who refused to lower the United States flag at Charleston harbor, delivered a lecture last night, pursuant to an invitation from many prominent citizens, on the Hartstene Expedition in search of Dr. Kane, of which he was a member. The lecture proved a complete success, Clinton Hall being well filled with respectable auditors, who applauded with much spirit the closing remarks of the speaker touching the seizure of the steamship *Marion* by the South Carolina authorities, with a view to pursuing the *Star of the West* and sinking her with all on board. Captain Whiting gave all the circumstances of this affair. During twenty-five years, he said, he had been a world-wide rover, and he had never seen the stars and stripes floating to the breeze without a feeling of pride and love which he could not describe. [Applause.]

In April 1861, a week after the surrender of Fort Sumter, a celebration was held in New York to honor Major Robert Anderson and his men, who had defended the fort. As witness of the esteem in which he was held, Captain Sam was chosen to be the bearer of the fort's flag that he had so famously saluted months earlier. The man being promoted as the new consul for Nassau was a brave man, a true patriot, and an experienced maritime adventurer. What

Grinnell and Tappan likely did not know was that Whiting would also bring to the islands a bit of a drinking problem and that this would lead him into some unfortunate situations in the coming year. What they could also not have predicted was that dealing with wrecking and insurance fraud would be the least of Captain Sam's problems during his time in Nassau.

3

Heyliger Arrives

The troubles that would occupy most of Sam Whiting's time started before he arrived in Nassau. On June 24, 1861, Isaac Merritt received a letter signed by two American citizens living in Nassau. One was Charles Jackson, the agent of the New York underwriters on the island. He had been in Nassau since 1859 and took up residence in the Royal Victoria Hotel when it opened in late 1861. His upper floor room faced the harbor and gave him a good view of the comings and goings of the various vessels arriving and leaving Nassau. Originally from Massachusetts and thirty-five years old when the war began, Jackson was of medium height with brown hair, a beard, and blue eyes and became a painful thorn in Sam Whiting's side.

According to one observer, Jackson was "a typical Yankee, and possessed in a marked degree all the characteristic shrewdness of his nation. He needed all these smart qualities, for his position brought him into contact with some of the brightest, cleverest people, in their special line, on the face of the Earth—the Bahama wreckers." The *New York Times* described the wreckers as

> a peculiar class of men. Nearly all negroes or creoles, strong, daring and inured to hardships, good seamen, and well acquainted with every reef and current in the gulf stream and the adjacent waters, they will put out to sea in the darkest night and in the most threatening weather, lured only by the hopes of picking up a few boxes or bales from some stranded ship or perhaps only a few masts and spars.

The letter's coauthor was Epes Dixwell Sargent, the thirty-three-year-old brother-in-law of well-known Nassau merchant Timothy Darling (who had been US consul himself in earlier years). Trained as a physician, Sargent came to Nassau in 1849 and operated as a commission merchant before opening up a small hotel called the Sargent House. His brother, Daniel Sargent, was an employee of the consular office as the agent for the island of Inagua. During his time as consul, Darling had once called on Sargent to assist him in saving the lives of a boat full of yellow-fever victims in the harbor.

The letter called Merritt's attention to the presence of the schooner *William H. Northrup*, which had arrived from Wilmington, North Carolina, and was sitting in Nassau harbor flying the flag of the Confederacy. What did Merritt intend to do about this? Because of the British neutrality proclamation, Merritt could not expect much help from local officials. He did the only thing he could think of, which was to write a letter to Secretary of State William Seward complaining that the schooner had violated a law dating to 1803 that the master of any ship entering a British port in the Americas must immediately deposit his ships papers with the consul. Merritt had no way of knowing the significance of this first arrival from the South.

Whiting arrived from New York on the British mail steamer *Karnak* and took over the consular office from Merritt on July 1, 1861, and Merritt returned to New York on the same ship several days later. By this time *William H. Northrup* had departed and Whiting must have hoped this episode was just an anomaly.

He focused on getting set up in his new position. One of the first things he did was to rent a new building for the consulate closer to the center of town near the corner of Bay Street and Charlotte Street. He noted approvingly in a letter to Seward that the American men working on construction at the Royal Victoria Hotel celebrated the Fourth of July.

After settling in, he wrote Seward another note that included a statement that is laughable in retrospect: "There is utter stagnation in all branches of commercial life owing to the war and there will consequently be a great reduction in the usual fees of the consulate." Whiting would soon have more action in the harbor than he could handle.

It did not take him long to figure out that things in Nassau were not conducive to carrying out his work. He informed Seward on July 13 that *John Hancock* from New Orleans had been sold in the harbor and left under a now neutral British flag. This might have been the first indication to Whiting that a game would be played right under his nose. He also pointed out to Seward a depressing observation he had made in his short time in Nassau: "There is a strong feeling in favor of the rebellion army among British officials and merchants."

To Whiting's consternation, *William H. Northrup* reappeared in the harbor on August 7, 1861. Reporting to Seward, Whiting described the ship as a low black schooner of about forty tons displacement. The patriotic Whiting was clearly frustrated, saying that ship had "lain at the wharf in front of the U.S. Consulate all this day with the rebel flag prominently displayed" and noted that this display was "to the manifest gratification of British white residents of Nassau, who are nearly all rank secessionists."

Whiting sent a letter (which was signed by Charles Jackson as a witness) to Acting Governor Charles Nesbitt protesting the display of an unauthorized flag. He sent another letter to the master of the ship, threatening a $500 fine. Nesbitt's reaction was that this was an internal American issue, and the master of the ship, Joseph A. Silliman, ignored the letter. At this early stage, Whiting could see in *William H. Northrup* what was to come as he noted to Seward that the ship had run the blockade several times already. The schooner *Adaline* had also penetrated the blockade from Nassau twice by this time.

The more familiar Whiting became with Nassau, the more clearly he saw the hostile environment in which he was now residing. On August 24, 1861, he noted that at a dinner held for officers of a British ship in port, a toast had been given to Jefferson Davis's health and that many other toasts "offensive to Union ears" had been offered.

Early the next month Nassau merchant John Rahming, who had set up shop at 36 South Street in Manhattan, was arrested and imprisoned in Fort Lafayette. Rahming had been apprehended at Seward's direction and was charged with having attempted to have the master of the schooner *Arctic* sail to Nassau, pick up a cargo of cannons and convey them to Wilmington. The British consul in New York, Edward Archibald, protested strongly at what he deemed the arbitrary imprisonment of a British citizen and at Rahming having been put in a cell "not long enough for him to lie down in."

Rahming was released on September 18 after having posted $2,500 bond and sureties to the US attorney that in the future he would do nothing hostile to the government of the United States. When the news of the imprisonment of the well-known Rahming got to Nassau, the locals were indignant and directed their anger at Whiting and other Americans. According to Whiting, "The news of the imprisonment of Mr. Rahming, an old resident of this place, caused much excitement and feeling here and 'the old Northern scoundrels' were loudly cursed on the corners of the streets." When he learned of Rahming's release, Whiting told Seward he hoped the release had been made for good reasons, as "he has a brother in business here and I am persuaded his view of going to New York is to ship provisions and munitions to this port." Whiting was correct.

✦ ✦ ✦

Merchants in England were anxious to begin sending military supplies to the South, and Charles Prioleau offered the use of Trenholm ships to take cargoes across the ocean. The first such ship was the newly purchased *Czar*, now renamed *Bermuda*, which sailed on August 22, 1861. Her cargo consisted of as many as 50,000 shoes, 24,000 blankets, and a wide variety of cannons, muskets, and other military equipment. Demonstrating both the weakness of the Union blockade at this point and the advantage of steam, the *Bermuda* made it safely into the harbor at Savannah, Georgia, on September 18.

The ship left Savannah in late October and easily made it back to Liverpool with 2,000 bales of cotton. The captain reported that he had not seen a Union ship during the entire round-trip voyage. *Bermuda*'s successful trip made a small fortune for Trenholm's company. In addition to being the first ship to come through the blockade from England, the trip was notable for two more reasons. First, the profits made by Trenholm were so high that the Confederate agents in England decided to bypass the middleman on their next venture. Second, by shipping cotton back to England, Trenholm was violating the Southern government's position on exporting cotton. At this early stage, some still held out hope that withholding cotton might force British recognition or even entry into the war on the Confederate side. The British, however, were not keen to be blackmailed, and Trenholm appears to have been the first man savvy enough to realize this. Before long tons of cotton were flowing through Nassau on the way to England.

To promote Confederate diplomatic ideas abroad, Jefferson Davis appointed James Mason and John Slidell as commissioners to England and France. In October, the two men went to Charleston to take the large steamer *Nashville* to England. With the number of blockading ships growing around Charleston, the large, slow ship was having trouble finding a safe time to get out to sea. With Mason and Slidell in a hurry to get to work, Trenholm offered his services, for a fee of course.

Carolina, now renamed *Theodora*, under Thomas Lockwood (who had rescued Whiting) was in the employ of Trenholm. As she was much smaller and faster than *Nashville*, Trenholm offered her as part of a plan to get the men to England. Lockwood took the men and their families out on October 12 and headed to Nassau.

Just for the fun of it, he chased Charles Jackson's boat into the harbor on his arrival. Unable to find a vessel in Nassau headed to England, he took Mason and Slidell to Cuba. There he loaded *Theodora* up with pistols, lead, and cigars and made his way back to Charleston on November 4. The ease and speed with which Lockwood made this trip certainly got Trenholm thinking about using smaller boats between the Confederacy and the islands. As the blockade got stronger, it would make sense to bring supplies to the islands from England in large, slow boats and then get them to the South in small, fast ones.

Mason and Slidell boarded the British mail steamer *Trent* in Havana and headed toward England. Between Cuba and the Bahamas, the steamer was intercepted by USS *San Jacinto*, commanded by Captain Charles Wilkes. Wilkes sent Mason and Slidell as prisoners to Boston and was praised as a hero in the North.

The British, including the residents of Nassau, were outraged at this tampering with an official British ship. The ensuing diplomatic crisis brought England as close to going to war with the United States as at any point in the next four years. British troops began landing in Canada preparing for battle. President Lincoln wisely came to the conclusion of "one war at a time," and in January 1862 the two envoys were released and eventually made their way to Europe. Wilkes was not done annoying the British, and we shall see that the people of Nassau soon came to consider him a true villain.

Meanwhile, James Bulloch decided to bring military supplies to the Confederacy without having to pay what he considered the exorbitant fees charged by Fraser, Trenholm and Company. He wanted to command a boat himself so that he could confer in person with Navy Secretary Mallory about conditions in Europe. Using government funds, he purchased the steamer *Fingal* (under British registry of course) and had her loaded with fifteen thousand Enfield rifles, a million rounds of ammunition for the rifles, four artillery pieces with their ammunition, and clothing for Confederate sailors.

He appointed John Low, a Liverpool native and veteran of the merchant marine, as second officer. Low moved to Savannah at age twenty in 1856 and began operating as a commission merchant. James Bulloch came to know him there, and when the war started Bulloch recruited Low to come to Liverpool and help him acquire ships. To deflect attention, Low traveled to England with his wife Eliza and his uncle Andrew Low and Andrew's wife Mary. Andrew Low was possibly Savannah's wealthiest merchant and had been a mentor to John Low in getting started in business in the city. Eliza Low was the sister of Andrew Low's partner Charles Green.

Fingal arrived in Bermuda on November 2, and Bulloch found *Nashville*, which had finally escaped Charleston. On board *Nashville* was John Makin, an experienced pilot who had been sent by Mallory to guide *Fingal* into Savannah. Pilots were mariners who were experienced with navigating boats in and out of the treacherous waters of certain ports. During the next four years, pilots would be in high demand to get boats into Charleston, Wilmington, and Nassau. An old mariner's saying was, "If the Bahamas let you pass, then look out for Hatteras." Both ends of a blockade-running trip were tricky enough even without the presence of US warships.

After leaving Bermuda, Bulloch called his crew on board and announced to them that while they had cleared for Nassau, he was actually going to Savannah. He said he would drop off any men who did not want to continue to Savannah in Nassau, but everyone on board agreed to experience the upcoming adventure. He also said he did not expect much opposition from US cruisers, but if he met any, he intended to fight back. This would be impossible with *Fingal* flying under the neutral British flag, as the men would be considered pirates.

This inability to fight back would become one of the most frustrating things about running the blockade in coming years. But Bulloch said he had a bill of sale ready, and if the need arose he would officially buy the boat and run up the Confederate flag. The men then positioned the four pieces of artillery on deck in case that time came. With a few tense moments, including a rooster on board crowing as they tried to sneak into the Savannah River at dawn, Bulloch brought *Fingal* safely into Savannah on the afternoon of November 12.

Not to be outdone, George Trenholm and Charles Prioleau worked with Caleb Huse to fill the steamer *Gladiator* with over a million dollars of military supplies, far more than *Fingal* had carried. The ship's owner, Thomas O. Stock, was to be covered against loss by the financial backing of Fraser, Trenholm and Company. Captain George Edward Bird left London in *Gladiator* on November 10 with orders to make his way to a port in the Confederacy or to a neutral intermediate port. When he stopped in Tenerife in the Canary Islands for coal, he was able to secure only forty of the one hundred tons he had requested. Thus, he arrived at Nassau on December 9 to get information on the best Confederate port to approach and to secure more coal. Things in Nassau were about to get very interesting.

Though as many as thirty ships flying Confederate flags ran into Nassau from blockaded ports during the fall of 1861, in late November Whiting informed Seward, probably correctly, that he was "satisfied that no arms or ammunition have been shipped from this port." He had by now caught on to the intentions of a man named Henry Adderley. He informed Seward, "I have now, however, good reasons for believing that Mr. Adderley is a warm sympathizer with the rebels. He has large interests in the North which are in the hands of Messrs. Montell and Bartow, a most suspicious firm I am to believe."

As we will see shortly, merchant Henry Adderley was soon to be the most powerful man in the Bahamas. Though it was early in the game, Whiting had already recognized one of the key features of the way Adderley and others would operate. By using his pre-war connections in ports like Baltimore, Philadelphia, New York, Saint John, New Brunswick, and Halifax, Nova Scotia, Adderley would secure goods from the North and from England for shipment to the Confederacy and use these ports as false destinations on the manifests of the ships he sent to Charleston, Wilmington, and Savannah.

Henry Adderley and Company had been one of the more prominent shipping companies in the Bahamas for many years and was well known to merchants from New York to New Orleans. Because Bahamian business was done largely with the United States, British visitors to Nassau often exclaimed how American the island seemed while American visitors talked about how British it was. Recognizing a kindred spirit, George Trenholm reached out to make Henry Adderley his main connection in Nassau.

As early as August 1861, a Boston resident informed the government that the "feeling at St. John is very strong in favor of the Southern Confederacy" and that merchants in that city were already sending needed items (likely consigned to Adderley) to the Confederacy via the Bahamas. Montell and Bartow, mentioned by Whiting, were Francis T. Montell and John A. Bartow. Montell was born in Nassau in 1811 to a prominent merchant and slaveowner who had been Speaker of the House of Assembly. He was well known to Adderley and others of that generation.

Montell moved to Baltimore by the 1830s, where he ran a shipping operation called Montell and Company. He was accused there in 1840 of outfitting a ship to be engaged in the African slave trade (outlawed by Congress in 1807) but was acquitted after other Baltimore merchants attested to his high character. He was fined one dollar later that year for throwing snowballs, perhaps according to the *Baltimore Sun* because of his accuracy. While it seems the Montells might have been racist, Francis Montell's brother Charles drowned in Baltimore in 1837 attempting to save a black boy who had fallen out of a canoe.

In 1859 Montell was part of an interesting controversy concerning an obscure Bahamian island called Key Verd on which a Baltimore man, William Kendall, discovered a large quantity of guano, highly desirable then as a fertilizer. Kendall claimed the island as his own, not knowing it was part of the Bahamas. When he sent men back to claim the guano, they were met by an armed force led by Bahamian governor John Bayley's son-in-law, who informed the men that the guano was being claimed by the Crown and consigned to Francis Montell of Baltimore.

While dealing with Cuba, New York, and England, Montell's firm maintained strong commercial and personal connections to the Bahamas. In particular, Montell traded frequently with Adderley and merchant Robert H. Sawyer. Around the time the Civil War began, Montell moved from Baltimore to New York and partnered with Bartow, an established New York commission merchant. As Whiting correctly surmised, Montell would do a lucrative business shipping from New York to Adderley and Sawyer during the war, and Adderley would sometimes use Montell's company as a bogus destination for blockade runners.

Along with Montell, various other entrepreneurs in the North and in Canada made connections with Adderley and other Nassau businessmen for the purpose of profiting from the blockade. William Stockman was a well-to-do commission merchant from Philadelphia who had taken several trips to Nassau on *Karnak* in 1859 and 1860. Henry Adderley began using Stockman's Philadelphia business as another false destination for his blockade runners clearing Nassau.

Much farther to the north a number of companies got involved with the Nassau merchants as blockade running got into full swing. These included William Pryor and Sons and Benjamin Wier in Halifax, Nova Scotia, Nehemiah Clements in Yarmouth, Nova Scotia, and William Wright in Saint John, New Brunswick. Wier flew a Confederate flag over the entrance to his warehouse. The Canadians were ship builders and owners and operated large fleets of vessels headed south and across the Atlantic.

Because the Bahamas and Canada's Maritime Provinces were both populated by descendants of Loyalists who fled after the Revolutionary War, there were tight bonds between them. Even as early as the spring of 1862, Adderley, Robert Sawyer, and fellow merchant Henry Saunders made full use of their business connections in Canada to both acquire materials and as decoy destinations for vessels more likely headed to Charleston or Wilmington. A September 1861 letter from Whiting to Seward makes clear what was to come: "I am convinced that the rebels and their sympathizers have determined to make Nassau a depot from which supplies may be reshipped to the insurgent states. At all events large quantities of provisions are constantly arriving here from the North for other purposes than the supply of this market."

✦ ✦ ✦

Earlier in the year, John P. Baldwin of Richmond, Virginia, mailed a letter to Henry Adderley. Baldwin, a lawyer and member of the Confederate congress got right to the point:

RICHMOND, Virginia, July 30, 1861

My Dear Adderley: The secretary of the navy of the Confederate States of America has ordered from England, to be shipped to Nassau, a quantity of arms and powder. I have recommended them to be consigned to you, and I have to ask of you, as a favor to me, to take good care of them. I will be with you soon, and will expect your aid in transshipping the same.

I must request you to regard this as a confidential communication, and will explain the reasons when we meet. You need not write me at all on the subject.

Hoping to see you, I remain your friend,

JNO. P. BALDWIN

Henry Adderley, Esq.
Nassau, N.P. Bahamas

Union authorities intercepted the letter and in September Secretary of State Seward sent a copy of it to Charles Adams, the US ambassador in England. He asked Adams to bring this to the attention of British officials. Adams sent the letter forward to Lord Russell, and on November 15, 1861, a decree was issued by the Duke of Newcastle, British secretary of state for the Colonies. The circular made it clear that British merchants could ship anything, even arms and ammunition, as long as it did not violate the Foreign Enlistment Act.

Upon receiving the Duke of Newcastle's circular, Acting Governor Charles Nesbitt made some inquiries and responded to Downing Street within a week of the circular's receipt. With his reply, Nesbitt included a letter from Henry Adderley and one from Receiver-General Fletcher Whitley. Adderley stated that no warlike stores had been consigned to him for transport to the Confederacy and also took a swipe at the Americans for intercepting his mail. Whitley confirmed that no supplies for war had been received at Nassau, and none had been shipped from Nassau to the Confederacy.

As of the date of Nesbitt's reply, November 20, 1861, both of these letters might have been truthful. While it is clear that boats had been moving between Nassau and the Confederacy through the fairly flimsy blockade since the beginning of the war, the system was not quite yet in place for munitions to be moving through Nassau to the South. But everything would change in just a few weeks.

✦ ✦ ✦

Despite his growing concerns about the hornet's nest he had landed in, Sam Whiting did his best to welcome Prince Alfred to Nassau in early December 1861, decorating the consul's office and writing a poem in his honor. According to the *Bahama Herald*:

> The illuminations from the American consul's were in equal good taste with his other preparations. The transparencies in front of his piazza had the word "Welcome" in a circle at the top, underneath which was

We love thy mother and accord to one
So dear to hear a proper homage due
May QUEEN VICTORIA's noble SAILOR-SON
Be like his sovereign mother, good and true

Under that was "A Sailor's welcome to a Sailor Prince." All looked very pretty.

The next week brought several other arrivals to Nassau that changed the city and Captain Sam far more than had the visit by Queen Victoria's son. On the day after the prince landed, the first load of cotton came in from Charleston. In an interesting coincidence, the small boat bearing these 140 bales was named *Prince of Wales*, the same as the title held by Alfred's older brother. On December 9, Trenholm's *Ella Warley* came in from Charleston with a thousand bales of cotton, and the *Gladiator* arrived from London packed with thirty thousand Enfield rifles and two hundred tons of gunpowder. Clearly things had changed from several weeks earlier, when Nesbitt notified the Home Office that everything in Nassau was normal. Now cotton was coming in from the Confederacy and war supplies were arriving from England.

Possibly of even more importance to Whiting and the blockade-running enterprise in general, *Theodora* reappeared in Nassau harbor on December 10. Like *Prince of Wales* and *Ella Warley*, she had cotton on board. But she also carried a passenger who would play a critical part in the Great Carnival: Lewis Heyliger. Heyliger's trip from Charleston on *Theodora* was through a fierce storm that almost took his ship to the bottom. Given his importance in the coming years, it was fortunate for the Confederacy that he made it safely to the Bahamas.

Heyliger was born around 1816 in Ireland and came to the United States in 1836. By his mid-twenties, he had helped to start a newspaper business called Kursheedt, Heyliger and Company in New Orleans, publishing the *New Orleans Commercial Times* from 1845 to 1849. His partner was Gershom Kursheedt, one of the most prominent figures in a growing Jewish community in New Orleans. That community also included Judah Benjamin, a man who became a lifelong friend of Heyliger and played a key role in Heyliger's activities in Nassau.

Before the paper finished its run, Heyliger changed partners and the company was now called Bravo, Black and Heyliger. His partners were Charles Black and David Bravo. Bravo also ran Bravo's Commercial Exchange, and this might have given Heyliger the idea of trying a more lucrative field. By the mid-1850s he had become partners with James Wibray in the firm of Wibray and Heyliger, operating as exchange brokers selling a variety of commodities. Wibray was a native New Yorker who had come to New Orleans many years before. A slave owner, he also operated a brokerage business in New York.

Heyliger became a naturalized United States citizen in 1850 and was well-known to the power players in Louisiana during his years in New Orleans. In 1857 he became part of a business enterprise that included both of the state's US senators, Judah Benjamin and John Slidell (later Confederate envoy to France), as well as powerful politicians Pierre Soulé, Emil Lasere, and Duncan Kenner. Heyliger likely shared membership with these men in the influential Boston Club of New Orleans (named for a card game and not the city).

The business venture was called the Louisiana Tehuantepec Company. Many years before the opening of the Panama Canal, enterprising eyes were on the Isthmus of Tehuantepec in Mexico. This stretch of land, swampy and full of malaria-carrying mosquitos, was the shortest path through Mexico from the Gulf of Mexico to the Pacific Ocean. The company proposed to build a carriage road and railroad across the isthmus to carry passengers and freight, avoiding the long trip around Cape Horn at the tip of South America.

Financial complications prevented the firm from completing the project, but the connections Heyliger made would serve him well in the coming years. A *New Orleans Time-Picayune* article on May 9, 1857, gives some sense of Heyliger's stature in the community: "It give us great satisfaction to state that Louis Heyliger Esq. has been chosen Secretary of the Louisiana Tehuantepec Company. A better choice and one of more promising advantage to the company could not possibly have been made, Mr. Heyliger being in every way eminently qualified for the important and responsible trust to which he has been elected."

In addition to his business dealings, Heyliger also occupied some minor public offices, including being appointed by Governor Thomas Overton Moore to the Board of Currency and being part of the committee that led the efforts to erect a statue of Andrew Jackson in what then became known as Jackson Square.

It is no surprise that Moore remembered Heyliger when war broke out in the spring of 1861. Moore, an ardent secessionist, sent a message to President Jefferson Davis on May 1, 1861, asking whether he should attempt to buy a large quantity of guns and gunpowder then available in Havana, Cuba. Secretary of War Leroy Walker replied by telegram two days later telling Moore to go ahead with the purchase. That same day Moore gave Heyliger over $155,000 worth of Spanish doubloons to be used, according to Heyliger, "for the purpose set forth in my instructions." So it appears that Heyliger was charged with one of the Confederacy's earliest arms purchases. In late October of that year, Heyliger was appointed as aide to the governor and given the rank of lieutenant colonel in the Louisiana Militia.

A little over a month later Heyliger was on a different mission, one that turned out to be much more long-lasting than the Havana expedition. Judah Benjamin was now secretary of war, and in early October he proposed to Secretary of the Navy Stephen Mallory that an agent of "large experience" be sent to Havana to aid in the acquisition of arms and ammunition. This conversation eventually must have led to the nomination of Heyliger.

Arriving in Charleston on December 3, 1861, Heyliger made contact there with officials at John Fraser and Company, possibly Theodore Wagner and George Trenholm. He also sent letters to Benjamin and to Confederate Secretary of the Treasury Christopher Memminger indicating that he intended to leave for Nassau that night on *Theodora* under the command of the ubiquitous Thomas Lockwood. He then intended to make his way from Nassau to Havana. His career on behalf of the Confederacy was almost over before it began.

Theodora left Charleston loaded with several passengers and seventy-five bales of cotton and had a terrible time getting to Nassau. Heyliger described the trip in a letter written to Benjamin on his arrival: "I have just arrived here in distress. Twenty-four hours after leaving Charleston we encountered heavy weather, which increased to a gale, and during forty-eight hours we battled for life inch by inch, expecting every moment to go to the bottom. The water in the hold was up to our ash-pans. It was a terrible time and we had all given ourselves up as lost. The captain, engineers, and crew behaved nobly."

Heyliger's general mission as assigned by Benjamin was to proceed as agent of the War Department from Nassau to Cuba and there to help Confederate agent Charles Helm in facilitating cargoes through that port. Helm was appointed to this position on July 22, 1861, by Confederate Secretary of State Robert Toombs. While his most important mission was to secure goods through Cuba, Helm was also given the imposing task of facilitating trade through all the other British, Spanish, and Danish West Indies.

A lawyer and a Mexican War veteran, the forty-three-year-old Helm had been appointed commercial agent to the Virgin Islands in 1853 and consul to Cuba in 1858. When the war started, United States Secretary of State Seward attempted to keep him in place as Cuban consul, but Helm sided with the Confederacy and resigned to return to his home in Kentucky. A few months later, Toombs appointed him and he made his way back to Cuba through Canada and England.

The successful run by *Theodora* from Havana to Charleston a month earlier had shown the Confederates the merits of John Baldwin's idea of transshipping cargo to a neutral port instead of direct from England. To aid in the transshipment work, Heyliger was to bring to Cuba the cotton from *Theodora* and written credit for about £3000. Heyliger acquired the funds in Charleston by drawing on the Royal Bank of Liverpool on behalf of the Treasury Department.

In a cover letter to be handed by Heyliger to Helm, Benjamin provided an introduction: "You will find in Mr. Heyliger an active and accomplished business man, prompt to aid you in the disposal of cotton or the arrangements for the shipments to the best of his ability; and I also bespeak for him our courtesies, as toward a personal friend of mine."

Due to the severe beating it took in the storm, *Theodora* needed repairs and was unable to bring Heyliger and the cotton to Cuba. At this time Nassau did not have a dry dock for repairs so Lockwood would fix what he could and try to get back to Charleston. Heyliger was forced to sell the cotton, some damaged by water, in Nassau.

He left for Havana on the mail steamer *Karnak* on December 16 and met with Helm in Havana on the evening of December 18. At this point, the plan was for him to be of temporary service to Helm and was then to return home to New Orleans. In a letter written to Benjamin the day before he left for Cuba, he offered another possibility: "it may be worthwhile to consider whether my services here cannot be made available in some shape similar to the aim you charged me with." He told Benjamin that he was extremely anxious to return home but that it might be advisable to yield to other considerations.

✦ ✦ ✦

Helm had his hands full with his work creating a blockade-running hub from Cuba to Confederate Gulf ports and had not made his way to Nassau to meet Captain Bird of the *Gladiator*, who was expecting him. He and Heyliger decided that given the value of *Gladiator*'s cargo, Heyliger's skills would be better used in returning to Nassau. Heyliger did just that, leaving on *Karnak*'s return voyage from Havana to Nassau on December 21. Judah Benjamin approved of Heyliger posting himself in Nassau and told him he would write to Governor Moore to make sure his official position as assistant to the governor was preserved for him. But Nassau would continue to grow in importance to the Confederacy, and Heyliger, expecting an assignment of a few months, would not leave the city for good until the last months of the war.

Heyliger had written Benjamin regarding *Gladiator* when he had first arrived in Nassau on December 10. His first message indicated that *Gladiator*, having stopped in Nassau for coal, would leave Nassau to run the blockade for Charleston the next day. As pilot, Captain Bird would have the services of Robert Lockwood, the brother of *Theodora*'s master. Heyliger said he would gladly have had Thomas Lockwood himself go back as pilot if necessary as the cargo on *Gladiator* was "worth ten *Theodoras*."

During the two days it took to get the coal loaded onto the *Gladiator*, USS *Flambeau*, under the command of Lieutenant William G. Temple, arrived at the western end of Nassau harbor. Heyliger wrote to Benjamin indicating that as *Gladiator* was so slow (with a top speed of nine knots) Captain Bird was afraid to leave the harbor. Captain Bird was convinced that *Flambeau* was there just for him and that Temple was willing to let *Theodora* and *Ella Warley* go freely back to Charleston in order to catch *Gladiator*. He was correct. The arrival of *Gladiator* was anticipated by Union officials as no attempt was made to disguise the arms and ammunition when the ship was loaded.

Virginian D. T. Bisbie was a passenger on *Gladiator* and had been assigned as supercargo, the person on a boat responsible for overseeing the cargo. Bisbie also wrote to Benjamin describing *Gladiator*'s predicament and with suggestions for avoiding such situations in the future. Bisbie was prescient in his recommendations as they came to pass in short order. He suggested that all cargo be disguised and that the payment for the trip be contingent on the success of the run in order to maintain secrecy. He also suggested that the Confederacy start making use of vessels that could travel at least fifteen knots, and that slower boats loaded in England transship their cargo to these faster ships at ports in the West Indies. The smaller ships would be manned by captains and pilots familiar with the blockaded ports.

When *Gladiator* pulled into Nassau on December 9, Sam Whiting complained strenuously to Charles Nesbitt that the ship was carrying contraband of war. He then chartered a boat and had it sent to Key West with a message for Union naval forces there to come to Nassau and intercept the ship. His request was accompanied by his opinion that the arrival of a Union war ship "would have a salutary effect upon the minds of the deluded people here." Unfortunately for Whiting the boat returned a week later never having reached Key West. Whiting was convinced that the black skipper of the boat had been bribed by the local merchants to turn back. Luckily for Whiting, *Flambeau* had appeared unexpectedly from New York just in time.

Interlude: Why Nassau?

4

"This Remote Western Maritime Colony"

In February 1859 the British mail steamer *Karnak* made its way from New York to Nassau for the first time, beginning a monthly connection between the two cities that would last for decades. The establishment of such a regular link with the outside world had been a high priority for the British officials in the Bahamas for some time and an act of the Bahamian legislature in 1851 offered £1,000 to the provider of a "good, substantial and efficient" steamship service from New York to Nassau. A first attempt in 1851 failed when SS *Jewess* arrived from New York but caught fire and burned to the waterline. A severe cholera epidemic in the islands in 1852 also discouraged entrepreneurs from taking on the challenge.

In 1858 Samuel Cunard of the British and North American Royal Mail Steamship Company signed a five-year contract for £1,000 per year, in return for which the company would send a ship on a monthly roundtrip from New York to Nassau and then to Havana, and then back to Nassau and New York. Cunard's company (later to become the famed Cunard Line) also had weekly mail steamers traveling from either New York or Boston to Liverpool, so this contract meant that Bahamians would finally have a regular connection to both North America and Europe. There was also the potential for an additional benefit in luring Northern tourists to the islands for the mild winters and scenery.

When Prince Alfred paid his visit to New Providence in December 1861, Acting Governor Charles Rogers Nesbitt wrote an official welcome in which he referred to the Bahamas as "this remote western maritime colony." This phrase gives some sense of the perception those in the Bahamas had of their place in the world. A quick glance at their history will show that Bahamians are opportunistic people of the sea and embraced everything associated with a maritime lifestyle. But unless there were goods on a wrecked ship to pilfer, there was not much to do.

Blockade-running captain Tom Taylor described pre-war Nassau: "Everyone was poor and everyone was lazily hopeless of any further development." And the people, especially the British stationed there for official duty, felt the crushing remoteness of an island weeks away from news of anything else happening on the planet. Unlike our perceptions of the touristy West Indies today, being posted to Nassau in the 1860s was not seen as a choice assignment. Despite the great natural beauty, many saw the islands as hot, boring, lonely, and dangerous due to hurricanes and fairly regular bouts with yellow fever borne by multitudes of mosquitoes. While the heat and danger remained, Nassau would soon be anything but boring.

✦ ✦ ✦

The Bahamas are comprised of thousands of islands and rocks varying in size from a couple of feet wide to Andros Island, which is about a hundred miles long and forty miles wide. Tens of millions of years ago, coral reefs began building up in this part of the ocean and now have reached a height from the sea floor of several miles. In prehistoric time when sea levels were lower, much of this limestone platform was dry land. The Bahamas we know today are the projections of this limestone above the ocean. The water around most of the Bahamas islands is very shallow, though there are a few very deep passages. The name Bahamas most likely comes from the Spanish "baja mar" meaning shallow sea. Navigation here has always been very tricky and often deadly. Only the most experienced sailors can work their way through the maze of channels between the islands.

The Bahamas stretch about six hundred miles from Great Inagua, about fifty miles from the eastern tip of Cuba, to Grand Bahama and Abaco. The Biminis, just southwest of Grand Bahama, are about fifty miles due east of southern Florida. Only about thirty of the islands have been populated, and the population is distributed quite unevenly. More than half the population is located in the city of Nassau on the island of New Providence, a fairly small island almost directly south of Charleston and Wilmington.

Most of the land on the islands is an accumulation of sand, limestone, and rocks not suitable for cultivation. There are forests of Caribbean Pine on Grand Bahama, Abaco, and Andros, three of the larger islands. New Providence, the focus of our story, has smaller areas of these trees as well as extensive areas of shrubs and small trees. Native fauna on the land includes iguanas, flamingos, parrots, and various reptiles, and the turquoise waters hold coral, lobsters, and an amazing array of tropical and game fish. The Bahamas have long been called the "Isles of June" or the "Isles of Summer" due to their pleasant climate. The daytime high temperatures vary from around 90 °F in the summer to about 75 °F in the winter. The only interruptions to this tranquility come from the occasional hurricane or tropical storm.

The original inhabitants of the islands were Native Americans who worked their way from South America to Haiti and then to the Bahamas. Not long after Christopher Columbus made landfall in the Bahamian islands in 1492, the Spaniards began to enslave and kill off these peaceful people, and within thirty years they were completely wiped out.

For the next 130 years or so the islands were largely uninhabited until a group of Englishmen fleeing religious persecution in Bermuda established a small colony on Eleuthera in 1648. The going was tough for these pioneers as they attempted to live from farming the poor soil. In 1666, another group from Bermuda set up a settlement on New Providence and fared better as they turned their attention to the sea, eating fish and turtles, salvaging wrecks and making salt. In 1670 King Charles II granted oversight of the Bahamas to the Lords Proprietors of the Province of Carolina. This established a connection between the Carolinas and the Bahamas that lasted through the Civil War, but the lords themselves took little action or notice of the Bahamas.

In 1684, the Spanish burned the settlement at Eleuthera and the beginnings of one at Nassau on New Providence and both were abandoned for some time. During the 1690s, while England was engaged in another of her numerous wars with France, English privateers used what was left of Nassau as a base from which to attack French shipping. When the war ended many of these men and others turned to piracy. Nassau coalesced into a small lawless city run by pirates like Edward Teach (Blackbeard), who wreaked havoc on merchant ships for hundreds of miles around the islands.

By 1718 the British Crown had had enough and sent prominent sea captain Woodes Rogers and several armed ships to reclaim the city. Rogers drove off those pirates who did not wish to be pardoned and found himself appointed the first governor of the Bahamas. Rogers established order in the community, and it began to grow during the following decades.

The next influx of Englishmen into the Bahamas came in the early 1780s as a result of the Revolutionary War in the United States. These Loyalists did not wish to live under American rule and migrated out of the Carolinas and eastern Florida to New Providence. Included in this group were people like Abraham Adderley, grandfather of Henry Adderley. Within a few years the population of the Bahamas tripled. The Loyalists coined the somewhat derogatory name "Conchs" for those older inhabitants of the islands, but this term eventually became a common moniker for all the white inhabitants of the Bahamas.

Based on their experience in the southeastern states, many of the Loyalists attempted to set up cotton plantations in the islands, often manned by slaves they brought with them. The cotton did well for a few years, but as the early settlers on Eleuthera found, the soil was not conducive to long term cultivation. Their efforts were also hindered by insect problems, and by early in the nineteenth century many of the Loyalists accepted the inevitable and turned to the sea or other businesses to make a living. The large number of slaves they brought with them or imported from Africa remained.

In keeping with the rest of the British Empire, all slaves in the Bahamas were emancipated on July 31, 1834. Although most of the black inhabitants retained second class status and were barely acknowledged with common courtesies by most whites, the emancipation in the islands was far less cataclysmic than the events in the United States three decades later. To the astonishment and consternation of many Confederate sympathizers who ended up in Nassau in the 1860s, the black people of New Providence lived in relative harmony with the white minority and in some cases even had official positions of power. In his reminiscences, one blockade runner spoke of postmaster Stephen Dillet when commenting, "I was shocked to deliver my mail to a colored man." This same Southerner later saw a masonic funeral in Nassau: "When I found black and white arm in arm I had no wish to visit the Lodge."

✦ ✦ ✦

Imagine you are taking a trip on *Karnak* from New York to Nassau in late 1861. You board the ship on a chilly Thursday in November at the company wharf in Jersey City across the Hudson River from Manhattan. By Sunday you will be having dinner under palm trees in Nassau. You pass within sight of Cape May and by Friday you are passing Hatteras Island, North Carolina, about fifty miles to your west. The weather on the deck is just a bit warmer than it was in New York. As you head south, the coast recedes quickly westward so that by the time you pass Savannah, Georgia, you are four hundred miles from land.

By Saturday afternoon you can take your coat off on deck and the air and sun begin to warm your skin. You sight your first land since Cape May as you pass by the Bahamian island of Abaco to your west, catching a glimpse of your first palm trees and the famous rock formation known as Hole in the Wall on the southern tip. Finally on Sunday morning you can see Nassau on the horizon. At the highest point of the island a flag runs up the pole at Fort Fincastle, alerting the residents that the mail steamer's arrival is eminent. Although you cannot see it from this vantage point, the fort was built in 1793 in the shape of a ship.

The harbor of Nassau is protected and framed by a long, low island about three miles long known as Hog Island. Many years later the locals would rename it Paradise Island and put up resort properties on it, but in 1861 it is still largely uninhabited and serves as a nice day trip for picnickers. A lighthouse built in 1817 sits at the westernmost point of the island and as you round the lighthouse you can see Fort Charlotte's white walls on a hill rising above the western edge of the city. The fort was built in the 1780s in honor of King George III's wife and has a moat and dungeons.

Entering the harbor is tricky due to a large sand bar and other shallow areas. Larger ships like *Karnak* sometimes come to the western edge of Hog Island and wait for smaller boats to come assist in getting passengers and cargo to shore. As you wait for the tender to arrive to bring you in, you can see almost the entire city. It extends about three miles east from Fort Charlotte and about a quarter of a mile back from the water to the high point of the island, a ridge reaching a height of about a hundred feet. Nassau is located on the northern coast of New Providence Island, which is about twenty-one miles long and seven miles wide. Only about 20 percent of the city's ten thousand residents are white.

Upon securing the Cunard contract, the Bahamian government made the decision to build a hotel to lure Northern tourists and provide a new revenue stream. The legislature decided to go in debt to the tune of £25,000 to build the hotel, not knowing at the time that this seemingly risky venture would be paid off very quickly by the revenues from blockade running. The Royal Victoria Hotel was completed during the summer of 1861 on land bought from merchant Timothy Darling.

The hotel, which has just opened for its inaugural winter season, sits prominently along the ridge behind the city just to the west of Fort Fincastle. Before the construction of the Royal Victoria, there were just four small boarding houses downtown to accommodate visitors. The proprietor of French's boarding house, the most popular at the time, added to his income by selling milk from the cows he kept in the yard.

At this time in American history, the idea of a vacation is still frowned upon as it violated the Protestant work ethic, so the hotel advertises the restorative health benefits of getting out of the frigid northeast and recuperating in the tropical climate. Over the next few winters, many amused visitors and Nassau residents will note the large number of seeming invalids who are immediately able to swim, fish, and move about with ease as soon as they step off *Karnak*.

The Royal Victoria is built of stone four stories high and is the largest building in the Bahamas. Like Fort Fincastle, it has a nautical theme: the eastern end is rounded somewhat like the bow of a large ship. The lower three levels have ten-foot-wide verandas all around, and a cupola on top of the hotel affords a beautiful view of the city and neighboring islands.

The many amenities inside include ninety well-appointed bedrooms, a large dining room on the first floor with a high ceiling and walls adorned with palmetto leaves, a billiard parlor and barber shop, and numerous sitting spaces for impromptu soirees. In the lobby, you will see people lounging on comfortable couches as a band plays outside on the lawn. Native Bahamians of all ages fill the area outside the entrance hawking sponges, coral, baskets, and sugar cane. Fresh flowers occupy various spots around the hotel. The hotel is contracted to be open from November 1 to May 31, but during the next few years it will stay occupied through the summer as it becomes a central meeting place for those involved in the Great Carnival. But even with the addition of this grand structure, there will not be nearly enough housing for all the people swarming the city.

Running along the harbor in an east to west direction is Bay Street, the business artery of the city. The northern side of Bay Street, closest to the harbor, consists in 1861 mostly of wharfs and open lots, while the southern side is lined with shops. The tender carries you from *Karnak* across water perfectly transparent to the bottom and lands you at a public wharf nearly in the center of town and just down the hill from the Royal Victoria. The public wharf is made of limestone and Prince Alfred's steps bring you up level with Bay Street.

This main thoroughfare and the side streets leading south are paved with crushed limestone and are bright white in the sunlight, as are many of the buildings. Other buildings are in pastel colors that are a bit easier on the eyes. Many of the elite merchants wear tinted glasses and a wet sponge under their hat to deal with the glare and the heat. Disembarking on the wharf, passengers are besieged by young black men offering to carry luggage to the hotel or dive for coins in the crystal-clear water, and by adults seeking to sell fruits or trinkets. The policemen on the street, wearing blue jackets and white pants, are also black. More than one Confederate casually uttering a racial epithet in the coming years will find himself in the astonishing position of being arrested by a black policeman and brought before a black magistrate to be fined.

After settling into the Royal Victoria, you can hire a carriage for a tour of the city and get a sense of the layout. There are four streets, including Bay Street, running parallel to the waterline. Each one of these is a little higher up the ridge. Crossing these are about a dozen streets that run down the ridge to the waterline. All these streets are lined by shops and the residences of the white population.

Many of the merchants live above their shops with verandas on the second story. None of the homes have chimneys since there is no need. Heading down

Parliament Street from the Royal Victoria until it intersects Bay Street, you encounter the three public buildings that house the legislature. Flamingo pink with white trim, the buildings are arranged in a U-shape around a paved area known as Parliament Square. Almost directly across Bay Street is the office and residence of Henry Adderley.

Heading east down Bay Street you reach the outskirts of town and a large open area known as the Eastern Parade. Used for sporting events, military processions, and recreation, it was also used for public hangings until a jail was built in the 1860s. Next to the parade ground is St. Matthew's Anglican Church, built in 1802, the original church of many of the prominent white residents of the city.

Farther to the east, you reach the remnants of tiny Fort Montague, built in the 1740s to defend the residents from the Spanish. Near the fort is a fine old estate called The Hermitage, built in the late 1700s and later owned by merchant Timothy Darling. Finally you reach the manor known as Waterloo and the strange lake adjacent to it. Known as the Lake of Fire, it is about one thousand feet long and three hundred feet wide. When you move your oars in the water or watch fish swim by, you'll see phosphorescent trails of light streaming behind. The light is said to be bright enough to allow you to read the newspaper.

Turning around and heading back west through the city, you pass shops on the south side of the street ranging from modest spaces to opulent stores carrying the finest European merchandise. Most of the stores open by 6:00 a.m.

Dogs are everywhere, and it was once said that everyone in Nassau has a dog and they all bark all night. One observer of the time said, "Just imagine ten thousand or more of them, throughout the city, and up the sides of the bluff, even to the forts on the summit, all barking, howling, squalling, and making other noises for which there is no name." Just when people finally doze off from this caterwauling, a cannon goes off at 4:00 a.m. to signal the start of a new day. Another is fired at 8:00 p.m. every night and is followed by the 2nd West India regimental band playing "God Save the Queen." In fact, cannons are fired off for pretty much any occasion.

As mentioned before, there is not a lot to do, but that will soon be changing. While you might encounter the occasional delicacy at the Royal Victoria, food on the island consists mainly of fruit and canned pickled beef and pork brought in from abroad. While lots of roosters roam around, there are few chickens, and thus eggs are rare, as is bacon. A typical breakfast will consist of fried bananas and other fruit. Standard meal times are 9:00 a.m. for breakfast, 3:00 p.m. for dinner, and 8:00 p.m. for supper.

You encounter some notable landmarks near the intersection of George Street and Bay Street. On your right is the Vendue House. This one-story building, open on all four sides, has been used since the mid-1700s for selling and auctioning all sorts of commodities, including slaves.

By the time of the Civil War, the wrecking industry has become the predominant source of income in the Bahamas and most goods salvaged from the wrecks end up at the Vendue House. Nearly half the able-bodied men in the islands are engaged in wrecking, and as the Civil War starts, nearly two-thirds of Bahamian exports are salvaged goods. Men lounge around for long periods of time waiting for the call of "Wreck!" One observer described the city as "a population of idlers with maritime tastes."

Nearby on Bay Street is the three-story brick Custom House, where many blockade-running ships will clear for false destinations with a wink from local officials, and the Bank of Nassau, the only bank in the city. The bank issues no notes as all transactions here are carried out with gold and silver coins. Also along the waterfront on the north side of Bay Street, and just a bit east of the Vendue House, is the public market. These three one-story wooden structures have shingled roofs and are mostly open. Adjoining them to the east are storage yards fenced by walls topped with broken glass to prevent theft. Between the market and the Vendue House is the ice house, where large blocks of ice packed in sawdust are brought from Canada. The area around the Vendue House is usually crowded and busy on a work day.

As you continue west on Bay Street, you'll see Christ Church Cathedral and Government House to your left up George Street. The cathedral, built in a Gothic style from large limestone blocks, has become the church home of most of the prominent Bay Street merchants. Formerly named Christ Church Parish Church, in 1861 it was designated a cathedral and mother church of all Anglican churches in the Bahamas. With this designation, Nassau officially became a city.

Government House, at the top of George Street and along the ridge, is the official residence of the governor and is pink and white like the parliament buildings. In front of the building and gazing out to the sea is a statue of Christopher Columbus built in the 1830s.

As you continue on to the west, in another block you come to the western parade ground, known as Fleeming Square. The oblong, grass-covered field, 90 yards wide and 160 yards long, was named for Admiral Charles Fleeming, who commanded the West Indies fleet in the late 1820s. On its north side are the barracks of the 2nd West India Regiment and the Navy Ordnance Yard, and on its east side is a long three-story building that houses the officers of the regiment.

Like the Eastern Parade, Fleeming Square is a popular recreation area, and the regimental band plays one or two concerts a week there to large crowds.

Everyone wears their finest, and the children run around the grass while being minded by their black nannies. The men of the regiment wear gaudy uniforms with scarlet jackets, blue trousers, yellow leggings, and white hoses. On their head each man has a red fez with white tassel, all surrounded by a white turban wound around several times.

Finally you come to Fort Charlotte, the western extremity of the city. The western part of the island is largely uninhabited. If you were to continue along Bay Street as it becomes an unpaved road headed into the countryside you would, after a half-day trip, come to the village of Adelaide on the southwestern tip of the island. This is the most remote community on the island. In 1831, Governor James Smyth designated this spot as a refuge for 157 enslaved Africans captured from the Portuguese vessel *Rosa*. They constructed thatched huts and now live much as they did in their western African villages.

The other black residents of the island are primarily concentrated in three suburbs of Nassau. The largest is called Grant's Town and is just behind the ridge from Fort Fincastle and the Royal Victoria. Early each morning many of the residents there make their way into Nassau to sell fruits, vegetables, and other goods at the public market and elsewhere. Lemons, limes, coconuts, pineapples, and oranges grow here in abundance despite the soil.

To the west of Grant's Town is Bain Town. Finally, a couple of miles to the southeast of Fort Montagu is Fox Hill, founded by freed slave Samuel Fox in 1801. The interior of the island is deserted and filled with fruit groves and the abandoned plantations from the era before emancipation. The people of all colors and means residing on this sleepy island will soon find themselves unexpectedly at the center of world events. Some will prosper and others will come to ruin, but few will be unaffected.

5

The Bay Street Boys

Despite the relative smoothness of the transition after the emancipation of slaves in 1834, Bahamian society in 1861 was still largely divided by color, and many of the most powerful players still held strong racist views. While people of color comprised 80 to 90 percent of the population, power was in the hands of a small group of wealthy white men. Many of these were merchants of Bahamian birth, while others were Englishmen appointed to high office on the island. Because of the locations of many of the shops, this merchant clique has often been referred to as the Bay Street Boys. While the men appointed by the Crown to oversee the island were nominally in charge, in practical terms it was the most powerful merchants who drove the important decisions.

The most notable exception to the rule of white power in Nassau was Stephen Dillet, born in Haiti in 1797 to a French army officer and a free black woman. By 1822 he had become a successful tailor in Nassau and a slave owner. His light skin color, intelligence, and character allowed him to be accepted into the upper crust. He served for twenty-seven years in the House of Assembly, as postmaster for twenty-six years, and also as inspector-general of the police force during the Civil War. An active Freemason and a vestryman of Christ Church Cathedral, Dillet's tailoring business catered to the upper class and middle class of both colors. His son Thomas followed in his footsteps in the assembly and other prominent governmental posts. His grandson James Weldon Johnson was the first person of color to be chosen as executive secretary of the NAACP.

At the beginning of the Civil War, the governor of the Bahamas was Charles John Bayley. Bayley had been governor since 1857 and was in his mid-forties as the war began. As desolate as the Bahamas were in the 1850s, it was certainly a step up from his previous assignment as colonial secretary on the island of Mauritius in the middle of the Indian Ocean. The governor's office kept a very formal relationship with the people of the Bahamas, and Bayley himself seems to have been an aloof and distant person.

Compared to other Bahamian governors, Bayley seems to have held fewer functions at Government House and apparently enjoyed them less than his predecessors and successors. The ranking woman at Government House was the leader of upscale social life on the island. While this was usually the governor's wife (as in Bayley's case), it could also be the governor's sister or daughter if he was not married. Bayley's stiff personality turned out not to be as problematic as the strong Confederate sympathies that eventually resulted in his removal by the Home Office in 1864.

The wealthiest merchants and their spouses were known as the Upper Ten, meaning upper 10 percent, the pinnacle of Bahamian society. They received an invitation to Government House for all occasions. Those slightly lower in stature were known as the Lower Upper Ten and were invited to official state occasions. Some especially respectable middle-class citizens, regardless of skin color, were invited to Government House for certain functions.

The white elite of Nassau did their best to pattern their behavior after the upper classes of Britain. Social life consisted of private visits, dances, dinner parties, clubs, and watching or participating in cricket and polo matches. There were two Masonic temples that attracted most of the wealthy men. The dress and the formal life were a bit pretentious to some observers.

Church life was important to almost everyone in Nassau, and the white elite generally attended Anglican services at Christ Church Cathedral, though some attended the Methodist chapel on the west end of town or the Presbyterian Church. People of color normally attended smaller churches in their neighborhoods, or in the case of the Africans, retained their native religious ceremonies. The rear seats and seats in the balcony at Christ Church were reserved for "the poor." The schools in New Providence were of inferior quality and not well attended. The House of Assembly delegated public education to the Anglican Church, but white people with money sent their children abroad or to private tutors.

Despite their superior numbers, the non-white population was too diverse to be unified in any constructive way. Creoles, born in the islands, looked down upon the Africans who had accumulated as a result of the slave trade. The Creoles imitated the white middle class in hiring black gardeners and domestic servants. The elite Conchs ignored almost all people of color and generally treated them with contempt except in their roles as domestics and laborers. One exception to the general divide was a universal celebration of Guy Fawkes Day every November 5.

The 2nd West India Regiment stationed in Nassau was a source of some power for non-whites, though there was tension between these men and the native-born Creoles. Though the officers were white and British, the soldiers were mostly of West African descent and well suited to serve in the environment of the West Indies as neither the heat nor tropical diseases bothered them. Their barracks were on the west end of the city near Fleeming Square, and their presence throughout the town would be a great aid to the police force during the raucous times between 1861 and 1865.

Crime was not prevalent before the Civil War, and those who were arrested and sentenced to imprisonment (and sometimes hard labor) were almost always people of color. There was a common saying that "no white man can go to prison in Nassau." Those crimes that were committed were usually of a fairly trivial nature. For example, in 1857 people flying kites in the streets was considered a serious enough issue that Inspector General Stephen Dillet was charged with having his police officers clamp down on the problem.

Communication was an important concern for everyone in the city during the war. Telegraph lines did not come to the island until the 1890s, so news came by ship and before the war was fairly sporadic. Once the arrival of blockade runners became a common occurrence, both Southern and Northern newspapers showed up on a regular basis, and the people in Nassau were generally only a week behind the events happening on the battlefields and two weeks behind news from England.

The two major newspapers in the city were the *Bahama Herald*, with editor Thomas B. Thompson, and the *Nassau Guardian*, with editor Edwin Moseley. Both newspapers came out on Wednesday and Saturday, and both took a generally pro-Confederate tone, not surprising given the boon to the city from blockade running and the similarities in culture between the Nassau elite and the Southern aristocracy. The Bahamian government seemed to consider the *Herald* to be a bit harsh in its criticisms, but both papers were popular around town.

The man tasked with managing daily life in the Bahamas was Colonial Secretary Charles Rogers Nesbitt. He spent more than fifty years of his life in public service in Nassau and often stood in for governors when they were away from the islands. Nesbitt was born in London on April 3, 1799, and came to the Bahamas as a teenager in 1814, when his father was appointed colonial secretary. He took over the office and position in 1831 when his father left the colony on leave of absence and did not return. So by the start of the Civil War in 1861, Nesbitt had been perhaps the most influential man in Bahamas political life for three decades. He was also elected to the House of Assembly in 1831 and began a tradition that the colonial secretary would advance the government's agenda in the House.

Nesbitt was a slave owner, but it appears that he played a critical role in helping ease the transition after emancipation in 1834. As colonial secretary, he was responsible for all official government correspondence and publishing proclamations, and he had access to virtually all information gathered about the islands and the people. With this stockpile of knowledge, Nesbitt became an extremely important advisor to the governors who came to Nassau. Between 1831 and the end of the Civil War, Nesbitt served under nine different governors. With the average term lasting just a bit over four years, the effectiveness of any government programs relied heavily on the continuity of Nesbitt's work. He was in sole control of the administration of the Bahamas for fifteen months during the Civil War due to Bayley being away from June 1861 to March 1862 and to the gap between Bayley leaving the island in June 1864 and the arrival of his successor Rawson W. Rawson.

Three other British officials played important roles in the upcoming events in Nassau. George Campbell Anderson, born in the Bahamas in 1804 to Loyalist parents, had been in the House of Assembly since the late 1820s and had been Speaker of the House since 1839. A lawyer, he had also been the colony's attorney general since 1837. In this role, he would be making decisions regarding the legality of actions by all the various players in the Great Carnival. Like Bayley, he was noted for his strong support of the Confederate cause.

John Campbell Lees was chief justice of the Bahamas and justice of the Bahamas Vice-Admiralty Court. Born in Middlesex, England, in 1793, Lees had been chief justice since 1836. He was also an amateur meteorologist, keeping weather journals that have proven useful to modern researchers studying the climate of the islands. After his wife and adult daughter both died in the 1840s, Lees remarried in 1849 and despite his rather advanced age fathered five more children between 1851 and 1859. His ruling in the summer of 1862 regarding *Oreto* had major repercussions for the remainder of the war and beyond.

Fletcher Whitley and John Dumaresq (after Whitley's death in 1862) were the receivers-general and treasurers for the Bahamas. A receiver-general is responsible for accepting payments on behalf of the government. In this role, these men oversaw the collection of duties at the Custom House, a duty that became complex as the number of ships coming into the harbor increased rapidly and the character of the cargoes on the ships became more and more questionable. During the height of the craziness, there would sometimes be more than 100 ships in the harbor. By 1864, custom duties had tripled from 1860 and the number of ships entering the harbor had risen from 219 to 910. By 1864 custom duties accounted for 73 percent of the total governmental revenues. This dramatic change would transform the city.

The legislature of the Bahamas consisted of two councils whose members were nominated by the governor and an elected House of Assembly. The Executive Council was chaired by the governor and usually consisted of the colonial secretary, attorney general, and receiver-general as ex-officio members and three more members nominated by the governor. The Legislative Council had nine members nominated by the governor. Members of the House of Assembly could also be on one of the councils but no one could be on both councils simultaneously. The governor was bound by decisions made by the Executive Council. The House of Assembly had twenty-nine members representing all the various districts of the Bahamas. Because their families once lived in the out islands, the elite white merchants living in Nassau often assumed the assembly seats for those districts. Robert Sawyer, for example, represented Harbour Island, and Timothy Darling represented Inagua.

The preeminent merchant in the Bahamas was Henry Adderley. Adderley transformed his modest pre-war shipping operation into a blockade-running tour de force that made his name known on both sides of the Atlantic. The *New York Times* prefaced the name of his company with the word "notorious" so often that it seemed part of the brand. He appears to have become the Bahamas' first millionaire.

Henry Adderley was the grandson of Abraham Adderley, a Loyalist who had come to the Bahamas from St. Augustine, Florida. Abraham Adderley was granted land on Bay Street fronting the harbor and bordered by East Street and the public wharf. Henry was born to Abraham's son Nehemiah in Nassau on October 2, 1803. Nehemiah was a planter and slave owner and at least one of his slaves would later be registered in Henry's name. Henry married Mary Ann Perpall at Christ Church in 1825, and they had twelve children.

Henry began his mercantile career by taking over the trading business of a Mr. Elliott, and by the 1830s he had achieved some stature in the community as a merchant and was involved as an officer in the local Masonic lodge. As early as 1834 he was taking trips to New York to build business connections there. During this time he began to conduct sales at the Vendue House, most likely including the auctioning of slaves. When it became apparent that slavery was on the way out in the Bahamas, he was fined and threatened with imprisonment due to the strenuous objections he made to the governor.

Over the next couple of decades, Henry built his business based on trade with England, New York, Baltimore, Philadelphia, Charleston, Savannah, New Orleans, and the Canadian Maritime Provinces and by being a prominent player in the wrecking and salvage industry. Not only were many of the goods salvaged from wrecks brought to Adderley to be auctioned, but he was also appointed by the legislature (of which he was a part) as president of the Bahamas Marine Insurance Company. So he was able to make a profit whether a ship wrecked or not.

As our story will show, Henry Adderley came to personify the opportunism exhibited throughout the Civil War. He was sympathetic to the Confederate cause, but more importantly he had already built the infrastructure and trading connections to jump on that opportunity. While several other merchants also had massive businesses associated with blockade running and many smaller operators tried their hand at the game, none could rival Henry Adderley.

While they did not rise quite to the level of Adderley, other Bay Street Boys already in business at the start of the war were also prepared to take advantage of the situation. Many of these merchants operated retail shops on Bay Street, but like Adderley they also conducted sales at the Vendue House or at various warehouses or wharfs on the north side of Bay Street. A brief review of the key players will show how intimately their businesses, power, and families were entwined. All of these men were involved with blockade running by the summer of 1862.

- **Robert Henry Sawyer** and **Ramon Antonio Menendez** operated as Sawyer and Menendez. Sawyer, born in Nassau in 1832, was a member of the House of Assembly and the Executive Council. Menendez, born in Spain, was Sawyer's brother-in-law.
- **Henry Rowland Saunders**, born in 1814, operated Saunders and Son with his son **Pembroke Saunders**, born in 1838. Henry Saunders was a member of the House of Assembly. Their store was on Bay Street opposite the public market.
- **George David Harris**, born in London in 1827, was Henry Adderley's son-in-law and operating his own shipping company as the war started. He later joined Adderley's firm, and some claimed that he was the real brains of the operation during the war. Harris was a member of the House of Assembly and Executive Council.
- **Augustus John Adderley**, son of Henry, born in 1835, member of the House of Assembly and Legislative Council. Both George Harris and Augustus Adderley became partners in Henry Adderley and Company early in the war.
- **Charles Robert Perpall**, born in 1824, was Henry Adderley's brother-in-law and operated Perpall and Company with a store on Bay Street.
- **William James Weech**, born 1803, and his son **Robert William Henry Weech**, born 1826, both operated thriving shipping operations. William Weech was a member of the House of Assembly.
- **John Gray Meadows**, born around 1810, was another brother-in-law of Henry Adderley, though his wife Eliza Adderley Meadows died years before the war. A member and former Speaker of the House of Assembly, he operated a shop on Bay Street.
- **Gustave Renouard**, born in France in 1811, came to the Bahamas as the

survivor of a shipwreck about twenty years before the war. As well as running his business Renouard and Company, he was also appointed to be French consul to the Bahamas. His exportation of sponges to Paris is often credited as the beginning of that industry in the Bahamas.

- **Alexander Johnson**, born 1829, son-in-law to Henry Saunders.
- **William Daniel Albury**, born 1811.
- **John Josiah Turtle**, born 1822.
- **John Saffery George**, born in 1825 and son-in-law to William Weech. His business at the corner of Bay Street and East Street continued in operation until the twenty-first century.

Some other merchants seem to have come into the game a bit later on, perhaps lured by the lucrative profits being made by those first to take part. These included:

- **Abraham Turton Holmes**, born 1820, and his son-in-law **Manuel Menendez** (Ramon's brother, born around 1823), who operated his own trade business and shop. Both were members of the House of Assembly. Holmes's shop was on Market Street.
- **Samuel Otis Johnson**, born 1828, operated Johnson and Brother (his brother George had passed away in 1859). Johnson was also a member of the House of Assembly. He married Timothy Darling's daughter.
- **Charles Henry Edward Kemp**, born 1834, a member of the House of Assembly.
- **Thomas Kingsbury Moore**, born around 1817 and half-brother of Robert Henry Sawyer, member of the House of Assembly.
- **Michael C. Knowles**, born in 1837, his shop was on Market Street.
- **Charles Tyldesley Rhodes Sands**, born 1832, his shop was on Frederick Street.
- **Daniel Shepherd Farrington**, born 1822.

A couple of other prominent merchant families were involved in blockade running, but with a slight twist. Tight connections existed between Nassau and New York, and two families actually moved part of their operation to the latter city. John Christopher Rahming spent most of the war in New York while his older brother Walter handled the Nassau side of operations. Elderly Antonio Eneas was born about 1787, and his two sons Joseph (born 1824) and George (born 1835) went to New York years before the war. Both John Rahming and Joseph Eneas spent time in federal prisons during the war due to their involvement in the illegal trade.

A quick perusal of the merchants listed above makes it clear that there must have been abundant opportunities for all. These merchants formed the core of the trade with the Confederacy, but many others would come from Europe and the Confederacy to Nassau during the war to get in on the action. Given the intimate family ties, it is not surprising that the core merchants often cooperated with each other. They often sold goods at each other's warehouses or conducted business on behalf of others in the inner circle. Given the strong representation in the Bahamian parliament by these Bay Street Boys, it is not surprising that it would be very tough for any laws to be passed that would hinder the trade.

Merchant Timothy Darling was an esteemed member of the white elite but an outlier in terms of his politics. In some ways his stature and strong opposition to the blockade-running business made him a counterweight to the power of Henry Adderley. He was born in New Brunswick, Canada, in 1810, and he married Lucy Sargent in 1835 in Sullivan, Maine. In 1839, Darling reached Nassau inadvertently when, on a trip to Galveston, Texas, his ship was wrecked off the Berry Islands about fifty miles northeast of Nassau. Transported to the capital city, he liked it so much that he decided to make Nassau his home.

Darling was friends with influential politician Daniel Webster, and through Webster's influence Darling became US consul to the Bahamas in 1842. It seems a bit odd for a British subject to hold the position, but Darling was born in St. Stephen on the Canadian-United States border and actually grew up in Calais, Maine, across the St. Croix River. He held the consular post from 1842 until 1845 and in a second term from 1853 to 1857.

In his first year as consul, he had to deal with a very sticky situation when the *Creole* came into Nassau harbor. The boat had been carrying 135 slaves from Richmond to New Orleans when a group of the slaves took over the ship, overwhelming the ten-man crew and killing one of the slave traders. Furious Southerners demanded that the slaves be returned, but they were freed and most sent on to Jamaica. In his role as consul, Darling tried to have the mutineers brought to trial for piracy, but the admiralty court in Nassau released them.

Over the next twenty years Darling became a well-established merchant and ship owner, making his living largely from selling wrecked goods. He was a member of the House of Assembly and Executive Council and the Upper Ten. He also stood out in his compassion for the less fortunate, gaining notoriety for his efforts to help the poor during the 1852 cholera epidemic. When the war came he was a strong supporter of the Union cause and stood out as the only high-profile Bay Street merchant who did not leap on the opportunity that the war provided. He refused consignments associated with blockade running "to his great personal injury and pecuniary sacrifice," as the *Nassau Guardian* stated years later in his obituary. The Nassau correspondent of the *New York Times* singled out Darling in a July 1862 article on blockade running:

> We have but one house of importance in Nassau who have stood entirely aloof from the secession business. That is the house of T. DARLING & Co. While they

could have made a fortune out of the business they have acted from principle rather than for profit, and refused all consignments of Southern goods or vessels, or to be in any way connected with the dirty business.

Darling's interactions with Henry Adderley must have been fascinating given their proximity and relatively equal social status. When Adderley was appointed president of the Bahamas Marine Insurance Company, Darling was appointed Vice-President. The insurance company board of directors also included a number of other men heavily involved in blockade running: Robert Sawyer, John S. George, Robert Weech, and William Albury. Darling also served side by side with Adderley in the House of Assembly and with Adderley's son Augustus and son-in-law George Harris on the Executive Council.

Because of his loyalty, Darling's business was the official agency for the New York underwriters. It is not clear if Darling was able to offer much advice to the US consuls who served in Nassau during the war since his tenure occurred under such different circumstances. Despite his status as an outlier, Darling appears to have been held in very high esteem on the island. His obituary in the *Nassau Guardian* on October 30, 1880, stated, "To a powerful intellect, he added the charm of gentle manners and a most generous disposition."

✦ ✦ ✦

It is important to note why Nassau became the most important transshipment point for the Confederacy. While Bermuda, Havana, Matamoras in Mexico, and even Saint John and Halifax in Canada all played important roles, Nassau had significant advantages. In addition to experienced and opportunistic merchants like Henry Adderley who had already built connections to the main Southern ports, Nassau was considerably closer to Charleston, Savannah, and Wilmington than were the other locations. Charleston and Wilmington were in turn closer to the military action in Virginia than the far western ports of the Confederacy. From Nassau to Charleston was about 560 miles and two to three days' travel, and Wilmington was about seventy miles farther away. Given the relative scarcity of coal, a shorter distance became important. Using less coal also meant more room for revenue-generating cargo. While the other intermediate ports all played vital roles in keeping the Confederacy alive, in the height of the blockade-running years, Nassau was clearly the leading port.

The nature of the Bahamian archipelago also lent itself to the blockade-running trade. For centuries, international maritime law had proclaimed that a nation's territorial waters extended three miles from shore. This was roughly the distance a large cannon could fire a shell, and also about the distance the horizon appears for a person standing at sea level who is gazing out at the ocean. The basis of the law was that a nation had the right to protect the waters it could defend and within which it could see enemy targets. Given the thousands of land masses that comprise the Bahamas, it was quite easy for the master of a blockade runner to slip within the British territorial limits very quickly. Leaving Nassau, these small islands gave the ships running contraband about a 100-mile head start toward the southern coast.

This normally offered protection from Union ships but as the story of *Margaret and Jessie* in 1863 will show, the captains charged with stopping blockade runners did not always adhere to the rules. Protection was also afforded only to ships of the country who owned the waters, so most blockade runners flew the British flag while in Bahamian waters. The ships were sold in Nassau, sometimes in legitimate sales to British owners and sometimes in sham sales that just changed the registry to allow the British flag to be flown. The ships were largely manned by British or other foreign seamen, as any Confederate citizens captured would be imprisoned for the duration of the conflict as prisoners of war while foreigners could expect to be released in a couple of weeks. As the *New York Times* commented in July 1862, "In this mongrel port of Nassau they are allowed openly and defiantly to complete their outfit, whence they will sally forth and throw away their English nationality."

One other aspect of maritime law that affected Nassau's role as an intermediate port was the doctrine or law of continuous voyage. This was an application of the general rule of law that a person is not permitted to do indirectly what he or she is forbidden to do directly.

Arising from the Seven Years War of 1756–1763 (the American portion of which was termed the French and Indian War), the law stated that stopping at an intermediate port did not legalize an otherwise illegal voyage. Prior to the Civil War, the United States did not abide by this rule and the American interpretation was that a neutral ship traveling to a neutral port could not be harmed. Once cargo was landed at a neutral port a belligerent nation could not inquire as to the ultimate destination. Any goods shipped directly from a neutral port to a belligerent were fair game to be captured. This interpretation went back to the French Revolution and Napoleonic Wars when England and France were at war and vessels traveling from the French West Indies to France could be captured by British ships and brought to British prize courts.

A prize court filled the role of a belligerent's duty to neutral countries by determining if a ship had been lawfully captured. If not, the ship was returned to her owners. If so, the ship and cargo could be sold with the proceeds going to the captain and crew of the seizing ship. So while Union sailors in the Civil War blockade were in part motivated by patriotism, they also stood to make money from ships they captured. A number of the ships sold at the prize court in Key West were immediately bought back by British subjects and returned to Nassau.

During the conflict between England and France, American shippers attempted to evade the doctrine by shipping goods from the West Indies to American ports and from there to France, hence creating a legal voyage. The British courts disagreed with this interpretation, and it was not until 1861 that American courts began to come around to accept the doctrine of continuous voyage, as it was now imperative that they do so. The shoe was on the other foot at this point as British merchants began to use Nassau and other intermediate ports in the same manner that Americans had done years before, and these led to many tense situations.

For example, the *Springbok*, headed from neutral London to neutral Nassau in 1863, was captured about 150 miles east of Nassau by USS *Sonoma* and taken to prize court in New York. The ship was filled with military contraband, and the court ruled that Nassau could not be considered an ordinary neutral port. While this case and others caused a furor in England, some savvy men in London realized that this new interpretation by the United States might one day work out in their favor, and they were right. Fifty years later in World War I, the then-neutral United States was prevented by this same interpretation from sending supplies to Germany.

A nice summary of the answer to the question "Why Nassau?" was given about forty years after the war by Judge Charles B. Elliott:

> If the vessel was not subject to capture until after it left a neutral port such as Nassau, the danger line was brought within a few miles of the coast of the belligerent. A small island near the coast of Florida, therefore, soon became the center of an important trade. Its harbors soon swarmed with innocent looking trading vessels and the U.S. government was asked to assume that they had no improper relations with other craft of race-horse type and notorious character which so frequently called at the port.
>
> It was in fact common knowledge that the entire trade was a gross manifest and palpable evasion of the recognized rules and requirements of the law of neutrality, that Nassau was a mere outpost for attack upon a friendly belligerent by theoretical neutrals; a rendezvous for vessels engaged in a forbidden trade. The greater part of the transactions were conducted by, or under the immediate supervision of confederate agents.

In June 1861, Governor Bayley and his wife left on *Karnak* for New York and then to England. It was customary for the governors of remote outposts to be granted an occasional "return to civilization" as a reward for overseeing the empire's business in the middle of nowhere. At this point, Bayley was probably as oblivious to the coming importance of the Bahamas in the Civil War as were most people not named Trenholm or Adderley. By the time Bayley returned to New Providence in the spring of 1862, the Great Carnival had begun to transform his island.

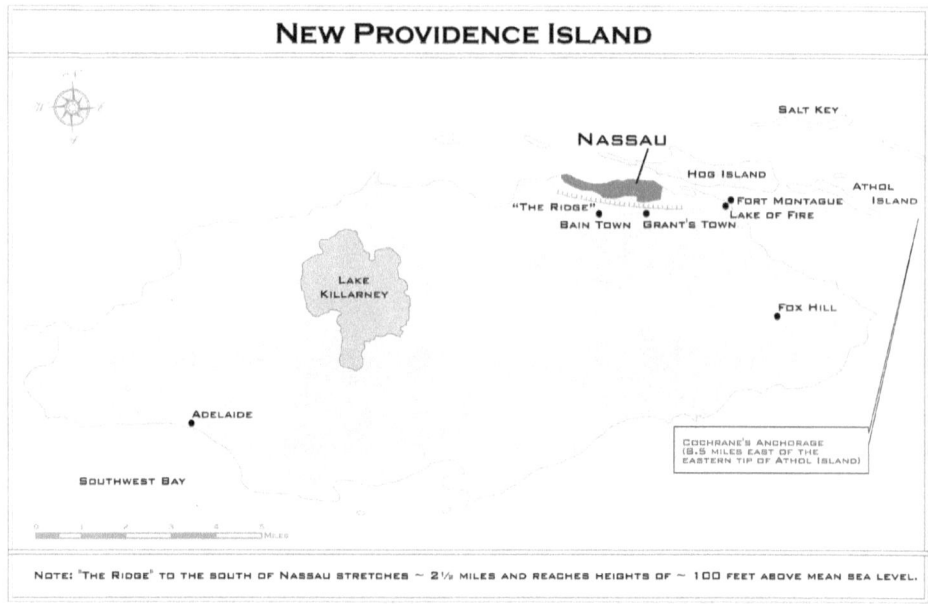

New Providence Island: The map of New Providence Island, within the text, also uses UTM Zone 18N and WGS 1984 datum. The scale is 1:160,000.

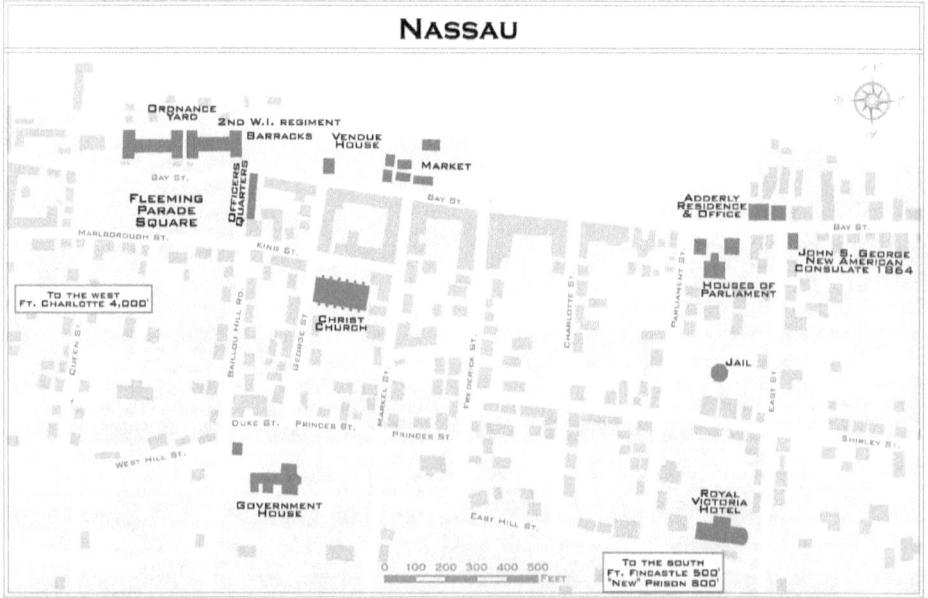

Nassau: The map of Nassau in the 1860s uses UTM Zone 18N, WGS 1984 datum, and a scale of 1:4,500. Building locations are based on material from IMRAY (1884), p0210, BAHAMAS, NASSAU, and other sources.

Royal Victoria Hotel

View down George Street

Bay Street, east of Parliament Square

Fleeming Square

Nassau harbor from the top of Christ Church Cathedral

Nassau harbor with blockade runners

Another view of Nassau harbor

Bay Street near Market Street

Cunard *Corsica*

John S. George warehouse

Henry Adderley's mansion

Adderley drawing room

The Great Carnival

6

Putting the Pieces in Place

With *Flambeau* waiting like a cat for *Gladiator* to leave Nassau, Sam Whiting realized that this standoff might be the first of many similar situations. He decided to acquire a stockpile of coal so that any Union cruisers that came to port would be ready to move on blockade runners when necessary. Blockade runners had a serious advantage in that they chose the time to make their move, while blockading ships had to always keep their steam up to have any chance of catching their prey. Keeping steam going on a nearly continuous basis required a lot of coal, and in his efforts to address this problem, Whiting ran headfirst into British "neutrality."

The schooner USS *Caleb Stetson* (named in honor of a Massachusetts politician) arrived in Nassau on December 7 with a load of coal from the Philadelphia Navy Yard. As more ships were relying on coal, it was becoming a strategic material. The technology and technique of blockade running evolved so that a particular type of coal, called anthracite coal, came into high demand. This coal is much harder than more common bituminous coal and burns with virtually no smoke. Blockade runners used sail or common coal to make their way toward ports and then on moonless nights burned anthracite coal on approach to make themselves as invisible as possible. Most ships would carry the minimum amount of coal necessary in order to provide more room for cargo.

The Bay Street Boys certainly had an interest in coal as another revenue stream, but they did not look kindly on the consul supplying Union warships from Nassau harbor. A contingent of merchants went to visit Government House to complain, after which Charles Nesbitt informed Whiting that the coal could certainly be landed but that in no case could it be used to fuel a warship such as *Flambeau* since this would violate British neutrality.

Whiting then tried another approach to get *Flambeau* fueled, claiming that *Caleb Stetson* was leaking and that to prevent her from sinking he wanted to put some of the coal on *Flambeau*. Nesbitt said again that he could land the coal but could not give it to *Flambeau*. Whiting was outraged, as outside the dock at his office he could see men working for Adderley coaling up the blockade runners *Prince of Wales*, *Theodora*, and *Ella Warley*. At the height of the craziness, merchants like Adderley, Sawyer and Menendez, and Saunders and Son accumulated mountains of coal on Hog Island for use by the blockade runners.

On this same day Nesbitt notified Whiting that *Gladiator*'s papers were in order for a trip from England to the West Indies and back, so there was nothing he could do unless Whiting had proof that the cargo was being shipped to the Confederacy. Lieutenant Temple of *Flambeau* wrote to Secretary of the Navy Gideon Welles on December 16 about the situation. His coal supply was not yet an issue, but he confirmed Whiting's take on the sentiments of Nassau residents: "My formal visits to the authorities have been courteously received; but it is evident from trifles, which I will not enumerate, that all their sympathies are with the rebels. Indeed, this is the tone of feeling among all classes here, and the common people barely fall short of downright insolence to our officers in the streets. Our presence is an evident source of embarrassment and distress to very many."

Word of the standoff between *Gladiator* and *Flambeau* quickly made its way into newspapers across the Union and Confederacy. Temple was aware that it was illegal to sit in a neutral port waiting on enemy ships, but he was ostensibly there to have repairs done on the ship's boilers. By December 19, *Theodora* and *Prince of Wales* had headed out to sea toward the Confederacy, hoping to lure *Flambeau* away from *Gladiator*, but Temple was not fooled.

While this was happening, Henry Adderley was busy filling the cargo space of *Ella Warley*. The cargo was being transferred from *Eliza Bonsall* (named for George Trenholm's sister-in-law), just in from Liverpool. Adderley first asked Receiver-General Whitley for approval to make such a transshipment, and Whitley referred him to Nesbitt, who approved the request.

Although such transshipment was done routinely on an informal basis before the war, this official approval set a precedent that Heyliger joyfully reported to Benjamin the week he returned from Havana: "We have succeeded in obtaining a very important modification of the existing laws, viz. the privilege of breaking bulk and transshipment." Heyliger had met with Adderley when he arrived in Nassau on December 10, and before the month was over they were forming a successful partnership.

When *Ella Warley* was loaded, Adderley wrote to Nesbitt indicating that the ship had cleared by customs for Saint John. But because there were now several other Union cruisers in the Bahamas he requested a Royal Navy escort. After consulting with Attorney General George Anderson, Nesbitt informed Adderley that a naval escort was only possible in times of war but that if *Ella*

Warley (now flying a British flag) was molested, the navy would take action. The ship left on December 28, "ostensibly bound for Saint John, New Brunswick" according to Heyliger. She arrived safely in Charleston five days later. *Ella Warley* was captured by Union forces in April 1862.

This ship provides another good example of the convoluted deceptions involved in getting cargoes into the Confederacy. While she was in reality owned by John Fraser and Company, she was registered to young Edwin Adderley, Henry Adderley's nephew. The *New York Times* correspondent in Nassau described Edwin as the "bogus owner" of the vessel and described him as "what we style a 'red-headed crab,' about eighteen years old, with but little brains and less money." The *Times* added, "Some of these steamers have been sold to boys who have never had money enough of their own to buy a small dingey. After all, it is not much to be wondered at—persons who are engaged in such dirty business will say anything but their prayers."

Ella Warley was about one hundred miles north of Abaco when caught in 1862, but her papers said she was headed to Canada with a cargo for William Wright. The pilot on board told Union sailors he had no idea where the ship was headed and claimed they were making for the Gulf Stream and not steering for any place in particular. The cargo, consigned by Henry Adderley and Company, consisted of rifles, muskets, lead, and saltpeter.

✦ ✦ ✦

Flambeau, keeping her boilers running, had finally gotten low on coal and headed to Key West. Whiting, frustrated at his inability to coal up the Union cruisers, sent *Caleb Stetson* to Key West to offload her coal there. But with various Union cruisers now prowling around both channels heading away from New Providence, getting the valuable cargo of *Gladiator* to the Confederacy would take some ingenuity. Sending the slow *Gladiator* herself was out of the question as the Union blockade was already getting harder to penetrate for anything but fast steamers.

Just as rifled muskets were making Napoleonic tactics obsolete on the battlefields, steam was bringing the days of sail to an end. Trying to enter the harbor of Georgetown, South Carolina, on Christmas Eve, *Prince of Wales* had been burned by a Union ship and Merritt and Whiting's old nemesis *William H. Northrup* had finally been captured at Little River Inlet, North Carolina, the next day. Not surprisingly, George Trenholm and Henry Adderley were prepared to offer their services, and as usual there was a fee.

Trenholm wrote to Judah Benjamin on December 30, 1861, offering the use of two of their steam-powered vessels, *Cecile* and the *Carolina* (a newly purchased ship, not the vessel now named *Theodora*), into which the cargo of *Gladiator* could be transshipped. Trenholm suggested that the vessels be cleared for Saint John and assured Benjamin that "our agents, Messrs. Henry Adderley and Company, will manage everything with the utmost discretion."

By the end of 1861, dozens of ships had evaded the blockade to make their way back and forth from Nassau to the Confederacy. But the arrivals of *Prince of Wales*, *Ella Warley*, *Theodora*, and *Gladiator* in early December brought astute businessmen like George Trenholm and Henry Adderley around to a new way of thinking. With the release of Mason and Slidell by the United States in January 1862, any chances of England coming into the war on the side of the Confederacy had decreased substantially. The war was no longer looking like a short affair and the idea of withholding cotton would have to be jettisoned in favor of sending cotton to England in return for the materials needed for the Confederacy to fight and survive.

In addition to the money to be made from the war, merchants like Henry Adderley, Henry Saunders, and Robert Sawyer continued to do much of the normal trading they had engaged in before the war. This often meant transacting fee payments in Whiting's office for ships doing legitimate business in the Unites States. This "business as usual" with the very people responsible for the Confederate flags flying on the boats across Bay Street from his office must have caused Whiting considerable frustration.

This new way of doing business involved coordinating the shipping of goods from England with the arrival of cotton and other resources like turpentine from the South. The logistics and financial aspects of the enterprise were about to get much more complex. In early 1862, both Trenholm and Adderley made personnel adjustments that allowed them to handle the huge volume of business they saw on the horizon.

With the blockade running trade about to erupt, Henry Adderley began 1862 by announcing that his son Augustus Adderley and his son-in-law George Harris were now partners in his firm. Like Trenholm, he had an idea of what was coming, and to maximize profits he needed young, energetic help. Harris had been running his own commission merchant business since the late 1850s, and Augustus Adderley had been doing work for his father already.

Harris was already quite successful and was described later in the war as the "leading and active mind" of Henry Adderley and Company. While helping to lead that company, he also maintained his own business and warehouses. During the fall of 1861, when the action in Nassau really started to ramp up, Augustus Adderley was in New York. He was most likely working on arrangements for procuring contraband supplies from that port to Nassau for his father's business.

Augustus was a sportsman, involved with racing horses and boats in New Providence. He appears to have also had a short temper. In the spring of 1862, he was entering the Bank of Nassau with his young son when his son had some sort of altercation with the black sentry. The sentry, a soldier in the 2nd West Indies Regiment, responded by pressing his bayonet into Augustus Adderley's chest. The soldier later alleged that both Adderleys used offensive language against him. The sentry's commander, a white British officer, defended his soldier's action, but witnesses were on the side of the Adderleys. Not surprisingly, the matter was dropped.

Augustus was involved in another incident later that spring. Underwriter's agent Charles Jackson had raised a very large US flag at his business when Augustus walked up and said, "Well Jackson I see you have got your Union flag out for a victory." Jackson replied, "Yes," and Adderley responded, "I have a Secession flag which I mean to hoist next to yours in the adjoining lot." The incensed Jackson then shouted, "You may hoist whatever flag you please, but I think you have disgraced yourself quite enough already without hoisting a Secession flag."

Augustus took this as an affront against the entire firm, and he, George Harris, and his father filed a suit against Jackson in court. The firm was defended by Attorney General George Anderson, while Jackson had the services of Stephen Dillet's son Thomas. Anderson made a mockery of Jackson hoisting the flag, sarcastically pointing out the great Union "victories" at Ball's Bluff and Bull Run. Given the local environment, few were shocked when Judge Lees found for the plaintiffs and fined Jackson £5. Apparently willing to litigate anyone who offended him, Augustus would also be involved in a lawsuit against fellow Bay Street Boy Robert Sawyer later in the war.

Sam Whiting might have been willing to come in as a character witness against Charles Jackson by this time, as the two Americans had had a serious falling out. Since Jackson worked for the underwriters who had secured the position for Whiting, the hostility did not bode well for Whiting's future in Nassau. Whiting had been brought to Nassau to get a handle on the losses being suffered at the hands of the wrecking industry, but he now had his hands full with the more serious problem of his country's enemies being supplied by boats moored right outside his front door.

Whether Jackson did not like Whiting personally or felt he was doing a lousy job, he began to complain to his bosses at the Board of Underwriters. He began by doubting Whiting's patriotism, a charge that seems ludicrous based on Whiting's behavior during the last year. But according to Jackson, in December 1861 Whiting was walking down Bay Street with Lieutenant Temple of *Flambeau* when they encountered Thomas Lockwood of the blockade runner *Theodora*.

Encounters between men on opposite sides of the war would become common on Nassau streets as the war wore on, and the encounters sometimes ended in violence. This time, to Temple's amazement, Whiting greeted Lockwood warmly and introduced him to Temple as "one of the best fellows in the world." When Temple reported this strange encounter to Jackson, neither man was aware that Lockwood had gotten Whiting out of serious trouble in Charleston harbor when he ran his boat aground earlier that year. Temple ended up writing a letter to Secretary of the Navy Welles about the encounter, and Welles forwarded the letter to Secretary of State Seward.

Jackson also began to infer more serious charges against Whiting related to his inability to hold his liquor. Thomas B. Ells, an insurance colleague of Jackson who was vacationing in Nassau, wrote a letter to Seward. The letter, which was probably written at Jackson's prompting, praised Whiting as "brave, noble and generous and as good a sailor as ever trod the deck of a ship." But Ells added that because of Whiting's habitual drinking problems, he "has lost the respect of everyone and is even pointed at by the negroes."

Two incidents seem to have prompted this charge. In the first instance, Whiting became inebriated after dining with a friend in early January 1862 and got in a loud argument on the street while walking home. During that same month, Whiting gave a party on the water and became intoxicated. After the party, he got into an argument in a local store that resulted in the police being called. News of both of these events traveled around the small city very quickly.

A concerned Seward asked Whiting to give his side of these stories. In his reply written on January 19, 1862, Whiting began by telling Seward that he had been a teetotaler and volunteer in the temperance cause for six years before coming to Nassau. In fact, his efforts had resulted in him being given the nickname "Reformer of the West." He then explained that he had continued total abstinence until the night he dined with the friend. Convalescing from a fever, he said that the wine they drank had "surprising effects." While walking home through a vacant lot he encountered "Buck" Saunders, known locally as "the Wrecker King."

This was thirty-five-year-old John Henry Saunders, who lived on Harbour Island but was often in Nassau. His schooner *Galvanic* was considered the queen of the fleet of hundreds of wrecking vessels that roamed the islands. Portly and illiterate, Saunders was as shrewd a bargainer as they come and well known to the merchants and to underwriter's agents like Charles Jackson. He had been at the wrecking game for a long time.

There was an oft told story that a ship insured through Jackson had run aground near the Berry Islands and been saved by the heroic actions of Saunders. While leaving the ship in its spot, the one thousand crates on board had been carefully transferred into *Galvanic* and brought back to Nassau in perfect condition. Saunders and the captain of the wrecked ship came to Jackson's office where the captain told of Saunders's valiant effort. Jackson was known to be tough on cases that appeared fishy, but he believed the captain on this one. He stroked his beard and asked Saunders what he wanted, and Saunders asked for $4,000 ($4 per crate) so as not to cause the captain too much trouble for having wrecked the ship. Jackson happily paid. Several months later the true story came out. The ship had run slightly aground and Saunders had come to investigate. While having a private conversation with the captain, Saunders had a load of bricks on the wrecked ship transferred over to the *Galvanic*, freeing the ship. Leaving the ship there in case any of the crew were to talk, the captain returned with Saunders and the cargo to Nassau, where they happily split the payoff from Jackson.

Whiting, who described Saunders as a "well known Conch Secessionist," claims that in passing Saunders called him a "damned Northern Scoundrel." Whiting replied that "he was a Northern scoundrel good for seventy Conch Secessionists." The shouting match degenerated from there and was considered somewhat beneath the dignity of a foreign consul, especially in full view of the citizenry.

In the second incident, Whiting threw a party on the water on January 7, 1862, and drank wine for what he claimed "was the last time in his life." He described himself as having become "considerably excited." After the party, he entered the store of a local man named Robins, described by Whiting as "having no social status and married to a colored woman." Robins made some derogatory comments about the North, angering Whiting. The police were called and though there were no arrests, it was again considered unbecoming of a foreign dignitary.

After six months in Nassau, Whiting and Jackson were through. In his letters to Seward, Whiting stated that Jackson had "no social status" and was universally disliked. Considering Jackson's job in Nassau, this was probably pretty accurate. He also describes Jackson as "a miserable, suspicious fellow." He said that while Jackson professed friendship, he was going behind his back to make unfavorable reports to the Board of Underwriters. Whiting had heard from Jeremiah Tappan of the Neptune Insurance Company that people were now talking badly of him in New York. Whiting also threw a jab at Lieutenant Temple's patriotism. At a dinner with Timothy Darling, Temple had apparently remarked that bombarding Charleston would upset him as much as bombarding Boston.

Fighting for his job, Whiting also pointed out that there seemed to be a number of people with a vested interest in getting him fired. The Board of Underwriters sent a representative to Nassau in the spring to assess the situation, and the report they received indicated that the reports of Whiting's incompetence were exaggerated. Rather, it seems that some locals wanted Whiting removed and replaced with someone of more Secessionist leanings. Whiting claimed that Isaac Merritt, his predecessor, was not happy with being bumped out of the job and could be behind some of the accusations.

He also said two other men were vying for the position. One was a man named George Barney who arrived in late 1861 and opened up a grocery store in a space he rented from Bay Street Boy Henry Saunders. The other was Otis Kimball from Maine, who ran the local ice house near the public market on Bay Street with another American citizen, Augustus Arnold. The ice they sold for three cents per pound was brought by ship from the Great Lakes to Boston and then to Nassau. Customers could either buy it from the store or it could be purchased from men and boys working for the ice house who carted it door to door in wheelbarrows.

Whiting did not disagree that he was generally disliked but attributed this to his patriotism and his diligence in doing his job. "There is a large class here to whom the sight of my consular flag is a considerable annoyance. The great Secession party here, with the rich old King Conch Henry Adderley at its head ... they frowned on me from the first."

Another issue for Whiting was that he was supposed to have put up a $5,000 bond when taking the position. William Seward's son Frederick was assistant secretary of state and in charge of consular positions. Frederick Seward had asked Whiting about this bond when he first arrived and then again in February 1862. To get rid of this peripheral problem, Whiting promised Seward that he would send his wife back to New York to deal with the issue. She traveled to New York on the *Wild Pigeon*, arriving on March 9.

A group of US citizens living in Nassau finally signed a testimonial that Whiting sent to Seward attesting to his patriotism and performance of duty. This seems to have quelled the uproar for the moment. However, Whiting's friction with Charles Jackson and the animosity of the Bay Street Boys toward him would not make his life in Nassau easy.

One of the men signing the petition supporting Whiting was John Sands Howell, the lessee of the Royal Victoria Hotel. Howell was thirty-six years old and accomplished at the construction of both buildings and boats. The 1860 New York census lists his occupation as master builder. He was also well traveled, having sailed to Australia and to England several times. He traveled to Nassau for the first time on *Karnak* in the summer of 1861 in preparation for taking over the hotel. His wife Mary died in September 1860, leaving him with a five-year-old daughter and perhaps looking for a new start. After the fall of

1861 he lived at the hotel, but continued to make an annual trip back to New York each summer during the war.

It seems that he did a first-class job on both the construction and the operation of the hotel. Daily activities at the Royal Victoria were overseen by Superintendent Eugene D. Thompson. During the first season both Nassau newspapers reported lists of the visitors to the hotel and carried ads for nightly game suppers and for ice cream, a rare treat in the tropics. A piano player named John Powell entertained in the lobby. In mid-February, many of the American visitors walked from the hotel down to Parliament Square to watch the pageantry associated with the opening of the legislative session. Though he was an American, Powell fit in nicely with the opportunistic Bahamian culture. Living in and managing the hotel, he was a key source of information about the comings and goings of the blockade runners. However, he was not above making a buck. He would leave the hotel later in the war to set up a new facility that was actually beneficial to those running contraband goods.

Despite the cold shoulder he was receiving from the Upper Ten, there were Conchs who seemed pleased with Whiting's presence on the island. In mid-February he gave a lecture titled "A Voyage around the World, with a Visit to the Islands of the East Indies, Archipelago, and a Horseback Ride over the Monumental Isle of St. Helena." He gave the lecture at the Bahama Institute, a society dedicated to the advancement of literature and science that was formed in 1854 with Judge Lees as the first president.

Publisher Thomas B. Thompson of the *Bahama Herald* expressed his great pleasure at Whiting's lecture and remarked that it was as good as an earlier speech he had given at the Institute. But Whiting's troubles must have been widely known, as Thompson added,

> Most sincerely do we also regret that it is the last time we are likely to have an opportunity of hearing Mr. Whiting nor can we help expressing the satisfaction we felt in listening to the short speech given by our esteemed friend at its close. His noble vindication of himself, and the warm sentiments of loyalty expressed by him towards England, added to the deep enthusiastic feeling for the ultimate success of his own native land over her foes, cannot fail to have won the admiration and good feeling of the large audience present.

Thompson also published a poem Whiting had written for the occasion and commended "his beautiful manner of recitation."

✦ ✦ ✦

While the various dramas involving Whiting were playing out in Nassau, the saga of *Gladiator* continued. No longer under the watchful eye of Lieutenant Temple and *Flambeau*, the boat was still too slow to pierce the blockade. In the first week of January 1862, Heyliger had the boat moved to Cochrane's Anchorage, a deep-water anchorage about eight miles east of the northeastern tip of New Providence and just south of narrow Rose Island. He was compelled to do this because ships were not allowed to anchor in the harbor with a cargo that included gunpowder, and *Gladiator* had tons of it on board.

Heyliger began to transship some of *Gladiator*'s cargo to the blockade runner *Kate* on January 28. *Kate* was the *Carolina* promised by George Trenholm the previous month but with the name changed and now under British registry. Before heading out to Cochrane's Anchorage in *Kate*, Tom Lockwood took a number of the Bay Street Boys and other Southern sympathizers (most likely including Heyliger) on a pleasure cruise around Hog Island, as reported disgustedly by the Nassau correspondent of the *New York Times*.

The partial cargo transferred over to *Kate* included six thousand Enfield rifles and five hundred barrels of cannon powder, giving some idea of the immense worth to the Confederacy of the ship's contents. By this time, *Flambeau* was back in town but because Heyliger had gotten British approval for transshipping, there was little Temple could do about it. While he did not observe the transshipping (likely carried out at night), Temple did note that *Gladiator* was sitting several feet higher in the water. He complained to Attorney General George Anderson but Anderson read him a circular from London written by Secretary to the Admiralty William Romaine. The circular instructed colonial officials not to interfere with the transshipment of any merchandise, even arms and ammunition.

Seeing there was little he could do, Temple and *Flambeau* left Nassau once again. In a letter to Benjamin, Heyliger gloated a bit about the situation: "You may readily imagine how intensely disgusted the Yankees are at this partiality, as they call it. It is called another flagrant violation of neutral rights." Unlike Whiting, Heyliger was fitting right in with the Bay Street Boys. As he told Benjamin, "My relations with the authorities here are of the most friendly character. I receive many marked attentions, which I value as going to show the increased cordiality of feeling toward the Confederate Government."

Heyliger filled out false bills of lading that indicated *Kate* was headed to Saint John. Instead she headed for the rather obscure location of Mosquito Inlet near New Smyrna, Florida. It was less than forty-eight hours from Nassau and a ship headed there could ride the Gulf Stream up and avoid any US ships headed south. The cargo was landed safely on January 31 and most of the munitions made their way to the armies in Virginia.

Mosquito Inlet had been suggested earlier in the month by John Maffitt. Maffitt was a lieutenant in the Confederate navy, but had been working as an aide to Robert E. Lee in strengthening the defenses from eastern Florida up through South Carolina. Before the war, Maffitt spent fifteen years on the US Coast Survey and probably knew the southeastern coast of the Confederacy better than anyone alive. His work in 1854 surveying what later became one of the paths used by blockade runners into Charleston led to it being named Maffitt's Channel.

In addition to his official role, he had also been advising John Fraser and Company in regards to their blockade-running endeavors. The forty-three-year-old Maffitt was the consummate seaman, having been born at sea and entering the US Navy at the age of thirteen. When the war started he resigned his commission and joined the Confederate navy. He was not only a widely respected and extremely courageous sailor, he enjoyed life and was a bit of a prankster. One former shipmate described him as "the warmest-hearted and most generous friend and the most genial companion I ever knew. He was always the life of his mess, full of fun and tender sympathy for all around him. He was a born sailor and a splendid officer, and I have never known one more beloved."

On January 2, 1862, as Trenholm communicated with Judah Benjamin about the Mosquito Inlet plan, he also appears to have suggested that Maffitt be shifted away from working with Lee to duties related to blockade running. On January 7, Maffitt was assigned to take command of *Cecile* and to use his experience with the coasts to run supplies from Nassau to Charleston and Wilmington. On January 27, Judah Benjamin asked Maffitt to head to Nassau in *Cecile* and talk to Heyliger to determine what was happening with *Gladiator* transshipment plan. If there were any problems transshipping her cargo, Maffitt was to take control of *Gladiator* and find a way to bring her to a Confederate port.

By mid-February, the *Kate* was back for more of *Gladiator*'s cargo. In addition, she brought another man sent to the rescue by George Trenholm. John Baptiste Lafitte, 39, was employed as an agent for John Fraser and Company and had a long history as a commission merchant. He became a key partner for Heyliger in facilitating the flow of material through Nassau. Lafitte proved to be an excellent choice as an important link in helping produce the twenty million dollars made by the Trenholm firms over the next three years.

Lafitte was born in Augusta, Georgia, and his family moved to Charleston when he was boy. He was sent to Spring Hill College in Mobile, Alabama, graduating at age sixteen and returning to Charleston to begin a career in business. He and his older brother Edward (who had raised the palmetto flag to a cheering Charleston crowd in December 1860) operated as commission merchants and became prominent enough to be elected to corporate boards and public office. While his brother was a slave owner and engaged in the slave trade, John Lafitte claimed after the war to have never been involved in the trade and to have opposed it. Still, both men were ardent supporters of secession, and John Lafitte might have had a somewhat distorted view of race relations in the South. During the war he wrote to Charles Prioleau that "there is not a particle of animosity between the two races. We have simply been asking them to advance their own intended purpose."

John Lafitte was not only a good businessman but a widely admired person. One observer speaking of him said, "He had an intellect of no small caliber. He loved truth and was always able to declare it. He was simple in greatness, and great in his simplicity." After the fall of Fort Sumter, John Lafitte did not wait long to begin helping the Confederacy acquire supplies from overseas. In early August 1861, he traveled with veteran Charleston Captain Daniel B. Vincent to Saint John to deal with the cargo of *Alliance*. The ship sailed from Liverpool in early May but was ordered off from Charleston by the fledgling blockading squadron there. She headed to Canada with a partial cargo of railroad iron and coal. Lafitte and Vincent traveled to Saint John by way of Boston and their conversation on the steamer from Boston was overheard by an informant from the US Marshal's office. Vincent and Lafitte's names eventually made it all the way up to Secretary of State William Seward. Arriving in Saint John, Lafitte and Vincent began having empty space on the vessel (which was now sporting a Confederate flag) filled with pig and sheet iron, percussion caps and other war contraband. Vincent, who was very familiar with the Carolina coast, must have served as pilot to bring the ship safely into Charleston.

By early September, Lafitte was selling the materials off *Alliance* to the Confederate War Department. Vincent continued to run the blockade until he was captured off Charleston in *Emilie* in June 1862. In addition to running their own company, the Lafittes were also partners in Bowie, Lafitte and Company with merchant John Andrew Bowie. This company had a dock right next to that of John Fraser and Company at the base of Cumberland Street along the Charleston wharf. The Lafitte brothers each had large houses on Wentworth Street, not far from George Trenholm's mansion on Rutledge Avenue, and had been doing business with John Fraser and Company before the war. At some point in early 1862 Lafitte apparently traveled to England to discuss logistics with Charles Prioleau before heading to Nassau.

Henry Adderley would be a fruitful partner for Trenholm, but since Adderley always put his own business interests first it became imperative for Trenholm to have an experienced representative in the location where the deals were taking place. Given their pre-war relationship and Lafitte's reputation, it is not surprising that Trenholm recruited him to be his agent in Nassau.

Lafitte and Heyliger became friends and close allies in the ensuing chaotic years. They might have made an unlikely pair as Lafitte seems to have been warm and outgoing while Heyliger was described as brusque, businesslike, and overworked. They often handled each other's business when necessary, and because of the close linkage between Trenholm's firm and the Confederacy, observers often assumed Lafitte was an official Confederate agent. And in a way he was. Lafitte and Heyliger worked on a regular basis with Henry Adderley and Company, and Lafitte also kept a regular correspondence with Charles Prioleau in Liverpool and Theodore Wagner in Charleston.

Lafitte arrived in Nassau with his wife Euphrosine and her seventeen-year-old niece Mary Virginia Fourgeaud. The Lafittes had two children, fifteen-year-old James and fourteen-year-old Marie, both of whom stayed in Charleston. Before the war was over James enlisted with the 27th Battalion of the Georgia Infantry.

Virginia (as she was called by family) made quite an impression on the people of Nassau and especially on young Confederates passing through. She was noted for her singing, and the *Bahama Herald* reviewed a concert she gave at the Royal Victoria: "'See 'tis the hour' was sung by Miss Fourgeaud, whose bird-like notes elicited the most intense admiration only to be deeply more felt when she warbled forth her second song 'Twas within a mile of Edinburgh Town' when the applause could only be appeased by her reappearance."

At least a couple of Confederates left a record of their enchantment with Virginia Fourgeaud. Richard S. Floyd was a nineteen-year-old officer on CSS *Florida*. From Tennessee, he had gone to Annapolis but resigned from the US Navy at the beginning of the war. As we shall see, during the late spring and early summer of 1862 *Florida* had its origins in Nassau and Floyd spent time there with the other officers of the ship. With time on his hands, Floyd made a series of sketches of Nassau life and people and gave them to Virginia. She also came into possession of a later sketch he made in 1864 of himself at sea on board *Florida*.

Another possibly smitten suitor was Douglas French Forrest, a twenty-five-year-old Virginian who started out in the Confederate army but later transferred to the navy. He arrived in Nassau in late May 1863 aboard another ship that will be part of our story, *Margaret and Jessie*. In Nassau he was introduced to the Lafittes and to Virginia by Alfred Trenholm, George Trenholm's son. Alfred had been in the army but was discharged due to severe pneumonia and had come in on *Margaret and Jessie* with Forrest. His father was sending him to England by way of Nassau to convalesce at the Liverpool home of Charles Prioleau. George Trenholm told Prioleau, "He was always delicate though not sickly and hardly fit for military service. He is the best boy in the world and will give you no trouble." Forrest accompanied Alfred Trenholm to England on the same steamer *Trent*, from which Mason and Slidell had been pulled by Charles Wilkes. From there Forrest continued his career in the Confederate navy on board CSS *Rappahannock*.

During his month in Nassau, Forrest spent a good bit of time with the Lafittes. He seemed to enjoy talking with the couple and their frequent guests. Pierre Soulé, a prominent New Orleans politician and a friend of Heyliger, was in town and Forrest bested him in a game of chess. That board game was especially popular with New Orleans natives as young Paul Morphy of that city had recently beaten all the best players in Europe and been proclaimed world champion.

Most of all, Forrest seemed to enjoy spending time with Virginia. Along with seeing the tropical sights, they took carriage rides, played card and board games, and had pleasant conversations. In his journal he spoke fondly of the young lady, who he remarked "looked very pretty." He also confirmed Whiting's assessment of the city's sympathies: "Astonishing how thoroughly Southern public sentiment is here. If there is entertained any feeling of hostility it is perfectly contained. The Yankees you see here are either boisterous Southern sympathizers or perfectly silent enemies. Men are sometimes pointed out to us as spies, correspondents, & c. They are villainous specimens & have the hang dog look, furtive, stealthy, sneaking."

Virginia ended up marrying another young man she met in Charleston after the war. Frank Dawson was born Austin Reeks in England, but when his father said he would ruin the family name with his intent to travel to America and join the Confederate cause, he changed his name. He went on board *Nashville*, which had run out of Charleston in October 1861 and burned an American merchant ship on her way to England. The ship, with Dawson on board, made its way to Beaufort, North Carolina, in February 1862, taking two more prizes on the way. Once in the Confederacy, he took the opposite path of Douglas Forrest by leaving the Confederate navy for the army. He fought at a number of important battles including Gettysburg and ended up on General James Longstreet's staff. He settled in Charleston after the war, marrying Virginia and becoming a well-known newspaper editor. He described her as "very handsome and accomplished, a charming singer, a polished woman, and a devoted and affectionate child."

The Lafittes took up residence in the Royal Victoria while Heyliger rented a house from Adderley on Bay Street. Adderley set Lafitte up in an office on Bay Street across from George Harris's residence. He and Euphrosine were very socially active, hosting parties and being warmly received by the Upper Ten. They hosted numerous old friends from the South who traveled to Nassau on their way to Europe or elsewhere.

With so many key players (including Charles Jackson) living there permanently and various blockade runners living there temporarily, the Royal Victoria became a lively place indeed. Virginia seems to have acclimated quite well to her new surroundings. In addition to young soldiers like Forrest and Floyd, she also befriended other teenagers traveling with their parents. One example was Ruby Senac, whose father Felix was taking his family to Europe where he became a Confederate purchasing agent. Ruby, just as attractive as Virginia, later married Henry Hotze, the noted Confederate propagandist in Europe and publisher of the *Index*.

Another companion was Charles Passailaigue, former privateer of the *Savannah*. Passailaigue was Virginia's cousin and Euphrosine's nephew, and after his release from New York he ended up as a clerk for Henry Adderley and Company, likely through the recommendation of John Lafitte. He lived with the Adderleys. Florence Emily Perpall, Adderley's niece and the same age as Virginia, was probably another friend. Florence and Charles Passailaigue married late in the war.

✦ ✦ ✦

It turned out that Lafitte's business skills were needed as soon as he stepped off *Kate*. The cargo of *Gladiator* had been consigned to John Fraser and Company, and now Captain Bird was having second thoughts about how he was making out financially in the current scheme. His original contract called for him to get a bonus of £1,050 for running the blockade. Now that the cargo was being transshipped, he said he wanted the bonus anyway or he would refuse to let any more cargo be removed. In addition he wanted the Confederacy to buy *Gladiator*. How he could demand this was unclear since the boat was owned by Thomas Stock in England. Bird said that if his demands were not met, he would run the blockade and sink the vessel if chased, thereby still earning the bonus.

Lafitte joined Heyliger in trying to talk reason into Bird, with Lafitte emphasizing how difficult the approach to Charleston was. But Bird would not budge, and finally Lafitte and Heyliger agreed to pay his demand. This cargo was too valuable to let anything happen to it. A sum of £15,000 eventually made its way from Lafitte to Stock, later to be reimbursed to John Fraser and Company by the Confederate Treasury Department.

The next day *Kate* went up to Cochrane's Anchorage to get the rest of the cargo, and to Heyliger's dismay Bird now had another demand. As Heyliger informed Benjamin, "To say that I was annoyed beyond measure would be a feeble expression of my sensations." Bird now stated that he wanted the whole transaction guaranteed by Henry Adderley and Company, as he apparently did not trust the solvency of any Confederate operation. This guarantee would of course require a commission to be paid to Adderley's firm. In his attempt to milk every transaction dry, one of the Adderleys or George Harris had almost certainly given Bird this idea during the previous twenty-four hours. Lafitte ponied up another £2,405 for this "service."

Heyliger and Lafitte had no time to negotiate, and after consultation they agreed to concede to Bird's demand. *Karnak* would be reaching New York that day, bringing news of *Kate*'s arrival in Nassau, and perhaps increasing the pressure on finding her as she tried to get through the blockade. To prevent any additional demands, they wrote out an agreement for Bird to sign. In the document they pointed out that Bird had no right to sell the boat, but that under the conditions, they were agreeing anyway. Half of *Gladiator*'s remaining critical cargo was transshipped to *Kate*, and she left on February 23, arriving safely shortly afterwards. Before departing, the *New York Times* correspondent had the chance to ask Tom Lockwood what cargo he had carried over on *Kate*'s previous trip, and Lockwood replied sarcastically, "Food for the North," meaning arms and ammunition.

In addition to the commission for guaranteeing Confederate payments, Henry Adderley and Company also requested a 2.5 percent commission for transshipping *Gladiator*'s contents. During this same time period, the two thousand bales of cotton Adderley had accumulated in Nassau in the first two months of the year were being transshipped in Nassau harbor onto *Eliza Bonsall*, leaving for Liverpool on February 27. Adderley requested 2.5 percent on this as well. Heyliger opined to Benjamin that this was an "exorbitant demand" but that John Fraser was willing to pay it "in consideration of retaining the interest of the most influential mercantile establishment in Nassau. Undoubtedly Adderley & Co. have lost northern business in consequence of their southern sympathies, and they are certainly doing their best to make up for it by taking a good slice from us."

Throughout the war, Adderley and Company added on fees wherever possible as the cotton came through. In addition to the standard 2.5 percent, charges for labor, storage, drayage (moving the cotton on the wharf), wharfage (use of the wharf), supplies like rope and twine, and hiring night watchmen would move the normal cut on each shipment closer to 4 percent.

Despite the sometimes-contentious business negotiations, Heyliger, Lafitte, and Adderley would form a formidable team in support of the Confederate war effort. In addition to finding offices for both men and a residence for Heyliger, Adderley helped make them a part of the Upper Ten. Sam Whiting took note of Lafitte's arrival, informing Seward in late April that "Mr. Lafitte of Charleston, owner of the steamer *Cecile*, has taken up his quarters here for the summer with his family. Both he and a Mr. Heyliger of New Orleans are agents of the Rebel states and have for some time been engaged in transshipping." While Whiting thought Lafitte was there on temporary business, he was there for the long haul.

On February 23, the same day *Kate* left Nassau for New Smyrna, Maffitt arrived in the *Cecile*. His charge to command *Gladiator* was no longer needed, but Heyliger wrote to Benjamin that he was thoroughly impressed with Maffitt and that he was "in every way competent, resolute and trustworthy." After a brief stay at the Royal Victoria, Maffitt supervised the transshipment of the remaining *Gladiator* cargo into *Cecile* and departed, arriving in New Smyrna on March 2 and just in time. By the middle of March, Union forces captured Jacksonville and the Confederates were forced to evacuate New Smyrna.

Finally empty of her precious cargo and now owned by John Fraser and Company, *Gladiator* finally sailed back to Liverpool on May 2. Not fully recognizing yet the importance of Nassau to the cause, Judah Benjamin wrote Heyliger in March praising him for his work on *Gladiator* and then offering to send him home. Another boat, *Southwick*, would be arriving from Liverpool and Benjamin told Heyliger that after dealing with that cargo that his service in Nassau would no longer be needed. He added that "I hope to be able to take advantage of your kind offers of service in some other sphere." The pace of events quickly showed both men that Heyliger needed to stay right where he was.

Trenholm's push to get Maffitt and his expertise in charge of blockade running seems to have had effect. On April 11, 1862, Maffitt received a letter from the War Department instructing him to go to Nassau in the ship *Nassau* (which was the new name for *Theodora*) and to "take the entire control of all vessels loaded with arms and munitions of war for the Confederate States which you may meet in your intended trip, and to bring them into such ports as you may select with their cargoes, or to transship such cargoes in other vessels."

He was instructed to confer in Nassau with Heyliger, so the arrangement might have been conceived as Maffitt coordinating the shipping aspects of the trade while Heyliger handled the financials. Or perhaps Maffitt would deal only with armaments while Heyliger would handle food, clothing, and other items. Whatever this rather vague order meant was soon be a moot point, as Maffitt would be redirected to a completely different assignment, and Heyliger would remain in Nassau coordinating all aspects of Confederate shipping.

✦ ✦ ✦

As winter turned into spring in 1862, Nassau began to change. A trickle of boats bringing over cotton from Charleston turned into a torrent as men began to understand the opportunity now available to them. It had taken almost three months for Henry Adderley to accumulate the two thousand bales he sent to Liverpool on *Elisa Bonsall*. By April 1862 he was taking in two or three ships per week and others like Sawyer and Menendez and Saunders and Son were also getting into the game in a significant way. Most of the cotton was coming from Charleston but some continued to get out from Savannah and other smaller ports like Fernandina, Florida and Georgetown, South Carolina.

In early May, Adderley took in his first shipment of cotton and tobacco from Wilmington, North Carolina. The ships were also becoming more efficient. *Cecile*, under Maffitt's command, made it to Nassau from Charleston on March 7 after a trip of only forty hours. Cotton would soon fill all the warehouses in the city and would crowd the docks and even the homes. To one stunned visitor, Heyliger commented that even all this cotton could not supply 5 percent of British demand.

In the winter of 1861–1862, Thomas Thompson of the *Bahama Herald* often used the arrival of entertainers to the island to point out how boring life was in Nassau. A company of glass blowers arrived in February to "relieve the dull monotony of our island." A week later Thompson commended local citizens for creating a regatta club, "something to relieve the dull monotony of the Island."

In an amusing use of current events, in the club's first race the boats ran out of the harbor to the east toward Cochrane's Anchorage and used *Gladiator* as the turn-around point. A performance at the theatre offered "pleasant relief to the monotonous existence we who reside in this little sea girt, are, in general, obligated to endure." In another month or so, even Thompson would have to admit that Nassau was anything but boring.

In mid-March Governor Bayley finally returned from the extended leave that began in June 1861. In his absence he had not only missed the visit of Prince Alfred but the eruption of the Great Carnival. As *Karnak* approached Nassau harbor with Bayley aboard, the weather was too severe to disembark her passengers. In order to get the governor home, *Karnak* traveled to the southwest bay near the village of Adelaide, where the water was calmer. A carriage met him there and brought him back to the city.

The African residents of the primitive area were likely stunned to see the governor in their midst. Bayley was most likely equally uncomfortable being among these subjects as he was widely seen as a racist and did not care much for them. In his 1862 annual report he stated that his effort to "inculcate habits of industry, thrift, decency and submissiveness, has been I regret to say, wholly unavailing." He told the home government that he would rid the island of them if he could. He did not care much for the black people born on the island either, commenting that "the negro Creole is entirely destitute of that persistent will and energy, physical no less than mental, by which alone he could raise himself in the social scale."

Kate, in once again from Charleston, traveled down to meet *Karnak* and take off the passengers while *Karnak* continued on to Havana. Quite a bit of liquid refreshment was loaded onto the *Kate* to make the voyage a bit more pleasant. Along with the crew, a number of Nassau notables including John Maffitt and Sam Whiting joined on board. Whiting was intent on getting to *Karnak* to pick up any important dispatches from Washington that might be in the mail.

On the ride back from *Karnak*, Whiting fell asleep, due to overconsumption of alcohol according to some, and his dispatches were stolen. When he awoke a huge argument ensued in which he accused Maffitt of stealing them while the crowd mainly looked on in amusement. According to one biased observer, Whiting was disliked by everyone in Nassau and "had winning ways to make everybody hate him." The papers were returned to his office the next morning, certainly after having been read by Maffitt, Adderley, and anyone else who cared to take a look.

But the fun was not over. When Whiting came downstairs from his apartment above the consulate for breakfast, he saw that someone (everyone agreed it was Maffitt) had replaced the US flag in front of the consulate with the Confederate flag. To make matters worse, the perpetrator had greased the pole so that the flag could not be removed. According to an observer Whiting "performed a war dance around that pole which was one of the most interesting spectacles ever witnessed by the Confederates in Nassau." When a US cruiser appeared off the harbor the next morning, Whiting got into his small boat outside the consulate to make his way out for discussions, but found that he was stuck by his rear end to his boat. Carolina tar had been applied overnight to his seat.

✦ ✦ ✦

On April 14, 1862, *Karnak* rammed the sand bar coming into the harbor from Havana. Within an hour, she had ten feet of water in her hold. Smaller boats streamed out and took off the sixty or so passengers, and then the wreckers came to salvage what they could of the cargo. Within three days Henry Adderley was selling cigars and sugar from the wreck at John Thomson's warehouse. A bit of controversy ensued over what caused the wreck. Most blamed the pilot, J. M. Cooke, though he wrote a letter in the *Bahama Herald* defending himself. In response many Americans who had sailed with Captain Frederick Le Mesurier on *Karnak* signed a testimonial attesting to his skills and claiming that the captain had warned the pilot that they were off course. A similar testimonial was drawn up and signed by many of the passengers, including John Lafitte, who had been on the boat traveling from Havana to Nassau when it wrecked. Sam Whiting wrote to Seward that rumors abounded that Cooke had been paid to wreck *Karnak* in order to prevent news from reaching New York about the huge number of blockade runners now entering Nassau.

In a little over three years *Karnak* had made the run from New York to Nassau to Havana and back thirty-six times and carried almost 1,500 people from Nassau to New York. Everyone from Governor Bayley to Henry Adderley had taken advantage of the convenience of the ship for traveling to New York and from there to England.

She performed her service without incident except perhaps for a tragic event on March 11, 1860, when a black crew member of a boat towing *Karnak* out of Nassau harbor fell from his boat. *Karnak* stopped and an oar was thrown overboard for him to hang onto, but as he cried, "For God's sake save me!" a large shark carried him underwater. Fairly large sharks were a common sight in the harbor. The shark was killed a few days later and in his stomach was found the man's right hand, a goat's head with nine-inch horns, and the head of a sea turtle. The hand was given to the poor man's family.

The Cunard line played a key role in building the connections necessary to make the Great Carnival of Nassau operate. In addition to transporting people, once the war started the boat also began carrying contraband. The *New York Times* reported that the February 1862 trip brought $75,000 worth of material to Henry Adderley, including a number of twenty-four-pound cannons. The passengers stranded from the wreck made their way back to New York over the next couple of weeks on cargo steamers like *Vigilant* and *Evelina*.

Scrambling to replace *Karnak*, the Cunard line sent over a ship from England called *British Queen* that displaced only 772 tons compared to 1,116 tons for *Karnak*. In a year, *British Queen* would be replaced by a newly built ship of comparable size to *Karnak*, called *Corsica* (1,134 tons). It appears that both of these ships were also used by Adderley and others to procure contraband from New York. *British Queen* would make her first trip to Nassau from New York in early June 1862, a trip that would be accompanied by some major complications. But the most serious uproar in Nassau in the summer of 1862 would involve a new boat that appeared in the harbor from England in late April.

7

The Lions of the Royal Victoria

After bringing *Fingal* safely into Savannah back in fall, James Bulloch met with Stephen Mallory in Richmond before returning by rail to Savannah on November 23. *Fingal* was to be filled with cotton by John Fraser and Company, and he and John Low were charged with bringing the cargo back to Liverpool. Bulloch was also officially charged by Mallory with taking command of either of the commerce raiders *Florida* or *Alabama* once back in England. Because the trains were occupied moving troops, it took another month before *Fingal* was loaded with cotton.

Unfortunately for Bulloch, this delay was disastrous as Union warships were now accumulating in preparation for assaulting Fort Pulaski, which sat at the mouth of the Savannah River. After two unsuccessful attempts to break through, in mid-January Bulloch decided he had best get back to England even without the cotton. As it turned out *Fingal* never could escape Savannah and was later cut to the decks and turned into the ironclad CSS *Atlanta*. Because of his lengthy unintended stay in Savannah, Bulloch and Mallory also decided that he should plan on taking command of *Alabama* since *Florida* might be ready for sea even before he returned.

After arriving in Savannah on *Fingal* on November 12, John Low received some surprising news. His wife Eliza and his uncle Andrew Low and aunt Mary had been arrested as disloyal persons on their return to Savannah from Liverpool. They had been detained while en route from Montreal to Savannah in the first week of November. Eliza, who was pregnant, was taken to Greenhow Prison in Washington, DC, while Andrew and his wife ended up in Fort Warren in Boston. Eliza was released on November 13, and an ecstatic Low found her in Richmond when he and Bulloch arrived there.

Low brought Eliza back to Savannah, but Andrew Low and his wife would stay behind bars quite a bit longer. Within a few days Union authorities realized that although Andrew Low had gone abroad earlier that year, it was actually his nephew John Low who was involved with *Fingal*. But their suspicions did not stop there. Seth Hawley, a special agent for the State Department, interrogated Andrew Low and determined that he was clearly dangerous. "The man who can raise the money to carry on a war is of more consequence than he who commands armies. I consider Andrew Low the most important man in Fort Warren—to keep—unless it be Commissioner John Slidell!" Andrew Low had powerful Northern friends, including prominent New York lawyer William Evarts, and he and his wife were finally released in March 1862. Seth Hawley would take his forceful manner and anti-Southern fervor to Nassau as US consul in 1863.

John Fraser and Company offered Bulloch and Low passage to Liverpool on their ship *Annie Childs*. They left Wilmington on February 5 and arrived in Liverpool on March 10 to find *Oreto* (soon to be *Florida*) ready to go. The ship was given the working name *Oreto* (for an Italian river valley) in the Liverpool shipyard to divert attention from its ultimate destination. Progress on the ship had been closely watched in Liverpool by US Consul Thomas Dudley. Dudley let both the British and his own government know that a "formidable and dangerous" ship was being built and was headed for the Confederacy.

The boat was supposedly meant for buyers in Palermo, Sicily, but the Italian consul knew nothing about it, and Dudley did not buy it for a minute. The ship was almost two hundred feet long, with twin stacks and clearly designed for war. The hull was pierced to hold four large guns, and the interior had spaces identical to a British man-of-war. However, the ship was at this point just a shell waiting to be outfitted. As such, the British claimed she had broken no laws.

Bulloch expected to find Captain Robert B. Pegram of *Nashville* in Liverpool and was prepared to give him command of *Oreto*. But *Nashville* (with Virginia Fourgeaud's future husband Frank Dawson aboard) had left days earlier. Because of all the Union spies swarming the Liverpool docks and pressure being raised by US diplomatic officials it was important that the *Oreto* get to sea quickly.

Knowing that John Maffitt was now running the blockade back and forth to Nassau, Bulloch ordered John Low to take the ship to Nassau and turn it over to Maffitt. Low, the Englishman, had been appointed on Bulloch's recommendation as master in the Confederate navy. To maintain appearances of neutrality, the man who actually took the boat to Nassau was a citizen of Scotland, James Allen Duguid. Bulloch told Low that if he did not find Maffitt in Nassau, he should contact Lewis Heyliger through the offices of Henry Adderley and Company to determine what to do.

Oreto cleared for Palermo and left Liverpool on March 23 with fifty-two men under Captain Duguid and one "civilian" passenger, John Low. When the ship left England it held a small cargo of liquor and food items that had been consigned to Adderley. The ship could not have held a normal merchant load as the typical cargo space was now configured for magazines intended to hold gunpowder and shells. All her weapons and ammunition had been packed on another ship, *Bahama*, which also left Liverpool for Nassau in mid-March. *Oreto* arrived in Nassau harbor on April 28.

Low took a room in the Royal Victoria, and after determining that Maffitt was not in Nassau he met with Heyliger, who let him know that Maffitt would be arriving from Wilmington within a week on the blockade runner *Nassau* (formerly *Theodora*). He also told Low that Whiting and various Union spies in town were very interested in *Oreto* and that they should move it to Cochrane's Anchorage to make it less conspicuous. By this time, everyone from Governor Bayley to the dock workers knew the purpose for which *Oreto* was intended. But even in this strong pro-Confederate climate, equipping the ship in the harbor below Government House was likely to create an international incident.

Heyliger accompanied Duguid as they moved the ship out to Cochrane's on April 30. Whiting was already clamoring for the Bahamian government to search the ship so Heyliger felt it was imperative that they get the boat out to sea with Maffitt as soon as possible. But in addition to prying eyes, the Confederates faced another problem: lack of coal for the huge number of ships now crowding the harbor. *Economist*, *Cecile*, and *Nashville* had all faced delays due to lack of the precious fuel. Without a fresh supply of coal, *Oreto* was not going anywhere.

By late spring 1862, the number of boats entering and leaving Nassau was growing each week. When Lord Russell attempted to downplay the British role in this activity by asserting in Parliament that only nineteen boats had broken the blockade since the beginning of the war, Heyliger took the time to write a letter to the *Nassau Guardian* showing how low this estimate was.

With an accompanying table compiled from official customs reports, Heyliger stated that "it is not with the view of expatiating on the effectiveness of the [blockade] that we have compiled this table, but to show our merchants the importance of the trade that has recently grown up, and which, if properly fostered, may attain much wider proportions." He also pointed out that "it is a notable circumstance that the arrivals from Southern states are much more numerous than those from the North with which our intercourse is free and unrestrained." Heyliger's table showed that after four blockade-runner arrivals in the summer of 1861, the pace picked up to about one ship per week in the last part of 1861: four in September, five in October, six in November, and four more in December. This was probably an underestimate since in the first year or two of the war, small sloops continued to slip into Southern ports and come back with a few bales of cotton.

Things exploded when Trenholm started to export cotton. After four ships arrived in the rough weather of January 1862, seven ships came in February and fourteen in March. By the time Heyliger made his table on April 10, 1862, nine ships had already arrived from the Confederacy that month, almost one per day. In these last three months, almost every ship brought cotton. Heyliger sent a copy of the article to Secretary of War George Randolph (who replaced Benjamin in March 1862 when Benjamin became secretary of state). In the accompanying letter, Heyliger claimed that his article created quite a sensation in Nassau since some people seemed oblivious to the huge amount of activity that had arisen in the last few months.

Heyliger mentioned the scarcity of coal to Benjamin in April and in early May he noted that with half a dozen blockade runners in the harbor, he did not have any coal for them. *Gladiator*, in fact, had only enough to get to Bermuda, where she refueled before heading to Liverpool. With an eye toward future profits, Henry Adderley and Company began accumulating coal, receiving two large shipments of coal from Havana and one from Saint John by early July. Henry and Pembroke Saunders began building their own gigantic pile of coal on Hog Island with a shipment from Havana and one from Cardiff, Wales.

In early May, these shipments were still a ways off, so Lafitte asked Heyliger to go to Bermuda and see if he could get some coal moved to Nassau. Without fuel for his ships, Lafitte was watching potential earnings dissipate. Heyliger left for Bermuda on May 3 with the intention of staying a couple of weeks. The day before he left, he wrote to Randolph informing him that "Mr. Lafitte will direct everything in my absence." Having Trenholm's employee cover the duties of the government agent clearly reveals how closely the private business and the Confederate government were connected.

Heyliger had a second reason to go to Bermuda. *Herald*, a Trenholm ship, had arrived in St. Georges, Bermuda, from Madeira on March 24. At this point in the war, Confederate operations in Bermuda were being handled by commission merchant John Bourne (for a fee, naturally). Bourne reported that *Herald*'s captain had decided that the ship would not run into Charleston as planned. To make matters worse, the captain consulted with US consul Charles Allen about his situation. Allen, of course, recommended that *Herald* head back to England. The captain also consulted with the governor and attorney general, both of whom informed Bourne there was nothing they could do to remove the captain from the ship.

After arriving and assessing the situation, Heyliger began to work on a way to get *Herald* out of Bermuda and into Nassau. To assist him, James A. K. Wilson, an agent for Fraser, Trenholm and Co. arrived from England. In negotiations that took over a month, Heyliger and Wilson eventually came up with a payment to the captain for which he would agree to relinquish the ship. Once that was done, they smoothed over things with the governor to allow the ship to proceed. Eventually *Herald* headed for Nassau on June 13. From there she would join the ships making regular runs to Charleston.

Heyliger made it back to Nassau a short while later on *Leopard*, arriving in Nassau on June 21. Having intended a short trip, Heyliger was in Bermuda for almost two months. While dealing with *Herald*, he had also managed to work with Bourne to get coal, most of which was coming to Bermuda from Cardiff. Bourne's new price was £42 per ton verses the old price of £30 per ton. The war was only a year old and men like Bourne, Adderley, and Trenholm were already accumulating riches.

John Maffitt arrived in Nassau on May 4, the day after Heyliger left for Bermuda. He brought along with him his twenty-year-old daughter Florie, who likely befriended Virginia Fourgeaud and seems to have had much of her father's spirit. Like Virginia, she was attractive and such a good singer that she also serenaded at the Royal Victoria during her brief stay.

After it was clear that her father would soon have duties carrying him far from the Confederacy, she took passage on *Nassau* back to Wilmington. The boat was captured on May 28, and a newspaper reported Florie's response:

> Captain Maffitt of the Confederate States Navy has a daughter who is a "chip off the old block." Her father, it is said, is celebrated for his fighting qualities, and the daughter is worthy of her parentage. She was on board the *Nassau* when captured by a Yankee ship. She sat on the open deck of the *Nassau* during our firing at her to make her bring to, until the captain warned her of the danger and advised her to go to her cabin. She would watch our guns, and as she saw the flames and smoke jut out would manifest just enough excitement to give the appearance of being well entertained. And she continued to enjoy the amusement through the window of her cabin when she went below. It must be borne in mind that the *Nassau* had tons of powder on board, to realize the awful danger of the situation. A single shell exploding in that cargo would have blown her into a thousand atoms. Her family were told by some who were on board the *Nassau* at the time that Florie urged the captain not to surrender, and when he reminded her of the danger from the cargo of powder and his duty to her father, she exclaimed, with tears in her eyes, that her father would prefer her being blown up rather than that the steamer be captured.

John Low came to Maffitt's room at the Royal Victoria the night Maffitt arrived and handed him a letter from James Bulloch offering him command of *Oreto*.

Without coal there was nothing Maffitt could do for now but he informed the ship's consignees, Adderley and Company, that he would be taking command of the "lone Confederate waif upon the waters."

By this time, Whiting had reported to Seward that *Oreto* had steamed out to Cochrane's Anchorage (or "the rebel rendezvous" as Whiting called it) and that numerous patriotic citizens had reported to him that she was being fitted out as a privateer to prey on Northern commerce. At this same time, Whiting sent a letter to Governor Bayley requesting he do something about these infractions but quickly received a reply from Charles Nesbitt that in Attorney General Anderson's opinion there was not enough evidence for them to do anything.

Whiting's accusations about *Oreto* did concern Bayley enough to request an investigation and on May 26 Receiver-General Fletcher Whitley reported to Nesbitt that he believed the consignees of the ship (i.e. Adderley and Company) had the intention of using *Oreto* to ship large quantities of arms and ammunition. While not exactly correct, this information prompted Commander H. F. McKillop of HMS *Bulldog* to send some men to Cochrane's Anchorage to investigate. McKillop suggested that *Oreto* be ordered back into Nassau harbor to prevent any misunderstandings. Governor Bayley inquired of Attorney General George Anderson whether it was legal to require *Oreto* to come to the harbor and Anderson answered that it was not.

In early June, Henry Adderley had accumulated some coal and asked Fletcher Whitley for permission to load *Oreto* for a trip to Saint John. Whitley took this request to Bayley who then took it to the Executive Council. The council decided that the boat could be loaded but only under the supervision of a British vessel of war. This was a complication that Adderley and the Confederates had not counted on but they now had a bigger problem.

The crew of *Oreto*, all British, was threatening to desert the ship. They had signed up for a commercial trip to Palermo and now found themselves in Nassau with no certain destination and very likely to be serving on a warship. George Harris offered them a bonus and free passage back to England if they would stay with the ship but most declined. Duguid had the men charged with breaking their contracts and thrown in jail. One of the crew, Edward Jones, took the time to write a letter to Whiting from jail describing the ship in detail and calling her a "perfect man-of-war." John Maffitt described Jones as "an excellent rascal, a low, dirty, Liverpool dock-rat."

Scrambling to pull a new crew together, Henry Adderley called on his brother-in-law Charles Perpall for assistance. This was likely done as a diversion to keep the spotlight off Henry Adderley and Company. Idle mariners were already accumulating in Nassau and as one observer stated, Perpall could pick from "the motley crew of sailors that floated about town ready for any kind of work"

Perpall began personally recruiting men at his store to join the crew and he told them the truth about the ship: it was headed to Mobile to become a privateer.

Adderley and Company advanced the men money to join the crew, but it was still tough to find too many takers. Maffitt wrote Stephen Mallory that seamen, firemen, and engineers were hard to come by, perhaps because they had all been scooped up for more lucrative blockade-running work. He added, "I mention these circumstances with the hope that the department will perfectly comprehend the trying position I have all along occupied and that justice will be done me if all my efforts and those of our intelligent Government Agent Mr. Heyliger assisted by Mr. Lafitte should fail."

Whiting informed the governor of Edward Jones's letter and this seems to have concerned Bayley enough that on June 5 he asked McKillop to escort the ship back to the harbor so she could be loaded under the supervision of a customs officer. On June 7, McKillop towed *Oreto* (along with her supply ship *Bahama*, which had by then arrived from England) back to Nassau harbor.

Whiting and the newspapers assumed she had been officially seized for violating the Foreign Enlistment Act, but she had not. Harris and Adderley began to have the ship filled with cases of shells as "cargo for Saint John" but quickly had to backtrack. McKillop and *Bulldog* had left Nassau and been replaced by the HMS *Greyhound* under Commander Henry Hickley, who was not as attuned to how the game was being played in Nassau as McKillop. Hickley informed George Anderson that he intended to search the ship. The next morning the ship was being frantically unloaded. This was no surprise since Anderson was also the attorney for Adderley and Company as well as being close personal friends with all three members of the firm.

This turn of events caused the creation of a new plan: the ship would clear "in ballast" for Havana. Ships sailing in ballast carried something like stones or sand to keep the ship upright, but no cargo. After getting the ship out of the spotlight of Nassau harbor she would be outfitted at one of the out islands.

Hickley and a search party came on board that afternoon and stopped the unloading of the few cases of shells left on the ship. He demanded that one of the cases be opened but Duguid protested. At that moment, George Harris and Yorick Webb came on board. Webb was the customs house's landing waiter, whose task was to oversee the landing of goods from vessels. Webb held the clearance papers to Havana in his hands. This seemed to satisfy Hickley but he indicated that he intended to search the ship once more before it departed the next morning.

Three days later, on June 13, the ship was still in the harbor. Harris informed Hickley at 6:30 a.m. that she would be leaving in an hour and half. Feeling that there had been a lack of good faith, Hickley immediately boarded the ship.

After searching it, he was so convinced of the military purpose of the boat that he requested again of Anderson that the ship be seized but Anderson again demurred for lack of evidence.

When Whiting heard of Hickley's actions, he realized he might have an ally. He rounded up Edward Jones (who he most likely was supporting financially) and several of the other original crewmen and had them present their case to Hickley. Maffitt was unable to get the entire new crew on board fast enough to depart, and Hickley seized the boat on June 15. He essentially bypassed Bayley and Anderson and seized the vessel under the authority of his commander, Admiral Alexander Milne. Although Bayley was technically the commander in chief of all British military forces in the Bahamas, Hickley was authorized to act on his own authority in matters not related to local defense.

Duguid wrote an official letter of protest but Hickley responded that the boat was too suspicious to be allowed to leave. Bayley and Anderson did their best to dissuade Hickley, but he would not relent and *Oreto*'s fate was to be adjudicated in Nassau's Vice-Admiralty Court under Judge John Lees. The trial took most of the summer and garnered attention from around the world. The new crew that had been recruited and paid by Adderley and Company disappeared into the Nassau streets.

✦ ✦ ✦

Sam Whiting continued to rant at the hostile environment in which he was living. In early May he wrote to Seward that Henry Adderley's workers were loading kegs of powder and cases of muskets into *Kate*, which was docked right in front of the consulate. A week later they were at it again as they loaded muskets onto *Cecile* as Whiting looked out his window. Captain Allen, master of a schooner assigned to Adderley, and another inebriated mariner tried once again to run a Confederate flag up the consular flagpole. Whiting was away when the incident started but returned to find his servant vehemently protesting the proposed act to the drunken sailors.

The British military also got into the act. In early June, Whiting claimed that soldiers of the 2nd West Indies Regiment and sailors from HMS *Bulldog* were uttering "anathemas upon my flag" as they passed by his office. He also accused Captain McKillop of the *Bulldog* of passing information to blockade runners regarding the location of US ships and of flying a Confederate flag on his ship on a cruise to Turks and Caicos.

Whiting noted that known associates and agents of the Confederates had taken a pleasure cruise to Havana on *Ella Warley* and had also gone cruising on *Bulldog*. To annoy Whiting even more, the local theatre around the corner from his office opened a panorama of the "Bombardment of Fort Sumter," which consisted of thirty paintings painted in Charleston showing the events from South Carolina's secession to the fort's surrender. Whiting told Seward he had learned that "the shooting down of the stars and stripes was received with great enthusiasm."

Perhaps he was soothed a bit when later in the month another panorama opened, this devoted to Dr. Kane's arctic expedition, in which Whiting had been involved. And Whiting got a measure of revenge for having his mail stolen when a "loyal American" brought to him papers of John Lafitte that had been left unattended in the Royal Victoria lobby. The letters indicated that *Fanny Lewis*, also in from Liverpool and now sitting in the harbor, was filled with gunpowder. Whiting's protests to Nesbitt went nowhere.

By this time, Charles Jackson had completely disconnected from Whiting and was sending his information to Francis Lathrop of the Board of Underwriters. Among other things, Jackson pointed out to Lathrop that both Adderley and John Rahming were bringing in coal from New York that was immediately being loaded onto blockade runners. He also pointed out Rahming's location on South Street in Manhattan and encouraged Lathrop to do something about him.

One of the boats that Jackson saw unloading coal was *Time*, owned by Henry Adderley. At least twice during this period of severe coal shortage, she had traveled from New York to Nassau full of coal and immediately transferred her cargo into the coal hoppers of ships headed to the Confederacy. On one of these trips, the ship had been held up in New York. Customs officials were beginning to understand how the game was being played and asked the New York firm shipping the coal to put up $400 for a bond ensuring that the fifty tons of coal on board would not be given to Confederates.

In this case, the New York end of the connection was Adderley's old friend Francis Montell and his partner John Bartow. Montell and Bartow paid the bond and the coal was shipped but Adderley was furious and wrote a letter to Governor Bayley in protest of the bond. In his letter Adderley innocently stated that there was a great demand for coal in Nassau due to the presence of HMS *Bulldog* and to the "increased steam communication between this island and the mother country." He neglected to mention the dozens of steamers traversing the waters between Nassau and the Confederacy. While acknowledging that the United States could set any customs rules they wanted, the rules must have general application and could not single out one particular British colony. Adderley ended with an appeal to Her Majesty's government to secure restitution and protection from such insults in the future.

The dispute ended up at the highest levels of the respective governments. The bond seemed to have been legal based on an act of Congress passed May 20,

1862, that allowed Secretary of the Treasury Salmon Chase the right to refuse clearance to or require a surety bond on any ship with a cargo suspected to be headed for the Confederacy.

Two days after the act passed Chase sent a message to Collector of the Port of New York Hiram Barney indicating that he was to refuse clearance to any ships headed to foreign ports or to the three Southern ports now under Union control (New Orleans, Port Royal, or Beaufort) that contained anything on a long list of military-related items. He also gave Barney the authority to require bonds on ships carrying coal, telegraph equipment, metals, and sulfuric acid or engine parts to these designated ports.

Lord Lyons, British ambassador to the United States, asked the acting British consul in New York, Pierrepont Edwards, to look into the situation. Edwards reported that Collector Barney had great discretionary powers and they had been used "extensively for the annoyance and injury to British trade." He recounted cargos of fabrics being recalled to port to be searched, a refusal to clear a cargo of shoes and a situation where medicines intended for Nassau merchants had been denied clearance. Lyons took his complaints directly to Secretary of State William Seward. Seward forwarded to Lyons a reply from Chase that stated that it would be his pleasure to remove the restrictions on coal and other items when "the present necessity which has made them imperative shall cease." Later in the summer, while Lyons was on leave to England, his chargé d'affaires William Stuart wrote to Earl Russell that the US government was so angry about the role of Nassau in supplying the Confederacy that he saw little chance of the rules being loosened for some time.

As if Adderley and others were not annoyed enough, a much larger cargo was held up in New York in mid-June. For many years, Nassau merchants had made use of the regular steam travel between New York and London to acquire merchandise for their stores. With the advent of the Cunard monthly mail steamer in 1859, this became a habitual way of doing business. Each of the large Cunard mail steamers *China* (2,638 tons), *Scotia* (3,871 tons) and *Persia* (3,300 tons) made their way between New York and London once every two weeks. In addition to capacities exceeding 1,000 passengers, they each carried many tons of freight across the Atlantic.

Since 1859, merchandise for the Nassau merchants was transshipped onto *Karnak*. On her very first voyage to Nassau, *Karnak*'s replacement *British Queen* ran into trouble. Cunard was informed by Barney that part of the merchandise that had arrived on *China* could not be transferred to *British Queen* unless he paid bonds worth double the value of the goods ensuring they would not end up in Confederate hands.

British Queen was sitting in the harbor already cleared with a partial cargo to Nassau. In this cargo was opium cleared to Havana, but the custom house now demanded that this be removed or the boat could not leave. Customs officials feared the opium was destined for use as a Confederate pain killer. As *British Queen* was a mail steamer with a tight schedule, the crew decided the best course was to have the opium removed and sail without delay. The goods still sitting on *China* as *British Queen* left the harbor belonged to a wide variety of Nassau merchants. While most of the merchandise was likely in the form of legitimate goods for sale in Nassau, the New York customs officials had become hyper-sensitive to the passage of contraband. Newspaper reports had already touted the various illegal items that had made their way to Nassau on *Karnak*.

On this same day, the schooner *William H. Clear* cleared for Eleuthera with a cargo of lumber, flour, and pork, but was stopped leaving New York harbor. According to a protest letter filed by the captain, John Henry Bethel, the boarding officers used profane language in front of his daughter, personally searched the crew, and brought most of the cargo on deck and opened it. Personal letters intended for Bahamian residents were opened and read. After nine hours, when nothing suspicious was found the boat was released to sail. The boarding crew left all the opened cargo on deck to be dealt with by the crew of *William H. Clear*. Coming not too long after the indignation of the *Trent* affair with Mason and Slidell, the events in New York with *Time*, *William H. Clear* and *China* raised the anger of the elite merchants in Nassau toward the United States to new levels. Sam Whiting's difficult life was going to get even worse. As he noted to Seward shortly after *British Queen* arrived in Nassau with news of what had happened in New York, "The universal feeling here is most bitterly against the Union. One thing alone reconciles me to sojourn here, that I may yet see the forced acknowledgment of the Conchs that we yet have a country."

The cargo manifest for goods on *China* that were headed to Nassau included familiar names like John S. George, John G. Meadows, Robert Weech, Sawyer and Menendez, Henry Saunders, Abraham Holmes, Johnson and Brother, Michael Knowles, John Turtle, and Daniel Farrington. As most of these men were clearly involved in blockade running, it was probably a wise decision on the part of the customs officials to scrutinize the shipment very carefully. Still, much of the cargo was perishable, and it would be at least a month before *British Queen* would make another run to Nassau.

The merchants in England who had shipped the goods (Chalmers, Guthrie and Company; S. and H. Harris; and Shorter and Company) complained vehemently to Earl Russell in London. Edward Cunard, representing his father's company, wrote for assistance from Chase and Barney and wrote directly to

Henry Adderley to let him know the situation. The Nassau merchants involved with *China* cargo wrote a letter of protest to Governor Bayley.

The political jockeying between Seward, Chase, Lyons, and Russell went on for months. The British argument was that international law governing the trade between the two countries allowed ordinary goods like shoes and fabric to be shipped without restrictions. But Chase and Seward had come to see Nassau as too dangerous and were determined to stifle the trade to the Confederacy. Chase, who lost to Lincoln in the Republican primary in 1860, certainly wanted to appear strong in preparation for another run at the presidency in 1864.

The system of requiring bonds on cargoes to Nassau for virtually any reason continued for the rest of the war. In theory, the bond system worked so that when Whiting was satisfied that the goods in question had been disposed of in Nassau in a way that would not allow them to reach the Confederates, he would sign the bond certificate. The wording on the certificate read in part that "the Consignee has certified, under oath, before me, that the said articles were all imported in good faith, for home consumption in the Bahamas, and that, to the best of my belief they are not to be used in any way to aid and comfort those now in rebellion against the Federal Government of the United States of America." When the ship returned to New York with the signed certificate, the shipping agent would have his bond money refunded. Over the next couple of years, this system broke down on both ends.

The *Time* and *China* incident allowed the details of what was happening in Nassau to come into the sunlight at the highest levels in England and the United States. Collector Barney, a close political supporter of Chase's before the war, got to the point in a letter to Chase during the summer of 1862. He explained in detail how Adderley was blatantly receiving goods and coal from New York and depositing them into blockade runners in Nassau harbor. He discussed the role of John Lafitte and of Trenholm's companies.

Barney also exposed another operation that sprang up very quickly after the war started. Two businessmen from Atlanta, Sidney Root and John Beach, set up an operation that would almost rival Trenholm's in the number of ships running from Nassau to Charleston.

Before the war, Root and Beach became quite wealthy and prominent in Atlanta as dry goods merchants. In a conversation with Jefferson Davis in early 1861, Davis asked Root if he could help the cause by importing supplies. Even though both Root and Beach had Yankee roots, they had lived in the South for some time and were not averse to making more money. In the spring of 1861, Beach left on one of the last trains north to New York and made his way to Liverpool, and like Charles Prioleau he became a British citizen to make future business easier. Root remained to run things in Atlanta but also set up a facility in Charleston. He brought in businessman Edward W. Marshall to run that part of the operation under the name Marshall, Beach and Company. In England, Beach made connections with Liverpool businessmen Frederick North and Henry Jorss. This trans-Atlantic conglomerate eventually ran about twenty different steamers through the blockade.

In Atlanta, Root also rented space to the Confederate government for offices and a shoe factory. Barney had in his possession intercepted papers that included a contract in which Jorss and North agreed for $3,000 to procure a ship and insure it and its cargo to Nassau and then to Charleston. The papers also included a letter from Beach to Jorss that indicated that Jorss would accompany the ship. Beach indicated to Jorss that when he arrived in Nassau he should call upon Adderley and Lafitte and that he would then "have all the local information you need to act wisely." Adderley and Trenholm appear to have had their fingers in almost every pie. According to Barney, captured bills of lading indicated that by spring 1862 Beach and Root had already shipped over $140,000 worth of merchandise to the Confederacy. The goods had been shipped from England to Nassau on *Pacific* and consigned to Augustus Adderley, who shipped them to Charleston on *Memphis*.

In a July 6 letter to Barney, Sam Whiting warned him that *Time* was once again clearing Nassau for New York, presumably to get another load of coal to be fed into blockade runners. He also warned Barney that the primary merchants involved in this nefarious activity were the Adderleys and George Harris, Saunders and Son, John S. George, Charles Perpall, John C. Rahming, John J. Turtle, and Alexander Johnson. He somehow seems to have missed Sawyer and Menendez, who were also doing a booming business. Quite a few other Nassau merchants were getting into the game.

As summer arrived, Northern visitors to the Royal Victoria had sailed back to New York and Thompson of the *Bahama Herald* expressed hope that they had enjoyed their stays and would be back when the next season began in November. But unlike previous summers when the town became somewhat deserted as tourists went home, in the summer of 1862 the annual migration north was hardly newsworthy. People from both sides of the Atlantic were beginning to flock to this once quiet island for a purpose far different from health and relaxation.

✦ ✦ ✦

When Lewis Heyliger returned from Bermuda on June 21 he quickly set to work building a defense for *Oreto*. The Crown's case would be represented by George Anderson who as Whiting wrote was "bent on procuring her release."

In addition to dealing with serious business, Heyliger also had time to do some entertaining as the bustling city could now claim two celebrity mariners.

Joining Maffitt in town was Raphael Semmes, former captain of CSS *Sumter* and soon to be known worldwide as the commander of *Alabama*. After leaving the *Sumter* in Gibralter, he had taken passage on *Melita* from England to Nassau on his way back to the Confederacy.

Because of his experience on *Sumter*, most observers assumed that Semmes was in Nassau to take control of *Oreto*. In fact, his arrival on June 8 seemed perfectly timed with the ship's proposed voyage in ballast to Havana. In reality, Semmes had no association with the ship, but his presence in the city took attention away from Maffitt. Semmes was quick to note the change in Nassau. In his memoirs he stated that before the war, the island was "the rendezvous of a few wreckers and fisherman," where now "all was life, bustle and activity." He also noted the many Northerners at the Royal Victoria where he was staying, noting that "the Yankee, in obedience to his instincts of traffic, had scented the prey from afar, and was here to turn an honest penny, by assisting the Confederates to run the blockade!" He concluded his observations by saying, "The American war which has brought woe and wretchedness to so many of our states, was the wind which blew prosperity to Nassau."

To honor these men, Heyliger and John Lafitte hosted two lavish dinners at the Royal Victoria with about forty guests at each affair. Maffitt and Semmes appeared in full uniform, and the guest list included John Lees (soon to preside over the *Oreto* trial), George Anderson, and the partners of Henry Adderley and Company. The two captains held court during their stay at the hotel, with a disgusted Whiting referring to them as "the Lions of the Royal Victoria."

Semmes enjoyed his month at the hotel, complimenting the fare in the dining room and the pleasant company of fellow Confederate officers and Southern ladies. He and the proprietor of the hotel, John Howell, got to know each other and enjoyed many pleasant conversations. In particular, he seemed to have a good time with Maffitt, whom he described as the "life of our household. He knew everybody and everybody knew him, and he passed in and out of all the rooms, *sans ceremonie*, at all hours." He described his fellow captain as a great favorite of the ladies and present at every party and every dinner.

Shortly after his arrival in June, Semmes received word that there was indeed a boat in England awaiting his command (the *Alabama*), and on July 13 he headed back to England on *Bahama*. A disappointed James Bulloch had been told his work securing ships for the Confederacy was too important to put him to sea now that Semmes was free to take command.

In order to not have *Bahama* sit idle while the *Oreto* trial was ongoing, Adderley and Harris unloaded *Oreto*'s weapons and ammunition from *Bahama* to their warehouse and sent the ship back to England for more cargo. Henry Adderley himself joined Semmes on *Bahama*, heading to England to work on business arrangements on that end and perhaps scouting out a plush landing spot for his family when the good times had ended. George Harris was in charge until Adderley returned in November. John Low also left Nassau, heading back to join Bulloch in Liverpool on *Minna* on July 1. As June ended, Confederates in Nassau had reason to hold parties. Yes, *Oreto* was being held up, but the outcome certainly looked favorable. Blockade running was booming, and on the battlefield Robert E. Lee was having his way with George McLellan during the Seven Days Battles. But a frequent visitor to the tropics was about to throw a damper on the festivities.

8

Yellow Jack

Sam Whiting's frequent trips to Cochrane's Anchorage to keep an eye on *Oreto* put him in a financial hole and the one person he could count on for help, Timothy Darling, had traveled with his family to New York on *British Queen* on June 11. In what must have been a humiliating experience, Whiting was forced to borrow $200 from J. C. Rahming and Company. He begged Seward for quick reimbursement.

Lewis Heyliger was also experiencing some frustrations, these unrelated to *Oreto*. One of the many people who arrived in Nassau to make money from the war was Benjamin Woolley Hart, a representative of British company S. Isaac, Campbell and Company. The company was headed by two Jewish brothers, Samuel and Saul Isaac. Dugald Campbell appears to have been a silent partner and not actively involved with the firm's operations.

The company Hart represented was second only to George Trenholm's in the amount of material supplied to the Confederacy. The Isaacs had long been suppliers to the British military and were happy to deal with Caleb Huse. Along with years of experience, they brought a shady reputation to the table but Huse could not be choosy.

S. Isaac Campbell and Co. was involved in blockade running from the beginning, placing cargo on *Fingal* in October 1861 and on *Gladiator* in December of that year. As well as chartering steamers, they owned the ships *Southwick*, *Stephen Hart* (named for Benjamin's father), and *Harriet Pinckney*. Hart, Samuel Isaac's brother-in-law, was fifty years old and had been living in New York since the mid-1850s. He and Heyliger might have known each other already since Hart's wife was the sister of Gershom Kursheedt, Heyliger's former business partner in New Orleans.

In May 1862 Hart arrived in Nassau with Samuel's twenty-six-year-old son Henry Isaac to set up a branch of the business there. By this time Huse had been doing so much business with the Isaacs that they had advanced him over $500,000 worth of equipment. To avoid increasing his debt, Huse worked out a plan in which the Isaacs would ship their cargoes to Nassau and Bermuda to be purchased by Confederate agents there. Heyliger seemed to have been unaware of this development when Hart came to him in June with an offer for thirty-two cannons from the Vienna Arsenal and the implication that it would be up to Heyliger to figure out how to get them into the Confederacy.

Heyliger sent a letter to George Randolph describing the situation but exhibiting little inclination to accept an offer that removed all risk from Hart's company. His irritation with this firm was exacerbated later in the summer when Henry Isaac was boasting throughout the city that the Confederacy owed everything to his father's firm and that they would soon put Trenholm's company out of business. As Heyliger and Trenholm's agent John Lafitte had become close friends, this did not sit well. Hart would stay in Nassau until 1865, but as time went on his relationship with Heyliger deteriorated to the point where he only communicated with Heyliger through Henry Adderley and not directly.

In the midst of the *Oreto* trial and the blockade-running frenzy enveloping the city, life went on for the citizens. The elite went to the Sunday musical concerts at Fleeming Square and to horse races now being run on occasion. Those less well-off who wanted to work found opportunities aplenty on the docks. For those willing to spend six pence to see it, shopkeeper Thomas Tynes had an unusual mouse at his store with a white stripe down his back and another white stripe crossing that one. Thompson of the *Herald* suggested that Tynes ship the mouse on *British Queen* to P. T. Barnum.

Americans Kimball and Arnold of the ice house bought the wreckage of *Karnak* for $825 at auction in early July. After sealing all leaks, they borrowed fire pumps from the city to purge her of water and lift her to the surface. Since her machinery was damaged, they hired Benjamin Buck, master of *Despatch*, to tow her to New York for repairs. After leaving Nassau, Buck decided towing the boat was using too much of his coal and cast *Karnak* adrift near Port Royal, South Carolina, with several people aboard. Only with the aid of another ship were they able to get her into the harbor at Port Royal. Kimball and Arnold immediately filed suit for damages in US District Court against Buck and won.

The oppressive heat cut down on midday shopping, and the swelter was worsened by the delay in the delivery of ice. Through most of July the *Bahama Herald* gave updates on where the ice boat might be and commiserating with the people that "we all long for a cool drink of pure water." One citizen wrote to the newspaper to express his opinion that Kimball and Arnold should focus their time and attention on ice instead of on *Karnak*. Finally on July 30 the boat arrived. As if Sam Whiting's environment was not hostile enough, rumors circulated that his instructions to the US fleet had something to do with the ice shipment being delayed.

With the influx of business came changes, good and bad. As a result of the "fast increasing growth and commerce of our islands," the *Herald* noted with approval the "many improvements of late." As blockade running boomed, the city coffers were filling and the paper began to carry numerous ads for workers and bids on new projects. But the paper also carried many more reports of crime, some violent, and a letter to the editor decried rampant drunkenness on the Sabbath.

Robert E. Lee's victories in Virginia were noted with pleasure by most in Nassau. As Heyliger informed Randolph, "It is needless to say that these signal successes have produced the most beneficial influence on the public mind here. They cannot fail also to produce a powerful impression in Europe." While news of the battles in America was usually delayed by at least a few days, both the *Bahama Herald* and the *Nassau Guardian* kept everyone informed with all the details. Confederate sympathies were not hidden, as Thompson of the *Herald* wrote, "At last it appears the southern star is in ascendency, and their noble courage and fortitude is meeting some reward." So much of each paper was now taken up with war news that a little girl was overheard asking her father, "Did newspapers exist before the war?"

✦ ✦ ✦

On July 4 the trial of *Oreto* began and a variety of witnesses were called in front of Judge Lees. In his twenty-six years on the bench, Lees had never dealt with a case with this level of international attention. In a typical case in his court, in May he sentenced former Royal Victoria employee Charity Snooks to eighteen months hard labor for stealing from John Howell.

Now with *Oreto*, prominent eyes from Washington and Richmond to London and Paris were watching for his decision. As most were aware and many wrote, the trial was a farce. Over the next month Lees heard from eight former crewmen from the ship, from Duguid and several other ship captains, from Hickley and his officers and from George Harris. Most of the crewmen made it clear that this ship was not built like any other merchant ship on which they had served. But was that a crime? There were some other questions that needed to be answered. What exactly was John Low doing on the boat? And did the crew do anything after arriving in the Bahamas to prepare her for life as a cruiser?

Sam Whiting was convinced that there was plenty of evidence to convict *Oreto*. Before the trial started, he offered Edward Jones a commission in the US Navy and sent him to New York in the first week of July on *Lucy Darling* with a letter of recommendation to show Moses Grinnell. Thus Jones, who had offered the most damning testimony so far, would not be at the trial. It probably did not matter as Duguid, in his testimony, discounted Jones as a troublemaker and said he had demoted him part way through the voyage to Nassau. As usual, Whiting could not win: rumors circulated that for some reason he had paid Jones not to testify!

Lees was careful to limit the crewmen's testimonies to very short statements. Charles Ward, steward of the ship, proclaimed that she was a war vessel and that Low was really in command, but in his decree Lees said Ward was a "man of abandoned character" and intent on doing harm to Duguid. Duguid and George Harris (speaking on behalf of the absent Henry Adderley, then in England) were allowed to speak for as long as they liked. Lees was deferential to Hickley but did not put much stock in his position.

Anderson and Lees had several "master mariners" brought in for lengthy testimonies that indicated that *Oreto* was a perfectly legitimate merchant ship. These men were the captains of the blockade runners *Scotia*, *Leopard*, and *Minho*. There was no probing of Low's role or why the ship had stayed so long at Cochrane's Anchorage. Statements from the crew that they had been ordered to rig up gun tackle blocks (used for raising and lowering guns) were dismissed because Duguid said he had not given such orders.

Over the last month, Bayley had come to see the sham trial as beneficial since it would set a precedent for other similarly outfitted ships that arrived in Nassau. The outcome was certain enough that Heyliger wrote to Randolph on July 26 that "it will be favorable." Rumors began around this time and continued after the war that Lees, Anderson, and even Bayley were slipped cash in order to assure the verdict. John Howell testified after the war that Duguid had mentioned to him that he had brought money from Charleston over for this purpose. Confederate Secretary of the Navy Stephen Mallory requested that the Treasury Department send $50,000 in cash to Nassau to "fit out and equip" the ship. This was a bit strange since everything for the ship had been brought to Nassau on *Bahama*.

Whiting had pleaded for months to have United States ships in the vicinity keep any eye on *Oreto* and in the week before the trial ended he got his wish. USS *Adirondack* made an auspicious entrance as she came towards Nassau firing on the same *Herald* that Heyliger had been dealing with in Bermuda back in May. A huge crowd gathered on shore to watch the spectacle. *Herald* was hit three times but there were no injuries and she made it safely into the harbor. Heyliger and others clamored loudly that *Adirondack* had violated neutrality by firing within three miles of shore but US Commander Guert Gansevoort was able to smooth things over with Hickley and the British officials on shore.

Adirondack stayed in Nassau for three days and during that time Gansevoort made some observations about what he saw there:

> Concerning the condition of things at Nassau, I have to report that nearly all the feeling of the place with regard to our present national troubles is in sympathy with the rebels. As we passed through the harbor Dixie was played for our benefit; when we walked the streets occasionally a more impudent blackguard would, as he passed, hurrah in our ears for Jeff. Davis. The warehouses of the town, and very many private houses, are stored to the full with arms and munitions of war, notoriously intended for the South. Vessels arrive constantly from England loaded with these stores; in some cases they are trans-shipped into vessels engaged in running the blockade; in others they remain in the vessels that brought them. The practice of the blockade breakers is to paint these vessels of a bluish-white color, which is about the color of the sky at early dawn. When a vessel leaves to run the blockade everybody in or out of authority knows it. The officials all connive at the practice. In the daytime, at all hours, without pretense of concealment, boxes of arms and munitions of war, cannon and ammunition, marked in large capitals "C.S.A." are dragged through the streets to be shipped on board vessels known by everybody to be going to Charleston and other Southern ports.

Gansevoort also took time to list the blockade runners that were sitting in the harbor with *Oreto*. These included the ships *Melita, Stanley, Leopard, Pacific, Minho, Kate, Columbia, Minna, Herald, Scotia, Lodona, Nashville, Lloyd, Hero,* and *Tubal Cain*. The correspondent for the *New York Times* wrote on August 5 that at least ten million dollars' worth of goods for the rebels was currently in the ships and warehouses of Nassau.

On August 2, Lees made his decree and *Oreto* was released. Whiting wrote Seward that "Nassau has done more to aid and prolong the foul rebellion than any two, ay, three of the rebel states." Within a few days *Oreto* was loaded with 180 pounds each of beef and vegetables and numerous cases of wine and liquor from merchant John. J. Turtle and her weapons and ammunition were loaded from Adderley's warehouse onto a ship, *Prince Alfred*, which John Laffite purchased from Alexander Johnson in the name of Augustus Adderley.

On August 7, *Oreto* sailed just outside the bar of Nassau harbor. Maffitt had not had time to replenish his crew, but needed to get out of Nassau and get the boat armed before US cruisers made their way to stop him or before Whiting or someone else filed an appeal. Still, he needed a day or so to test the engines and sure enough on August 8 USS *R. R. Cuyler* showed up and began to prowl all around *Oreto*.

Another of Maffitt's British friends, Captain George Watson of HMS *Petrel*, sailed his ship out to confront the *Cuyler* and ordered her to either enter the harbor or sail out past the three nautical mile limit. Sam Whiting made his way in his consular boat to the *Cuyler* and informed Captain Francis Winslow of the new rules governing the harbor and that he should best move away. At this point, Whiting still did not associate Maffitt with *Oreto* and told Winslow that since Semmes and his men had left Nassau that the Confederates were likely going to use her unarmed to run the blockade. Hence, *Cuyler* left that afternoon for a spot near Abaco where she hoped to intercept the ship. During the night Watson let Maffitt tie up *Oreto* to *Petrel* because Maffitt did not have enough men to weigh anchor. On a ship meant for 130 men, he had only twenty-two. This included three junior officers, five firemen, and fourteen deck hands.

Three British seamen, Peter Crawley, James Lockyer, and Andrew Hagan were walking to their lodgings around midnight when they ran into a large group of sailors in front of the Matanzas Hotel on Bay Street. This group convinced the three to join them in transferring cargo from a schooner into *Oreto* and that the work should take all night but they would be paid five dollars. Instead of transferring cargo all night, an hour after they boarded the three men found themselves headed out to sea in *Oreto*. Around noon, she was joined by *Prince Alfred*, the boat John Laffitte had bought from Alexander Johnson to carry *Oreto*'s equipment. Maffitt put Lieutenant Christian Stribling, who had served with Semmes on the *Sumter*, in charge of *Prince Alfred*. Together, the two ships made their way to isolated Green Cay, about sixty miles south of New Providence.

✦ ✦ ✦

As *Oreto* pulled out of Nassau harbor, she was carrying an unintended cargo: yellow fever. This mosquito-borne illness, referred to as Yellow Jack by the sailors because of the yellow flag flown by quarantined ships, commonly arrived in Nassau during late summer. Some years were worse than others, and while 1862 would be bad, it would not compare to the outbreak that devastated the city two years later. Those who survived the disease gained lifelong immunity, while those who perished suffered terribly in their final days.

John Maffitt first noted the outbreak around July 20 when his British friend Lieutenant Brown succumbed, and he was constantly nursing patients at the Royal Victoria for the next few weeks before his departure. According to Maffitt, most of the cases he saw were fatal. Benjamin Wooley Hart's young partner Henry Isaac succumbed on July 29.

The disease struck all levels on the social strata. Governor Bayley may have been afflicted, as in mid-August the *Bahama Herald* reported that he was regaining his usual health. Charles Caufield arrived in Nassau in May on *Wild Pigeon* and was enthroned as the first Bishop of Nassau on June 17, but he died from yellow fever on September 4. Two of his nieces also perished that same week. According to Sam Whiting, about five people were dying in Nassau each day.

The new enterprise enriching the city also had a sinister component as the blockade runner *Kate* brought yellow fever with her to Wilmington, and by mid-August that city was also going through a devastating epidemic. The disease also found its way to Key West, Florida, and Beaufort and Port Royal in South Carolina. As the fever raged in late July, the amount of shipping arriving and leaving Nassau dwindled to pre-war levels and did not recover until the outbreak dissipated in October. When *Cuyler* returned to Nassau from Abaco, the crew was infected with yellow fever. Despite the highly praised efforts of Epes Sargent, several of the sailors, including Captain Winslow, died.

In the intense August sun at Green Cay, all the men including the crew, the hired (some might say kidnapped) men, Maffitt, and the officers stripped to their waists and started into the brutal work of getting six large guns and tons of shot, shell, and equipment moved from *Prince Alfred* to *Oreto*. The ordeal took seven days, and on the eighth day they rested from exhaustion.

One man had gotten sick on the second day and died, but most aboard attributed it to his intense revelry while in Nassau. Maffitt, however, noticed a particular yellow tinge to the corpse. On August 17, they brought down the English colors, hoisted the Confederate flag, and to loud cheers *Oreto* became CSS *Florida*. The exhausted men hired to transfer cargo headed back to Nassau on *Prince Alfred*. They were never paid. Sam Whiting informed Governor Bayley that *Prince Alfred* had helped in arming *Florida*, but when Bayley asked Whiting to provide evidence, it was not forthcoming. The testimonials that Whiting did obtain surfaced almost three years later. *Prince Alfred* later ran the blockade under the name *Pocotaligo*.

At daylight the next day, two men on *Florida* were ill. By sundown half the crew sick with yellow fever. Unlike an epidemic in the city where the healthy can flee, Maffitt noted that on ship there was no refuge from the screams, the black vomit, or the yellow corpses. Cruising for prizes was out of the question.

In desperation, Maffitt decided to head for Cuba. Confederate agent Charles Helm had written to Maffitt in June stating that *Oreto* would be welcome there and that the Cuban government had a "most liberal view of neutrality." Maffitt made his way to Cardenas with several of his crew dead and most sick.

On August 22, three days after arrival, Maffitt came down with the disease. He did not regain consciousness until a week later. He grieved when informed that his sixteen-year-old stepson John Laurens Read, on board as paymaster, had died the day before. Four more of his men died on August 30. Richard

Floyd, who had drawn pictures for John Lafitte's niece, seems to have come through unscathed. Worried that he would be caught in defenseless Cardenas, on September 1 the frail captain made his way to the forts of Havana.

After a day of rest, Maffitt and the few men still standing left Havana harbor to head to Mobile, where the relatively small blockading force gave the greatest chance of getting through. His chances were decreased tremendously by the realization that in the hurried loading of *Prince Alfred* at Nassau they had forgotten the rammers and sponges needed to fire the big guns. He would have to run the gauntlet without fighting back.

On the afternoon of September 4 *Florida* approached Mobile. It was broad daylight, but without a pilot and in such a weakened state Maffitt dared not wait for nightfall. In a true do-or-die moment, he steamed ahead. A shell pierced the hull, wounding nine men and taking the head off sailor James Duncan. Two more shells pierced the ship just above the waterline. In a tortuous two-hour run, *Florida* found herself within eighty yards of three Union men-of-war that pounded her relentlessly. Somehow, she made it to the safety of the guns of Fort Morgan. The exploit added to Maffitt's growing legend. He wrote his daughter Florie that he was thinking of home but "recently all thought my home must be the cold earth or ... the sepulchral grave of the ocean."

In addition to everything else on his mind that August, Sam Whiting had to once again deal with accusations against him. In early August, William G. Butler wrote a letter to Abraham Lincoln accusing Whiting of being a traitor. Butler had been purser on *Marion*, the ship from which Whiting had famously saluted Fort Sumter. Butler told Lincoln that while in Charleston Whiting had actually written a poem justifying South Carolina's secession. On top of the rumors about Whiting paying off Jones not to testify and delaying the shipment of ice, the letter prompted Seward to once again ask Captain Sam to explain himself.

On August 22, he wrote a lengthy letter expressing his "mortification that imputations upon my loyalty have again been attempted." He explained to Seward that no other consular officer had encountered anything like the difficulties he was experiencing. He was surrounded by a "community of secessionist sympathizers" and an "influx of the most rabid rebels." He indicated again that people craved his position and would do anything to hurt him. He and his wife were socially isolated, and when he walked down the street he heard, "There goes Abe Lincoln's spy!" In September, he had placed an ad in the *Bahama Herald* offering a reward for the malicious persons who had filled his personal boat with coal.

In his letter, he enclosed an editorial from the *New York Tribune* that voiced the popular opinion there that Whiting was a patriot and a hero and would be sorely missed. He also enclosed a copy of a poem he had published while in

New York that expressed fervent patriotic thoughts and asked Seward whether the author of such a poem could ever have justified secession. "No, no sir," Whiting answered his own question. He summarized his thoughts to Seward: "If any further doubts exist, put me on the first rank of the Potomac Army or on the deck of a gunboat and I will prove to the world that my love of country and my hatred of her foes are stronger than my love of life."

In a subsequent letter he offered a theory to Seward about what prompted William Butler to write Lincoln. Earlier in the summer, Whiting had publically denounced Samuel Dexter Bradford, a wealthy and influential New Yorker who was wintering at the Royal Victoria with his family and several servants. According to Whiting, his outrage stemmed from Bradford giving a pistol as a gift to Robert Lockwood, the blockade runner, an event reported to Whiting by John Howell. In Whiting's opinion, this confrontation led Bradford to get Butler to write the letter. By this time, Seward must have been thinking that he might need to make a change in the consular office. His hand would be forced in that direction in October when Whiting finally crossed too far over the line. But up until that time, Whiting would continue to be confronted with issues unique to his assignment.

On August 23, USS *Adirondack* wrecked on a reef off of Abaco, about a day's sail from Nassau. The ship might have been saved, but a large fleet of wreckers gathered and merely watched as the waves pounded the ship to pieces. Whiting received the news in a note from Commander Gansevoort on August 26, and he immediately attempted to hire the large steamer *Pacific* to tow *Adirondack* off the reef. *Pacific* was regularly shipping cotton and contraband goods back and forth between England and Nassau for Adderley and for Beach and Root.

After having agreed to the exorbitant price of $960 per day, Whiting was stunned to have the captain show up at his office and inform him that Henry Adderley and Company and John Laffite had intervened. They claimed to have cargo still on *Pacific* and objected to having the ship removed from the harbor. Whiting was able to rent another boat, *Star of the East*, and make his way to the site of the wreck on August 27. By the next day, he had managed to send a shipment of valuable items including brass and copper fixtures and military clothing back to Nassau and consigned them to Timothy Darling, who was back in town and the only merchant he completely trusted.

When Whiting returned to the city on August 31, he found that wreckers had managed to haul off quite a bit of other valuable equipment that was now sitting in a local warehouse. Whiting purchased what he could by promising that the US government would cover the costs. By the time the *Adirondack* salvage operation was completed, Whiting had gotten himself about $ 15,000 in debt. To his consternation, the Treasury Department refused to pay much of this amount, some because the department felt Whiting had been overcharged and some because he had neglected to fill out the correct forms. Despite his good intentions, the *Adirondack* episode managed to damage Whiting's reputation even more both in Nassau and in Washington.

About three weeks after the *Adirondack* wreck, USS *Dacotah* came to Nassau almost out of coal after cruising the out islands for blockade runners. Whiting, who had picked up a severe cold after his days at the wreck site, sent a note to Captain James McKinstry welcoming him to the port and letting him know that he had sent a note to Governor Bayley asking for permission for the ship to take on coal, permission that Whiting indicated "will undoubtedly be granted." He told McKinstry he could get coal from an American ship anchored near him or if that failed from J. C. Rahming's coal supply.

After borrowing money from Rahming, Whiting seems to have built some relationship with Rahming even though he was widely known to be running contraband out of New York. As usual, nothing in Nassau came easy to Captain Sam. He quickly received a note from Charles Nesbitt informing him that *Dacotah* had not asked permission from the governor to anchor. This was a new requirement put forth by Bayley, certainly intended to dissuade American cruisers from coming to Nassau. The mouth of the harbor was a dangerous place to anchor due to strong tides and shifting sands, so it seemed that few future warships would want to sit there waiting for Bayley's permission.

Later in the day Nesbitt let Whiting know that the governor was willing to let the ship make a brief stay but if she carried any cases of yellow fever she needed to anchor at Salt Cay three miles away. This spot had become a quarantine point for ships that had not received a clean bill of health. The governor would make a decision on coaling the ship the following day.

McKinstry assured Whiting that there were no cases of yellow fever on board and awaited the governor's resolution to his coaling request. When that decision came through a note from Nesbitt, both Whiting and McKinstry were outraged. *Dacotah* would be allowed to take on coal but only with a written guarantee from McKinstry that for the next ten days she would be no closer than five miles to any island in the Bahamas. Out of fuel, McKinstry reluctantly agreed to this request and with twenty tons of coal obtained from *Courant* steamed off to Key West.

Whiting wrote bitterly to Seward that Attorney General George Anderson could be "thanked for this act of discourtesy to the national vessel of a friendly government. Mr. Anderson is a bitter foe to the North, a violent denouncer of our flag and institutions, both publically and privately." Anderson was paid by American blockade-running companies during the war for legal advice and even appears to have consigned some cargoes himself.

In addition to the issues with the cruisers, Whiting continued to have financial issues. In theory, he was supposed to take care of consular expenses from the fees he collected from cancelling the bonds being issued to vessels going back and forth from Nassau to the United States. By the fall of 1862, his expenses far outweighed these fees.

One of the important duties of a consul was to assist US citizens and destitute seamen. As the port teemed with ships, taking care of seamen changed from what was a sporadic and routine task before the war to a serious responsibility. For example, in early 1862 five men loyal to the US were serving as crew members on *Ella Warley* but refused to cheer when another blockade runner passed by them in Nassau harbor. A fistfight ensued and the five men were put off the boat and ended up at Whiting's office. Whiting paid for their transportation to New York on *Levi Rowe*. It was not only an ethical duty to help these mariners but important to the war effort. When sailors found themselves stranded in Nassau for some reason, the money being paid to serve on a blockade runner was very tempting. The men Whiting tried to help included not only those from the United States but former Confederates who wanted to go north. Whiting did his best to help, but the Treasury Department proved to be a thorn in his side rather than an ally.

✦ ✦ ✦

In October, as the yellow fever epidemic was subsiding, the volume of shipping began to increase again. To reduce the number of bonds paid at the New York Custom House, Nassau merchants were now receiving some of their contraband directly from Philadelphia and Baltimore. And while Charleston and Wilmington continued to be the main Nassau connections for running supplies into the Confederacy, shipments still managed to find their way from Savannah, Port Royal, and even Florida.

At this point, things were going so well for the Confederacy in Nassau and on the battlefields that on October 2 Lewis Heyliger sent a letter to John Bayley officially announcing himself as the authorized representative of the Confederacy in the Bahamas. While Bayley obviously knew all about him, Heyliger let Benjamin know that he had not considered it necessary to "bring the matter formally to his attention until recently." In his letter to Bayley, Heyliger alluded to the recent military successes of Robert E. Lee and implied that it now seemed the time to establish a formal relationship. Somewhat surprisingly, his offer was gently rebuffed. Bayley obviously realized that officially recognizing the Confederacy might violate the queen's neutrality proclamation, and he had Nesbitt respond that Bayley "will always be happy to receive any unofficial representations which you or any other gentlemen of the Southern States may wish to offer him in his private and personal capacity."

A hindrance to the post-epidemic resurgence of the blockading bonanza was the appearance of Charles Wilkes, the US naval officer who had pulled Mason and Slidell off their boat almost a year earlier. On September 8, 1862, Secretary of the Navy Gideon Welles assigned Wilkes to command a squadron of seven ships to be named the West Indies Squadron. The mission was to destroy *Florida* and the new Confederate cruiser that had emerged from England in August with Raphael Semmes in command, the 290 (soon to be known as *Alabama*).

On October 6, Wilkes arrived outside of Nassau harbor in his flagship *Wachusett* along with *Octorara*. He did not test Bayley by anchoring, but instead the two ships maneuvered back and forth outside the harbor. Sam Whiting attempted to reach Wilkes in his small consular boat but was driven back by a squall. The next day Wilkes was able to get a letter to Whiting by way of a black wrecker. The letter outlined the plan Wilkes had developed for the operation of his squad. In addition to looking for the two Confederate cruisers, Wilkes intended to shut down blockade running from Nassau. He decided that blockading destinations like Wilmington and Charleston was too difficult and that the proper way to stop things was to blockade the point of departure. Never one for political correctness, Wilkes seemed to ignore that he was proposing to blockade a neutral port.

To accomplish his ends, he asked Whiting to provide him with two things. First, experienced pilots who could help his ships navigate the dangerous Bahamian waters and put them on equal footing with the blockade runners. There were a couple of small pilot rowboats used to get ships in and out of Nassau harbor, but Wilkes wanted men to accompany him and help navigate the pathways the runners took out of the islands. Second, he asked Whiting to provide him with a steady stream of information regarding the plans of the ships headed to the Confederacy.

Delighted to finally have some help in his efforts to stem the tide, Whiting replied immediately. While all the local white pilots had been scooped up by the Southerners, he could recommend some black pilots to Wilkes although he cautioned Wilkes to keep them away from liquor. As for communication, Whiting was emphatic that Nassau itself was not going to work. He and Wilkes decided that Stirrup Cay, a small island about fifty miles north of Nassau, would serve as a contact point. Whiting would send information to the island by way of a black wrecking captain named Loroda. To avoid the coaling issues that had hindered *Dacotah*, Wilkes established a coal depot at Turtle Harbor, Florida, about twenty miles south of modern-day Miami.

The presence of his squadron near Nassau caused consternation immediately. As *Wachusett* and *Octorara* prowled outside the harbor in early October, the *Bahama Herald* claimed, "Nassau is fairly under blockade." Wilkes left for Cuba in search of *Alabama* not long after communicating with Whiting, but by early November some of the other ships of his squadron had gathered near New Providence. The captains of *Octarara*, *Tioga, and Sonoma* spent the early part of the month cruising the waters and testing the new pilots.

On November 20, Wilkes arrived in *Wachusett* along with *Santiago de Cuba*. As he neared the harbor, he chased Captain Louis Coxetter's *Antonica* right up to the edge of the bar with some shots actually falling in the harbor. The citizens of Nassau had no love for Wilkes due to the *Trent* affair, and this dramatic reappearance was met with renewed hostility.

Wilkes did nothing to improve relations. As *Wachusett* neared the mouth of the harbor, a pilot named Lloyd rowed out and came on board with a copy of the proclamation stating the requirement to get Bayley's permission to anchor. Wilkes responded that he would anchor when and where he saw fit. When a small boat from HMS *Barracouta* made its way toward him, Wilkes toyed with them by staying just out of their range before finally steaming out to sea. The commander of *Barracouta*, George Malcolm, was furious and paid a visit to Whiting to impress upon him the gravity of this insult. It did not help matters that the pilot was in the city letting everyone know what Wilkes had said. Wilkes statement about anchoring where he pleased was in the local newspapers later that week.

Shortly after this incident, Whiting sent word to Wilkes at Stirrup Cay that the Bay Street Boys were extremely unhappy with the presence of his squadron. He enclosed a copy of a new proclamation from Bayley that provided for the arrest of any British citizen found to be aiding belligerents in the war. It was obviously aimed at the black pilots Whiting was now sending to aid Wilkes, and some of these pilots soon found themselves under arrest. Through the remainder of 1862 the Wilkes squadron put a bit of a damper on blockade running, but the size of the business was expanding so quickly that the overall effect was minimal.

With winter coming, the Confederacy had a large demand for woolen clothing, blankets, and shoes. To this end, James Ferguson of the Quartermaster Department's Richmond Clothing Bureau was sent to England in December to aid Caleb Huse in purchasing. Ferguson was a close friend of Robert E. Lee and designed the uniform that Lee wore at the surrender in Appomattox. Friction between Huse and Ferguson would have later repercussions, but for the time being the flow of material from England to Nassau expanded to the point that Heyliger and Lafitte began to be overwhelmed.

In November Heyliger wrote to Benjamin that his working force was not adequate for the "large amount of private freight that has accumulated at this point." Heyliger eventually received help when Major Richard Waller of the

Quartermaster Department arrived in Nassau the following summer. Until arriving in Nassau, Waller was in charge of the Richmond Clothing Bureau and had been James Ferguson's supervisor.

Around this same time, Edward Lafitte made a request in Charleston to obtain help for his brother John in Nassau. Edward wrote to Brigadier General Roswell Ripley on December 22, 1862, "My brother writes me from Nassau that it is absolutely necessary for him to have someone to assist him there as he has a great deal of government business to attend to. I would ask your assistance in having Pvt. Mahoney of the Palmetto Guard detached for special service so I can send him by the Antonica to Nassau." Ripley either ignored or passed this request on as Edward Lafitte made the same request of Brigadier General Thomas Jordan a few days later, including the comment that Mahoney's services were "indispensable" to his brother John.

Cornelius Mahoney was a young bookkeeper of Irish decent and had likely worked for the Lafittes before the war. At the time of Edward Lafitte's request, he was a private in Company A (often called the Palmetto Guard) of Manigault's Artillery Battalion defending Charleston. The amount of contraband passing through Nassau had reached such a level that John Lafitte obviously needed help with all the paperwork.

Edward Lafitte's request eventually made it to the top. Mahoney, who had enlisted on March 19, 1862, was detached to Nassau for sixty days by special order of General P. G. T. Beauregard on December 23, 1862. Mahoney must have served well with John Lafitte as Beauregard continued to extend his furlough every sixty days until the fall of 1864. Many of the cotton invoices from Laffite to Charles Prioleau in Liverpool were signed "J. B. Lafitte per C. Mahoney." On at least one occasion his company commander clamored that after the latest extension he must return to his company, but Edward Lafitte kept pushing to keep him in Nassau. In July 1863 Edward, who had relocated to Augusta, wrote to his clerk John Cay to talk personally to General Jordan and let him know that he had advertised and done everything else possible to find a replacement for Mahoney but had been unsuccessful. The company paymaster eventually dropped Mahoney from the roster in November 1864 when they apparently realized he was not coming back.

✦ ✦ ✦

During the time when Heyliger and Lafitte were beginning to have their hands full, the *Bahama Herald* apologized to its readers because all the merchant ad space was preventing them from printing all the news. Business was so good that some of the ads were now for people selling imported goods from their homes.

If the Northern tourists who began to fill the Royal Victoria in early November had been to Nassau before, they must have been shocked at the changes in the city. The hotel must have been quite an interesting place that fall. In addition to those visiting for pleasure or health, the residents included John Lafitte and his wife and niece, underwriter's agent Charles Jackson, hustlers like Benjamin Woolley Hart and his wife, and a rotating roster of blockade-running captains. The dining table and billiard room must have hosted some lively conversations.

Others besides Lafitte and Heyliger were making adjustments to the increased activity. On November 24, Henry Adderley returned from his business trip to England by way of St. Thomas on the mail steamer that regularly traveled from there to Southhampton (he was certainly not going to pass through New York). During 1862, Henry Adderley and Company had been the leading company in clearing ships in and out of Nassau. Sawyer and Menendez and Saunders and Son were close behind with many others jumping into the game as the year progressed. Even John Howell of the Royal Victoria was getting into the act. At the end of the year *Red Jacket* left New York with a cargo of lumber for Howell, and in a few months he teamed up with fellow American Epes Sargent to construct Nassau's first dry dock facility. The once sleepy harbor now had so many boats that there were many chances for profits on repairs and maintenance being missed. Their time in New Providence had infused Howell and Sargent with the Bahamian spirit of opportunism.

With the increased need for supplies and in an effort to stop paying outrageous prices for shipping, the Confederacy made an effort near the end of 1862 to start their own line of ships to secure goods from England. Secretary of War James Seddon (who replaced George Randolph in November) reached an agreement to form a partnership with the Crenshaw brothers of Richmond with the aim of creating a shipping line devoted to providing quartermaster and commissary supplies. William, James, and Lewis Crenshaw operated a woolen mill near Tredegar Iron Works until it was destroyed by fire on May 15, 1863.

The new company would be a strange hybrid of government with private enterprise. In November 1862, William Crenshaw traveled to Liverpool to begin work on the project. He became an ally of James Ferguson in Ferguson's later accusations against Caleb Huse. James Crenshaw would spend some of his time in Nassau overseeing the company's operations there. William Crenshaw partnered with Scottish shipping agent Alexander Collie to get the government steamer line started. In addition to making money off the war, Collie supported the cause by contributing to the costs of a statue honoring Stonewall Jackson that eventually ended up (and remains) on the grounds of the state capitol in Richmond.

On the battlefield, the Confederacy continued to have success, and Heyliger and others in Nassau were optimistic that either England, France, or both would soon be coming into the war on the Southern side. After brushing George McClellan away from Richmond in the Seven Days Battles, Robert E. Lee had taken the war north. He crushed John Pope at Second Manassas and then held McClellan to a draw at Antietam even though the latter had found Lee's battle plans. Most recently, Lee had easily defeated the Union forces under Ambrose Burnside at Fredericksburg in December 1862.

Confederate military fortunes would peak about six months later with the battles at Chancellorsville and Gettysburg, and much of the Confederate success was due to weapons coming in through the blockade. Up until April 1862, *Fingal*'s 15,000 guns had been the main contribution to the Southern cause. But between April and August, almost 50,000 more guns arrived, and by the end of 1862 a total of 157,000 guns had passed from Europe to the Confederacy. Trenholm's firms had raked in millions of dollars in 1862, and things were really just getting started.

With all the success and activity in the South and in Nassau, there were some signs that all was not well. On November 17, Benjamin Woolley Hart wrote from Nassau to Secretary of War Randolph (who had resigned that same day due to health concerns) offering that S. Isaac Campbell and Company was in the position to outfit 100,000 soldiers with clothing and equipment. When John Jones, a clerk in the War Department in Richmond, heard this news, he commented, "This looks cheering. We have credit abroad. But they are Jews."

Hart pointed out that his company had already advanced the Confederacy over $2 million to this point so that some portion of this new order needed to be paid in cash. He also made it clear that he would appreciate a proposal on how the growing debt would be settled. The Confederacy did forward about $400,000 dollars to the company in January 1863, but if the needs of the armies were going to continue, they needed to find some way to foot this bill.

9

A New Consul

On January 1, 1863, Abraham Lincoln issued the Emancipation Proclamation that promised freedom to millions of slaves in the South. Of course there was still work to do to make this ideal a reality, so what had been a war to preserve the Union was now also a war to abolish slavery. The proclamation confirmed many Southerners' belief that, despite his words, Lincoln's aim had been to abolish slavery all along. There was widespread feeling that the intended result of the proclamation was slave revolt, and this hardened Confederate resolve to endure and win the war.

The proclamation was reported in the Nassau newspapers and was the topic of discussion on the streets. The sympathies of the white population were likely aligned with those in the South. The merchants with the largest revenue streams were certainly in favor of anything that would extend the war. While most people of color in Nassau probably felt support for the Southern slaves, it was not something to be discussed in public.

The issuance of the proclamation coincided with an important change in Nassau: Sam Whiting was on the way out. Placed in a no-win situation with intense local hostility and little external support, Whiting had slowly unraveled. By January, the man who one observer described as "prim and stately" was a mess. After dealing with the August accusations against him by William Butler, Whiting had been busy in September dealing with *Dacotah* and other issues. Other than having his private boat filled with coal by a prankster, things had been relatively calm that month. But on October 4, 1862, Whiting's wife left on *British Queen* for New York and she never returned to Nassau. Adding the threat of yellow fever to the rampant hostility must have made her say enough was enough.

When the ship returned two weeks later, Whiting hoped to find her on it but instead found trouble. Secretary of State Seward received a letter written by

Enoch Turley, a ship captain then in Nassau, describing what happened next. The letter was written to Philadelphia merchant John Varree, who worked with Turley. Varree forwarded the letter to Seward and added his opinion that the enclosed story indicated that the consul was unfit for his post.

According to Turley, Whiting came onto *British Queen* "crazy drunk" and caused a "disgraceful scene" in the presence of a large number of ladies and gentlemen. He shook his fist under the nose of a British officer and called him a son of a bitch. The next day Turley was talking on the street with Charles Jackson when Whiting, drunk again, passed by and told Turley he was in "damned bad company." After cursing the people of Nassau, he said to Turley, "If you do not choose to pay me an official visit, you can go to hell!" Turley added his opinion that Whiting was the laughingstock of Nassau.

Soon after the incident Whiting wrote to Seward and offered his resignation: "I beg to tender to you my resignation of the office of US Consul at Nassau and to beg that my successor may relieve me from this disagreeable position as early as possible." About a week after that he wrote to Seward again, this time asking to rescind his resignation and offering an explanation for his behavior.

According to Whiting, the previous consul Isaac Merritt had been a personal friend of Governor Bayley's, and Bayley had always been haughty and almost insulting in Whiting's presence. He traced this to his initial meeting with Bayley in New York in June 1861. Whiting was getting ready to leave for Nassau, and Bayley was staying at the Clarendon Hotel in Brooklyn en route to England. Whiting said Bayley's reception of him on that day was of "a coolish character." He believed this set the tone for his generally hostile environment in Nassau.

The incident on *British Queen* involved Major James Mends of the 2nd West India Regiment and merchant Cornelius Lightbourne, who Whiting termed a leader of the "rowdy fringe of the upper crust." Both of these men had provoked Whiting before. Mends had supposedly encouraged his black enlisted men to make deprecating remarks when passing Whiting's residence. One night while Whiting and his wife were on their balcony reading, Lightbourne had pranced on his horse under the balcony shouting, "Hurrah for Jeff Davis and Beauregard!" When Whiting boarded *British Queen* that October day, Mends and Lightbourne yelled, "Here comes old Stars and Stripes, I wonder if he likes the news from Dixie?" While he did not mention being inebriated, Whiting told Seward that the remarks "made my blood boil and would have set my extensor and flexor muscles in motion but for the public position I occupied." He denounced Mends in particular and the Nassau population in general, shouting back that they were all "rank secessionists from the governor on down!"

After this scene it was obvious to Seward that Whiting, good man that he might be, had lost all credibility in Nassau. He began to look for a replacement and Whiting began to accept that his tenure in the Bahamas was coming to an end. In December he wrote to Seward acknowledging the acceptance of his resignation and asserting that he would continue in his duties until replaced and would give every assistance to his successor. He also expressed the hope that Seward might find him another appointment.

Seward would not have an easy task finding a replacement. Despite the importance of the position and the great increase in the cost of living in Nassau since 1861, the consular salary was still only $2,000 per year. Given the volume of activity, the office was understaffed, and Whiting had been forced to hire a clerk with his own funds. This rise in prices forced the British to give all the public officers in Nassau a 25 percent raise in 1864. Moses Grinnell referred Seward to a man named William Whetton as a candidate, but Whetton wrote Grinnell on November 20 that he had no interest in the position. Seward next offered the post to Lockwood L. Doty, deputy collector of customs in New York. Doty proudly accepted the position and took the oath of office on December 11. Seward urged Doty to get to Nassau as quickly as possible, but Doty dawdled and must have had time to change his mind. On December 29 he wrote Seward resigning the position.

While an exasperated Seward continued to hunt for a replacement who would accept the job, Whiting soldiered on. Given his status, there was little he could do to stop the onslaught of blockade runners coming and going other than to report back to Washington. As he told one visiting American tourist in the first week of January, there had been more successful blockade running in the previous three weeks than in any other period of the war. He apparently still had a few folks in the city who appreciated all he had done as on January 9 he placed a message in the *Bahama Herald* thanking the unknown gentlemen who serenaded underneath his balcony with national tunes "dear to every true American heart." He apologized that his "rheumatism" had kept him from coming to greet them but wanted to express his thanks for a "courtesy so rare."

On January 27 Seward finally found his man in the person of an old friend, Seth Hawley, the same fellow who had detained John Low's uncle Andrew back in 1861. Hawley, who had the somewhat ironic middle name Cotton, was fifty-two and the Chief Clerk of the New York Police Department. He had been on leave from the department and working as a special investigator for Seward since the war started. His position made him well aware of the trade between New York and Nassau and Seward had personally assigned him to investigate various men suspected of contraband activity including Andrew Low.

Hawley pointed out to Seward that he was aware of the woeful compensation for the position but hoped that might be changed. In any case, it appears he accepted the position mainly because he thought the tropical climate might benefit both him and his ailing daughter. After accepting the position, it took Hawley about six weeks to make it to Nassau.

During this same period, Seward received two letters requesting that he bolster up the Nassau position with higher pay and better support. The first came to him in January from Whiting's original supporters with the insurance underwriters including Moses Grinnell and Jeremiah Tappan. This letter requested that Seward find a way to double the consular salary and pointed out that Whiting had been paid far less than Charles Jackson and that this low salary had affected his stature in the city. The other letter came in March from Americans in Nassau including John Howell, Charles Jackson, and Epes Sargent. Their petition was actually addressed to Abraham Lincoln and pointed out the new importance of the city and the unenviable job of the consul there. They also asked Lincoln to ask Congress to increase the salary of the position. Unfortunately for Whiting and Hawley there would be no action on this request for some time.

The day before Hawley accepted the position, Whiting had the displeasure of watching John Maffitt sail into the harbor on *Florida*. When the pilot who came on board notified Maffitt that he had violated the new rule about getting the governor's permission before anchoring, he decided to see Bayley immediately. Lieutenant Charles Williams of the 2nd West India Regiment, a friend of Maffitt's, brought the regimental boat out with an honor guard to bring him to the governor. Bayley was delighted to see Maffitt again.

Sam Whiting could only fume at seeing all his efforts to stop *Oreto* go for naught and now the added indignity of the preferential treatment given to Maffitt only a few months after the cold shoulder that had been given to *Dacotah*. Maffitt met Lewis Heyliger along with John Lafitte and family at the Royal Victoria for breakfast. Maffitt noted approvingly in his journal, "On shore the demonstration was most friendly and congratulatory. Nassau is decidedly a Confederate stronghold." At 11:00 a.m. he went back on board the ship and entertained the officers of the 2nd West India Regiment and their friends. During his day long visit, Maffitt had quite a story to tell about his time since leaving Nassau in early August.

After arriving in Mobile, it had taken four months for the ship to be repaired, properly outfitted, and properly staffed. On the bitterly cold moonless night of January 16, *Florida* slipped back out past the Union blockade and by the next morning was one hundred fifty miles south of Mobile. Two days later she took her first prize, capturing the brig *Estelle*, bringing her crew on board, and burning the ship. The next day she entered Havana harbor, left *Estelle*'s crew there, and coaled up the ship to go cruising for more prizes. On January 22, she captured two more, but Maffitt got bad news from his engineer. The coal they had taken on in Havana was no good: the ship was barely able to make three knots. In a somewhat helpless condition again, *Florida* made her way northeast and arrived safely in Nassau harbor on the morning of January 26.

One of the sailors commented, "The town seems plentifully supplied with negroes, whatever it may lack in anything else. During the day an entire boatload rowed around us, singing the Bonnie Blue Flag. They are all southern sympathizers." When Maffitt met with Bayley that morning, the governor gave him permission to get new coal although he warned him that he could only stay twenty-four hours. Maffitt also recruited sailors to fill out his crew. In violation of port rules, laborers worked through the night, and by 10:00 a.m. the next morning the bad coal had been replaced with high quality coal. By noon the *Florida* was off to seek new victims.

Although the ship would never visit Nassau again, Maffitt returned to the city in a different role later in the war. Informed by Whiting of *Florida*'s visit, William Seward complained and got a response from Bayley defending his actions and his regret "that the Secretary of State should have given credence to the misrepresentations of a person of such infirm and excitable judgement as Mr. Whiting has proved himself to be."

The amount of contraband crossing the blockade was continuing to grow. Whiting wrote in February that three new formidable iron-hulled blockade runners, *Britannia, Georgiana,* and *Gertrude,* had arrived in Nassau harbor from Scotland within an hour of each other. As Hawley later estimated for Seward, a typical blockade-running ship that made four successful trips and was then lost with all cargo on the fifth trip would profit her owners almost $300,000. While the Wilkes squadron made captures, they were hardly putting a dent in the flow. Still, the greed was unbounded and any dent in the profits was unacceptable. Heyliger wrote to Benjamin that the British were going to make a formal demand that Wilkes be removed from command for facilitating an illegal blockade. The issue was important enough that Admiral Milne himself made a visit to Bayley in December to discuss the situation.

Although neither was due to Wilkes, two Union captures in the second half of 1862 led to interesting episodes involving Lafitte and Heyliger. On December 3, *Emma Tuttle* was captured off of Wilmington by USS *Cambridge*. The ship was owned by Augustus Adderley and was used frequently by John Lafitte to ship contraband consigned by Adderley and Company and by Sawyer and Menendez. Union commander William Parker placed a prize crew on board and *Emma Tuttle* started off for New York to be adjudicated in prize court. But off Cape Hatteras she ran into such a severe storm that the wooden boom along her main sail was torn off. In fear for their lives, the prize master turned the ship back over to the ship's captain who then immediately made way for

Nassau. Back in the city, Lafitte resumed control of the boat in violation of international maritime law. Whiting wrote Seward that he did not even try to protest as there was no reason to expect justice.

Another strange situation involved the blockade runner *Victoria*. She left Wilmington in July 1862 but was caught and taken to the prize court in Key West. After being condemned she was bought by longtime Nassau merchant Sylvain Haymann, a French citizen. He renamed her *Harkaway* and sent her on a run from Nassau to Wilmington with a cargo of salt. Salt was in high demand in the South for meat preservation and tanning hides, and in two years its price rose from one cent per pound to fifty cents per pound. Boats from Liverpool often came to Nassau with salt as ballast and returned with cotton. Haymann cleared *Harkaway* for Beaufort, North Carolina, which was then in Union hands and a legitimate port. But like most ships cleared for Beaufort from Nassau, she instead headed to Wilmington. On her return trip, she was to bring Haymann a cargo of cotton and rosin (a pine product with many uses including inks and adhesives).

When *Harkaway* arrived in Wilmington, a British subject named Davis reclaimed her, asserting that the decision of a US prize court had no validity in the Confederacy. In February 1863, Haymann went to Heyliger with a letter of protest which he also sent to the Duke of Newcastle. Heyliger wrote to Benjamin requesting that he remedy this injustice, not only because Haymann had lost about $120,000, but because it was bad for business. If prior owners could reclaim their ships when they arrived in Charleston or Wilmington, it would make Nassau merchants hesitant to buy vessels at prize court. As Heyliger said, such an outcome would diminish the means of finding suitable craft to run the blockade. The case dragged on in the Confederate district court until Wilmington was evacuated in early 1865 at which point *Harkaway* was likely destroyed.

As business boomed, the city continued to adapt and change. The town had new restaurants, a new theatre, and a new bowling alley. The Bay Street Boys advertised Cuban cigars and cases of champagne at discount prices. The three photograph studios in Nassau began taking photographs of blockade-running captains and crew members as mementos, but someone began selling copies to the US consul's office. When these photographs were forwarded to US cruisers, captured Southern captains who claimed to be English found themselves in federal prison.

One observer stated, "Money was almost as plentiful as dirt." The coffers were so full that money could be given away for the right cause. In February the news spread that Henry Adderley, William and Robert Weech, Henry and Pembroke Saunders, John S. George, Robert Sawyer, and Ramon Menendez had bought twelve hundred bibles to be distributed to Confederate soldiers. These same gentlemen and many others also donated to the Lancashire Cotton Famine Relief Fund. By the end of 1862 the cotton surplus in England was gone, and the mills there were feeling it despite new sources in other countries.

With the newfound affluence, the Upper Ten orchestrated ever more elaborate celebrations. In January 1863, the occasional horse races were formalized into the Nassau Races to begin in mid-February. The newspapers announced the guiding stewards of the event to be Henry Adderley, Augustus Adderley, George Anderson, Sylvain Haymann, and Lewis Heyliger. Being included in this group certainly shows Heyliger's prominence in the community. Horse racing was quite popular in New Orleans before the war, so Heyliger may have had an interest in the event beyond the prestige it brought him, and his involvement perhaps showed that he could occasionally put business aside. The races drew hundreds of spectators from all walks of life.

Of course, the influx of money and people into the city did not come without problems. According to one observer, it was "a stirring, colorful confusion of sailors, traders, agents and swindlers." The newspapers complained that the roads were now too narrow for all the people swarming them. So many shady boarding houses (which the *Bahama Herald* deemed "miserable hovels") had sprung up to house the sailors and hustlers that the government printed out rules for their cleanliness: floors swept daily and scoured weekly, bedding aired twice a week and privies "kept wholesome" by covering with two inches of sea salt in the summer.

The numerous bars and billiard parlors opening prompted the Royal Victoria to place ads reassuring potential customers that they had the best liquor and billiards in town. Only about one-third of the new drinking establishments were licensed, but rumor had it that the police were given free drinks in exchange for looking the other way. Custom duties on ale and porter rose from £544 in 1860 to £14,251 in 1864. The arrival of numerous foreigners was seen in ads for liquor and billiards now appearing in Spanish. The Royal Victoria was the scene of so much activity that the government appointed a committee from the House of Assembly that included Henry Adderley and Timothy Darling to make recommendations for making the place more sanitary.

Wherever money flows freely criminals are sure to follow. Burglaries and violence unheard of before the war were becoming common, and the newspapers began including crime reports that included assault, larceny, forgery, manslaughter, and murder. There were knife fights in the shipyards, and a fair number of sailors, presumably heavily intoxicated, drowned at night in the harbor. An argument in a billiard parlor on Christmas Eve that led to the fatal shooting of the owner as he tried to break up the altercation led to a law limiting billiard parlor hours and another that prohibited carrying loaded firearms. One observer noted just after the war,

> The excitement, extravagance, and waste prevailing at the time were extraordinary ... many a Dinah owed her ruin to the extraordinary temptations offered by reckless sailors, with more money than they knew what to do with, and with the very lowest notions of morality. A few undertakers may have profited, as disease became rather prevalent and fatal; and the Government was able to pay off a small debt; but what became of all the money made is a mystery.

As we shall see, most of the money ended up in England in the pockets of people like Henry Adderley.

The stores of Richard Sweeting and Alexander Johnson were burglarized. Police chief Stephen Dillet reported to the legislature that the police force was woefully "insufficient due to the influx of seamen." Still, Dillet had enough men to apprehend the black pilots who had been helping the Wilkes squadron. One such pilot, Alexander Price, was arrested on February 7 and charged with violating the Foreign Enlistment Act. The spirit of mayhem seemed to spread to the out islands where "Crazy Mary" Kelsol took over the jail in Inagua, was captured and then several months later took over the jail again.

✦ ✦ ✦

Seth Hawley left New York on *British Queen* on March 2, 1863, and touched down in this beehive of activity with his daughter on Saturday, March 7. He went to the consular office on March 10, but Sam Whiting was not there to conduct the required joint inventory of supplies. Hawley commented that the office was ideally located overlooking the harbor, but found it in complete disarray, with papers strewn everywhere and several windows broken out. Three days later the schooner *John Williams* attempted to get clearance for Beaufort, North Carolina, and Hawley set a new tone by refusing. He knew too well that these ships were headed for Wilmington.

William Seward was dismayed to receive a letter chronicling Whiting's final weeks in Nassau. The letter came from Robert Bowne Minturn Jr., the son of a wealthy shipping magnate and business associate of Moses Grinnell. One of American's most prominent men, the elder Minturn had donated the land that became Central Park in New York City. In an interesting aside, Grinnell and Minturn had lost money when a shipment of rice they owned was seized early in the blockade on the ship *Mary Clinton* headed from Charleston to New Orleans.

Minturn's son was vacationing in Nassau and had been one of the Americans who signed the letter asking Lincoln to raise the consular salary. According to his letter, on March 3 an inebriated Whiting led a mob of black men down Bay Street to the consular office. Whiting proceeded to the balcony where he harangued the crowd for singing Southern war songs and told them they should read the Charleston newspaper ads of "negroes for sale." He also disparaged the British Empire and the queen herself. When several passersby told Whiting to stop, he told them to make him stop. When they said, "Come down and we will," Whiting did just that and was arrested when police broke up the brawl that ensued.

Ten days later Whiting was at it again. He appeared at the Royal Victoria and after consuming some wine began yelling at various Southerners and their British friends. According to Minturn, who was there, these men endured Whiting's abuse with admirable patience until it was too much, and Whiting got the fight he wanted. Several men pulled Whiting away, but not until part of his clothing had been torn off. But Captain Sam was not done and came back for more. He shook his fist and continued to stream epithets at a Confederate captain, who finally drew his sword. Minturn and several other Americans saved Whiting and dragged him back to his room. Whiting was again arrested and given a heavy fine that he was unable to pay. He was only saved jail time by the generosity of John Howell, who paid the fine. By this time, Whiting's behavior had descended from embarrassing to ludicrous. As Minturn noted of the behavior, it was "harder for Americans here to bear as Mr. Heyliger, the Confederate agent, is such a gentleman."

Finally, to the relief of all, Sam Whiting boarded *British Queen* on March 23 and headed back to New York. He wrote to Seward attempting to explain the last incidents. He said the incident on March 3 at the consulate was a case of defending the national honor. As for the fight at the Royal Victoria, he said that he had not been there in months due to the insults he received. He did admit to drinking wine and said that its effects were exacerbated by opium he had had prescribed for his rheumatism by local doctor George Kemp. As he summarized for Seward, "I plead guilty to a considerable degree of excitement caused by drinking a little wine, and the memory of all the wrongs and insults heaped upon my country and flag during the past two years." Without his wife, the loneliness in such a frustrating and venomous environment combined with the humiliation at being replaced must have put him in a dangerous state of mind.

After the war Attorney General George Anderson contrasted Whiting's social stature to those of Heyliger and Laffite.

> In Nassau strangers are very generally hospitably received by residents, the only passport to social intercourse being gentlemanly bearing, combined with

propriety of conduct. At the particular period referred to Nassau was visited by numerous parties, almost all of whom were more or less interested in what was then considered the rising fortunes of a new nation. Many of them were persons of education and acquirements which gave them ready access to the best society of the place, while unfortunately, on the other hand, we had but few northern visitors; and the conduct of Mr. Whiting, the United States consul, being such as necessarily excluded him from social intercourse with respectable persons, he made such exclusions a ground of complaint to his Government, attributing to political motives and what was only the result of his own habits of inebriety and general misconduct, and building on such foundation charges of bias and corruption against all persons who, from feelings of self-respect, avoided his society.

While his drinking did him in, Whiting's low salary and his firm support of the Union cause would have likely finished him off eventually. Northern visitors expected the consul to be their entrée into local high society but his lack of money and opposition to blockade running made that impossible. Still, one must admire Whiting for what he did accomplish when confronted with such adversity. He had written hundreds of reports that kept Washington apprised of what was happening in Nassau. He also began the communication and intelligence system with the Navy that Hawley would soon refine. Captain Sam hoped Seward would find him another post to serve the country but not surprisingly this was not to be.

✦ ✦ ✦

On March 2, 1863, Governor Bayley opened the legislature for the season. This was always a significant event as there was a promenade from Government House to the Parliament buildings with salutes fired and American tourists gathering for a glimpse of the British rituals. Addressing the House of Assembly, Bayley gave a speech that exemplified the high spirits of all who were riding the crest of the blockade-running wave. Noting the great prosperity that had dropped in their laps, he said the merchants had the right of engaging in commercial operations with either of the belligerents. He acknowledged that those in the Union were not happy with them, but said "the people of the Northern States have awakened to a sense of their inconsistency and injustice, and that while they have not ceased to complain of the inconvenience to which they are subjected by the Neutral commerce of these islands, they have ceased to reprobate as moral delinquencies practices which derive their greatest authority from the example originally set by themselves." He pointed out that American naval officers must abstain from provocation or aggression within the jurisdiction of a friendly power and added that "the increased traffic and wealth of this city increase the importance ever attached to due protection of property."

If anyone needed proof that the Bay Street Boys were running the Bahamas, this speech was it. The House of Assembly, as always, made an official response to the opening speech. Surprisingly, as the body was almost completely composed of elite merchants, they asked that the government institute a higher tariff on goods entering and leaving Nassau to raise revenues needed for improvements in the city. In their opinion the current tariffs were not "framed to meet the exigencies which have arisen by the American War."

Bayley's speech provoked an immediate and angry reaction from his boss, the Duke of Newcastle. Noting his disapproval of Bayley's thoughts on blockade running, he pointed out that the Americans had every right to blockade the ports of their enemy. His final paragraph chastised Bayley for his exuberant remarks: "I have no doubt the language which you used was very acceptable to the inhabitants of the Colony, who are naturally anxious to make the most of their present position relative to the Seat of War. But I think you failed to observe that in using it, you were laying yourself open to a charge of unfriendly conduct towards a neighboring power, and were impairing the position of the Government which you serve." Bayley made an effort to defend his speech in a May 5 letter to Newcastle but seemed to only dig a deeper hole. This speech was the beginning of the end for Bayley. His strong sympathies for the merchants and the Confederates were causing too much friction for the men on Downing Street.

✦ ✦ ✦

Once Seth Hawley settled into his office on Bay Street, he could see his challenge out the front window. The harbor was packed with boats, many of them the long, low gray steamers running "like smoke" back and forth to Charleston and Wilmington and nearly invisible in the open sea. The shipyards in England and Scotland were busy producing dozens of "Clyde steamers," the sort of boat Hawley mentioned in a letter to his friend George Gorham.

Originally meant for fast transport on the River Clyde near Glasgow, they were modified to be perfect for the run from Nassau to the Confederacy. Hawley told Seward that it was easy to tell which ships were running the blockade, but very difficult to get the word to the navy. He and Commander Wilkes would soon remedy that.

The sense of relief over Hawley's arrival seemed to be universal. Wilkes told Gideon Welles that Hawley was a "great improvement on his predecessor, who was entirely unfit for his situation, and brought disgrace on our country by his habits and conduct." The *New York Times* correspondent said, "Our new Consul entered upon the duties of his office last Monday. He is a very gentlemanly, quiet man, and spoken highly of by all who have made his acquaintance." Even Governor Bayley seemed willing to give him a chance. In his first week in the city, Hawley attended a grand ball at Government House in honor of the marriage of the Prince of Wales to Princess Alexandra of Denmark. Hawley was one of one hundred sixty guests that included all the Upper Ten and their wives and many prominent Americans. If he had still been the consul, Sam Whiting would likely have been home alone.

Since the war started, the number of ships engaged in blockade running had been steadily growing except for a brief downturn during the yellow fever epidemic. Despite Bayley's ebullience, Hawley's first two months as consul coincided with a second decrease in shipping, this one due to events on both sides of the Atlantic. In Nassau, Hawley, Wilkes, and two American residents of the city would finally form a team that had a real impact on the Bay Street fun. As soon as Hawley was set up in his office, Charles Jackson paid him a visit to reestablish contact. During Whiting's last few months, the underwriter's agent had been hiring the pilots for the Navy ships as everyone seemed to have lost faith in the consul.

During his visit, Jackson asked Hawley to take some immediate action. Jackson had gotten inside information on the time of departure and route of the blockade runner *Granite City*. Jackson encouraged Hawley to hire black wrecking captain Matthew Lowe to find USS *Tioga*, one of the ships in Wilkes squadron, to forward the information.

Hawley hired Lowe and *Tioga* was lying in wait for *Granite City*, capturing her easily on March 22. This same system resulted in the capture of two more steamers in the coming weeks, and Hawley started to get the attention of the Bay Street Boys. Hawley and Jackson began to conjure up a plan to build a spy network as extensive as that already set in place by Heyliger and Lafitte.

Because the white men had been taken by the Confederates, this new network would need to consist primarily of black wreckers and other black residents. Since prize crews were given a cut from the proceeds of captured ships, Hawley suggested that black Bahamians whose information aided in the capture of blockade runners also be given some of the prize money as an incentive. Wilkes arrived off of Hog Island in mid-April after being gone for the last month in search of *Florida* and *Alabama*. Hawley took a small boat out to Wilkes's impressive new flagship, USS *Vanderbilt*, and met with the commander in his cabin. Wilkes was enthusiastic about the Hawley-Jackson plan and added that in addition to having wrecking captains providing information they should add to their spy network a series of "shore watchers." Hawley also told Wilkes about a new proposal that had come from American Epes Sargent.

Sargent wanted the US government to purchase a wrecker but use it for intelligence purposes. Sargent's plan was that he be in charge of the ship and report directly to the consul. Including a fee to him of $150 each month, the total cost would be about $500 per month, quite a bit less than either Wilkes or the Confederates were currently paying for information. Wilkes thought this was a great idea and forwarded the idea for approval to Gideon Welles.

It would be easy enough to disguise the ownership of the ship as the Bahamian government was very lenient about allowing sketchy ownership arrangements. For example, the *Harkaway* that was owned by Sylvain Hayman was registered to fellow merchant Richard Farrington. Another blockade runner that ran in and out of Nassau during much of 1863, *Wild Pigeon*, had owners in England, then in Hong Kong, and was supposedly bought in late 1863 by Frederick Chauncey of New York, who was a trustee of Moses Grinnell's Sun Mutual Insurance Company! She was actually owned by Joseph Eneas, one of the Bahamians heavily involved with running contraband from New York to Nassau.

Jackson and Hawley, along with Wilkes's cruisers, were starting to be an actual impediment to the blockade runners leaving Nassau. Along with *Granite City*, the runners *Rosalie*, *Five Brothers*, *Florence Nightengale*, *Brothers*, and *John Williams* were all taken during Hawley's first three weeks, followed by *Harvest*, *W. Y. Leitch*, and *Justina* in April. Profits were significantly affected, and it seemed that the tide might finally be turning.

Lewis Heyliger was concerned enough that he wrote to Benjamin in April lamenting the constant US violations of neutrality. He heard through the grapevine of Wilkes stating that his orders were to seize every vessel that came in his direction. He told Benjamin that he was apprehensive that any ship coming to Nassau would be captured regardless of the nature of her cargo. Heyliger wrote Benjamin again in the first week of May to tell him that "we are without news from any quarter and have not had an arrival from home in nearly a fortnight." For Heyliger, going from multiple arrivals on many days to no ships in nearly two weeks was a major problem.

✦ ✦ ✦

In addition to Hawley's arrival, the second hindrance to business was a financial problem among the Confederate agents in England. Since the beginning of the war Caleb Huse had been procuring most of the goods in England being shipped back to the Confederacy. When James Ferguson of the Quartermaster's Department and William Crenshaw of the new government shipping line showed up in late 1862, there was immediate friction as Huse refused to relinquish his duties to buy all supplies. This put Ferguson, Huse, and Crenshaw in the position of sometimes competing against each other for the same goods.

Ferguson, who had many years of experience in the textile industry, wrote his superior Abraham Myers that not only was Huse being seriously overcharged for the fabrics he was buying but that he was also accepting a personal commission on each purchase. Crenshaw wrote to Secretary of War Seddon that Huse insisted on buying only from S. Isaac Campbell and Company and added that this company had a reputation in England as being a bunch of crooks. The accusations upset Huse to the point that he later wrote Seddon, "I have not only been personally annoyed by the conduct of Major Ferguson and Mr. Crenshaw, but my efficiency as an agent of the C.S. War Department has been seriously impaired."

As the fall 1862 letters from Benjamin Woolley Hart had revealed, an additional complication in all of this was a general lack of funding for purchasing anything. The Confederacy was cotton rich and cash poor. To rectify that situation, March 1863 brought a new financial instrument into play. Working with the French investment bankers Erlanger and Company, the Confederacy began to issue unusual bonds. They sold for 90 percent of face value but were redeemable in cotton owned by the Confederate government. The catch was that the bond holders needed to pick up the cotton at a Southern port.

The overall idea was to give Confederate agents in Europe an infusion of money while simultaneously stimulating blockade running. Colin McRae, a merchant and Confederate congressman from Alabama, was appointed to oversee the loan. One of the first things he did on arrival in England was to get S. Isaac Campbell and Company to accept these bonds as payment of the Confederacy's outstanding debt. McRae was also appointed as chief financial agent and given the charge of coordinating the allocation of resources from the bond sales to Huse, Ferguson, and Crenshaw. Finally he investigated the allegations against Huse and eventually determined that he did not have criminal intent but was naïve for trusting S. Isaac Campbell and Company. McRae found that the company, who had provided much of the South's needs in the first two years of the war, was keeping two sets of books and was definitely gouging Huse. Alexander Collie, William Crenshaw's shipping partner, was later found to also be taking advantage of the Confederacy.

As part of the financial reorganization that had Colin McRae cleaning up the mess in England, Treasury Secretary Memminger appointed Heyliger as depositary of the Confederate States Treasury at Nassau. This appointment meant that Heyliger would serve a role in Nassau similar to that of McRae in England. With Richard Waller of the Quartermasters Department and James Crenshaw representing the Crenshaw/Collie Line soon to arrive in Nassau, officials wanted to avoid any confusion by allowing Heyliger to allocate all resources as he saw fit. As depositary, he would receive a commission not to exceed $2,500 per year on the funds passing through his hands. Heyliger replied with his gratitude at this mark of confidence. Heyliger also officially appointed Judah Benjamin as his attorney so that Benjamin could endorse Treasury Department drafts for him in Richmond.

The aggressive tactics used by Wilkes continued to irritate the British. There had already been contentious arguments at the highest levels of government over a capture by the Wilkes squadron in late 1862 of *Mont Blanc*. The British contended that the capture near Sand Cay, a tiny spit near Grand Bahama, violated the three-mile maritime limit. Wilkes argued that there were so many tiny patches of rock and sand in the Bahamas that the law was irrelevant. His argument did not hold up and *Mont Blanc* was eventually released and her owners compensated.

This same scenario played out in a much more high-profile incident on May 30, 1863, when *Margaret and Jessie*, returning from Charleston with sixteen passengers (including Douglas French Forrest, soon to be enamored with John Lafitte's niece, and Alfred Trenholm, George Trenholm's son) and seven hundred and thirty bales of cotton, was chased by one of Wilkes's ships, USS *Rhode Island*. The blockade runner headed for the shore of Eleuthera, the nearest island, but *Rhode Island* kept firing. With a range of five miles, the cruisers guns could pepper the ship from well outside the maritime limit, but witnesses later swore that the gunboat came within five hundred yards of shore. *Margaret and Jessie* was hit in one of her boilers and ran ashore while other shells from the gunboat peppered the homes on the beach.

As soon as he heard the news, Heyliger borrowed one of Henry Adderley's steamers, *Raccoon*, and headed to Eleuthera. On the way, he met *Margaret and Jessie*, which had been repaired (her cargo removed by wreckers) and was headed for Nassau. On June 2, Heyliger sent notary public Ormond Malcolm to get testimony from witnesses on Eleuthera and had the crew and passengers, including Douglas Forrest, testify to notary Bruce Burnside in Nassau. All accounts confirmed that *Rhode Island* had violated the three-mile limit.

Heyliger wrote to Benjamin on June 6 to inform him of the "disgraceful outrage perpetrated" by *Rhode Island*. He also enclosed a copy of the latest *Nassau Guardian* that included an article about the incident. The article, without a byline, appeared to be written by the editor Edwin Moseley but was actually written by Heyliger. He wrote that the attack was an "unjustifiable outrage" and pointed out the danger to the female passengers on board and all the residents of the island. As if he was a British citizen, he wrote that "it is high time indeed that the home government should act energetically with respect to these aggressions."

Not long after, the British government filed a formal protest. In this same issue of the *Guardian*, Heyliger also took the unusual step of having a letter in his possession published. As he told Benjamin, "through some influence it is unnecessary to mention, I had the letter intercepted." The letter from Albert Clary, the commander of the *Tioga*, to Seth Hawley, outlined their communications system at the outer islands and the plan to use a wrecker for espionage. Heyliger said in the newspaper note accompanying the letter that "correspondence of this nature is not normally intended for the public eye, but when found in the open street . . ." He added that this espionage system was a clear violation of the rights of a neutral power, cleverly ignoring the superior system that he and Lafitte had created.

✦ ✦ ✦

Heyliger's exposure of the Union system turned out not to matter. Within a week of Heyliger's submissions to the *Guardian* both Charles Wilkes and Seth Hawley left Nassau for good. These departures must have been a real blow to loyal Americans like Charles Jackson, Epes Sargent and John Howell. Wilkes's aggressive attitude had not only offended the British, but also his superiors in the Navy. Gideon Welles reprimanded Wilkes for spending too much of his time dealing with the blockade runners while *Florida* and *Alabama* were running wild on US merchant ships. Since the beginning of the war up to June 1863, one estimate claimed that Confederate raiders captured or destroyed 148 US vessels and that insurance on merchant ships had gone up 10 percent.

Wilkes responded with a letter that Welles deemed to be insubordination. In the first week of June he was removed from command and court-martialed. Wilkes was eventually found guilty of insubordination and suspended for three years, though Abraham Lincoln reduced the suspension to one year. He was placed on the retired list and remained something of a public hero.

Hawley's short stay seems to have ended due to health and financial issues. He had warned Seward that he might not stay if something was not done about the low consular salary of $2,000 per year. In addition, before coming to Nassau he had a bad case of carbuncles. They seem to have reappeared, and he feared the warm weather might exacerbate them. In late April, after less than two months on the job he requested a leave of absence. Hawley left for New York on June 8, and for the next few months people in Nassau and the United States considered him to be on leave. But by August it was clear to Seward that

Hawley was not going back to the Bahamas. Finding a suitable replacement would take almost a year.

When Hawley requested his leave, he also informed Seward that he had arranged for attorney William Charles Thompson to take over his duties in the role of vice-consul. The appointment was most likely suggested by Charles Jackson, as Thompson was a partner of Jeremiah Tappan at the Neptune Insurance Company and a member of the Board of Underwriters. Hawley described Thompson as "a gentleman especially well qualified by education, ability, temper, manners and discretion to discharge the duties of the consul under the present circumstances." Two days before Hawley left Nassau, Bayley officially approved Thompson as vice-consul. Whatever Thompson's personal qualities might have been, he would not be able to match Hawley's performance in affecting the flow of contraband. With the removal of Wilkes, Welles decided to go back to the strategy of trying to stop the runners at Charleston and Wilmington instead of a de facto blockade of Nassau. Even before this the Wilkes-Hawley effort was beginning to suffer. The ships now coming over from England were faster and harder to see, and much of that early success in March and April had been in catching older and slower ships. The blockade-running captains were also becoming aware of Hawley's spies and taking alternate routes out of the islands.

In addition to health and money, Hawley might also have left due to frustration. In his last official letter to Seward from Nassau, he admitted that he had been in error in early May when he declared blockade running unprofitable. By the end of May things were as bad as ever or worse. He also reaffirmed for Seward that Governor Bayley was the "humble servant" of the blockade runners and rebels. In any case, the former policeman had had enough. With Hawley and Wilkes gone, the Great Carnival was about to grow even larger, and it eventually took factors outside of Nassau to slow it down.

10

Living for the Hour

With Seth Hawley and Charles Wilkes gone, blockade running from Nassau ran wild for most of the next year. While Confederate military fortunes reached their high-water mark in mid-1863 with Lee's victory at Chancellorsville and his bold invasion of Pennsylvania, supplies continued to flow through Nassau in great quantities almost to the end of the war. George Trenholm wrote directly to Governor Bayley to gloat about the volume of trade flowing through his islands. He pointed out that just the single ship *Margaret and Jessie* had made five round trips and delivered 3,714 bales of cotton. At several hundred dollars per bale, that was a lot of money for just one ship in a large fleet. William Thompson did not have the stature to slow things down, and the Union Navy now turned their attention to sealing off Charleston and Wilmington.

With such an unprecedented opportunity to make money, people of all sorts began to take up residence in Nassau. Many of them lived at the Royal Victoria, a hotel that had been a speculative venture by the Bahamian government but was now bursting at the seams and staying full all year. Some of the most interesting characters at the hotel were the captains of the blockade-running ships. These men risked their lives on a regular basis and spent their time at the Royal Victoria doing their best to enjoy their days of relaxation. John Maffitt, everyone's favorite, was far away on the *Florida*, but many others had taken his place. Regulars certainly included Tom and Robert Lockwood and James Carlin with various ships, Louis Coxetter of the *Antonica* (formerly the *Herald*), William Ryan of the *Syren*, Ferdinand Peck of the *Cecile* and *Carolina*, and Jonathan Steele of the *Banshee*.

Two interesting lodgers at the hotel were British naval officers who left the British Navy to cash in on the frenzy. Augustus Charles Hobart-Hampden, son of the Earl of Buckinghamshire, was forty-one and had served since he was a young teenager, chasing slave ships off the coast of Africa and commanding a ship in the Crimean War. He had at one time commanded Queen Victoria's yacht.

Charles Murray-Aynsley was the same age as Hobart-Hampden and had served in the British Navy just as long. These two, along with fellow officers William Nathan Wrighte Hewett (who would captain the blockade runner *Condor*) and Hugh Talbot Burgoyne, were granted furloughs to try their hand at running the blockade.

Hobart-Hampden was quite successful at it and eventually wrote a memoir called "Never Caught" about his exploits with the *Don* and other ships. He went by the nom de guerre "Captain Roberts" during his exploits. Running the blockade did not quench his love of adventure as he entered the service of the Ottoman Empire a few years after the Civil War. He won fame commanding a fleet that suppressed an insurrection in Crete, and the Sultan awarded him the high title of Pasha. He apparently enjoyed doing his own thing: when the British Admiralty sent him a letter indicating that if he did not leave the Turkish service he would be scratched off their officer list, he wrote back, "You may scratch and be damned!"

Like most captains running the blockade, Hobart-Hampden made sure to secure personal profits on the side. Before leaving England, he had a conversation with a Southern woman there and asked her what was needed most in the Confederacy. The woman proposed that stays (a type of bodice or corset) would be highly prized by Southern females. So Hobart-Hampden made a deal to buy a thousand stays at one shilling each before leaving England and was able to sell the lot of them in Wilmington for twelve shillings apiece.

He also bought a huge number of Cockle's Pills, a digestive aid popular in England. He found to his dismay that he could not convince anyone in Wilmington to buy the pills, so he decided to take the pills to Nassau, where "everyone was bilious from over-eating and drinking on the strength of the fortunes they were making by blockade-running." In Nassau he found a druggist who wanted the pills and gave Hobart-Hampden two chests of matches in return. The next time he was back in Wilmington he sold the matches for a huge profit.

Seeing Nassau after first seeing Wilmington made quite an impression on Hobart-Hampden. Where Wilmington was full of poverty and distress, in rose-colored Nassau everyone was prosperous and happy. He met with "calculating, far-seeing men, who were steadily employed in feathering their nests, let the war in American end as it might," while other men "careless and thoughtless, living for the hour, were spending their dollars as fast as they made them, forgetting that they would never see the like again." The streets and the hotel had "rollicking captains and officers of blockade-runners and drunken swaggering crews, sharpers, looking out for victims" along with Yankee spies and free blacks all crowding together to make "a most heterogeneous, though interesting crowd."

Like Hobart-Hampden, Murray-Aynsley worked under a false name (Captain Murray) and matched Hobart-Hampden's success with his ships *Hansa* and *Venus*. After the war he returned to his normal service and was eventually promoted to Rear Admiral. Murray-Aynsley was described as universally loved, gentle as a child but brave as a lion. Those British naval officers still in uniform who spent time in the Royal Victoria often expressed their jealousy of the adventure and profits their colleagues on furlough were enjoying. Some of the sailors on British warships could not resist the temptation and deserted their posts to join the blockade runners.

Both of the British captains on leave brought their wives to Nassau, and Mrs. Hobart-Hampden and Mrs. Murray-Aynsley became matrons of the Royal Victoria social scene. According to the memoirs of another captain, Tom Taylor, these two ladies "presided at our revels and tended to keep the younger and more reckless of our set in order." Taylor continued, "Every night our dinner table was filled to its utmost capacity, and once a week at least we had a dance, when the office furniture was unceremoniously bundled out into the garden under the care of a fatigue party of soldiers, and the band of the regiment discoursed entrancing music to those whose feet never seemed to tire."

Taylor was also British but twenty years younger than Hobart-Hampden and Murray-Aynsley. Prior to the war he was working as an office assistant for Edward Lawrence and Company, a large Liverpool shipping firm. In early 1862 Taylor's employers decided to get into the blockade-running game and bought a steamer for that purpose. Taylor's supervisor asked him if he would like to go on the steamer as supercargo, and the young man jumped at the chance. The vessel on which he left Liverpool was the *Despatch*, a "second-hand cattle boat."

The rickety vessel was so loaded with coal for the voyage that she was almost swamped in a strong storm on the way across the Atlantic. Once in Nassau, captains who had experience running the blockade told Taylor that there was no way the boat would make it through. The young man managed to sell his cargo of silk and other luxury goods and decided to make the best of his situation by hiring the boat out to do something useful. He arranged to have his boat tow the *Karnak* back to New York. As described earlier, the captain of the *Despatch* cut the *Karnak* loose instead of bringing her to New York as promised.

Taylor followed the *Despatch* to New York, arriving on the *British Queen* on August 30, 1862, to find a seriously bad situation. The *Despatch* was not only quarantined due to yellow fever on board but was being sued by Kimball and Arnold for damages related to casting the *Karnak* adrift. After several deaths on board, the fever cleared, and the *Despatch* was moved from quarantine to the harbor under the custody of the marshal of the port. One night Taylor convinced his captain to make a run for it, but they were quickly turned around by Union ships. Eventually a friendly banker arranged to settle with Kimball and Arnold for $2,000, and Taylor was able to return to England.

His employers were so happy with his handling of the *Despatch* that they immediately put him in charge of a new ship they were having built, the *Banshee*. This was the first vessel built expressly for blockade running and would be the first all-steel ship to cross the Atlantic. He arrived in Nassau in early 1863 where the boat, an omen of things to come, caused a sensation. The ship made eight successful trips through the blockade, netting a 700 percent profit for her investors.

Taylor and his men were favorites on both ends of the blockade-running routes. His men appreciated his "coolness and daring," and they all seemed to have a good time in whichever port they were in. Taylor put his young purser Arthur Doering in charge of entertainment in Nassau, as "no one could mix a better cocktail." In addition to making the Royal Victoria livelier, they brought some cheer to Wilmington as well. That suffering city looked forward to his visits, when he invited citizens on board to enjoy champagne and food they normally could not obtain. The children of Wilmington called him the "Santa Claus of the war."

Taylor would manage his company's various ships, fifteen in all, and accompany many of them on their journeys back and forth. The blockade-running branch of the parent company was called the Anglo-Confederate Trading Company. He became good friends with Lewis Heyliger and after landing in Wilmington sometimes personally carried Heyliger's dispatches to Richmond.

One of Taylor's most interesting trips was on the *Banshee*'s successor, the *Banshee II*. Heyliger obtained a superb Arabian horse that was intended as a present for Jefferson Davis, and he asked Taylor if he would take it to Wilmington. As Taylor's boat quietly slipped through the federal cruisers outside Wilmington, the horse must have smelled land and began to neigh loudly. Several jackets put over his head were too late, and the boat narrowly made it to the safety of Forth Fisher under fire.

On arrival, they were immediately put into quarantine due to more yellow fever worries. During his blockade-running career, Taylor was twice in quarantine for fifty days. Taylor explained to authorities that they could not stay in quarantine, as they had no food for the horse. Shore officials telegraphed Richmond for instructions and were told to have Taylor come to port, unload the horse, and then return to quarantine. When Taylor approached port, half his men dove overboard and ran ashore. Taylor explained that putting him in quarantine now was no use, so he was allowed to offload his cargo, load up with cotton, and then steam out past the unhappy ships still sitting in quarantine.

Another notable British citizen who passed through Nassau was Frank Vizetelly, artist for the *London Illustrated News*. Vizetelly had been covering wars in Europe during the 1850s and arrived in Boston just as the Civil War was erupting. After a brief stint covering federal troops, he crossed the Potomac and for the rest of the war became both chronicler and supporter of the Confederate army. A number of his sketches were forwarded to England through Nassau by way of John Lafitte. He made a mid-war trip back to England and passed through Nassau on his return trip.

He wrote about Nassau, "The enterprise of British merchants has lined its quays with long light-colored, rakish looking steamers, discharging their rich freights of cotton that have run the gauntlet through the Federal cruisers of Wilmington." During his short stay he certainly joined in the Royal Victoria festivities. One observer in the Confederate army described him as "a burly-looking, reckless Bohemian of many accomplishments. He could write, could sing, could draw and paint, could dance and ride, could tell good stories (good only in the telling, not in the matter) by the hour, and, finally, could drink like a fish, and did so."

He was a big man. Tom Taylor had a fancy frock coat that others often borrowed to go to various formal affairs in Nassau, and according to Taylor, it was "a little wanting in the front" when Vizetelly wore it. During his stay, Vizetelly made a well-known sketch titled "Unloading Cotton from Blockade-Runners in Nassau, New Providence." In 1883 the adventurous artist disappeared in Sudan while covering British fighting against an Islamic insurrection. His body was never found.

While Tom Taylor managed things for the Anglo-Confederate Trading Company, 1863 saw many other British and Southern firms set up agencies in Nassau. The Erlanger cotton bonds were only of value if the owner could procure cotton from the Confederate ports, so a number of English firms were created to help in this process.

One notable example was the Albion Trading Company with Thomas Sterling Begbie as president. Begbie signed a contract with Colin McRae and John Slidell to take merchandise to the Confederacy and bring back cotton to help pay off the Erlanger loan. Begbie worked closely with George Wigg, who had an office in Nassau. Wigg was British but had been a cotton merchant in New Orleans for many years and was an old friend of Lewis Heyliger. He owned a number of steamers himself and also worked as an agent for Begbie and for two more operations that sprang up in response to the Erlanger loan, the European

Trading Company and the Atlantic Trading Company. Begbie contracted with Beach and Root as his connection on the Confederate end of things.

The new Crenshaw/Collie government shipping line also required agents in Nassau. William Crenshaw's brother James came from the Confederate commissary general's office in Richmond, while twenty-four-year-old Lewis Grant Watson came from England to handle Alexander Collie's side of that business.

In Charleston, a number of new firms were created to take advantage of the booming blockade business and the potential for astounding profits. For example, coffee could be bought in Nassau for $249 per ton and sold in Charleston for $5,500 per ton. Going in the other direction, $100 of cotton would bring $1,000 in Liverpool. Most of these new companies were offshoots of John Fraser and Company in one way or another.

The most prominent of these was the Importing and Exporting Company of South Carolina, with William C. Bee as president. Henry Adderley owned stock in the company, as did John Fraser and Company. Lewis Simons Jervey, teenage son of William Bee's partner Theodore Jervey, and bookkeeper Charles Gustav Mueller arrived in Nassau to handle the interests of the new company under the name Jervey and Mueller. Lewis Jervey was serving in the army but appears to have been furloughed and sent to Nassau at around the same time as Cornelius Mahoney.

Bee was something of a hero after the war as he did his best to sell clothing and provisions at reasonable prices and not let them fall into the hands of speculators. Many Southern citizens were aghast at the profiteering running rampant around them, so Bee's attitude was appreciated.

Other new Charleston companies included the Chicora Importing and Exporting Company with Theodore Wagner of John Fraser and Company as one of three directors, the Charleston Importing and Exporting Company, the Consolidated Steamship Company of Charleston, and the Palmetto Importing and Exporting Company. The Steamship Pet Company owned and operated only one ship, the *Pet*, but her nineteen successful trips made the owners a fortune. The stock opened at $3,200 in December 1863 and by March 1864 was at $5,750. Representing other small Charleston firms in Nassau were Oliver Hewitt representing Joseph A. Enslow and Edwin Bell representing Mcleod and Bell.

The seemingly endless list of men who now found themselves doing business in Nassau included Ernest Zachrisson, a Swedish native who had worked as a merchant and Swedish consul in New York for many years before setting up shop in Nassau in 1863. Liverpool merchants James Thompson and Isaac Rich added George Chambers as a partner and sent him to Nassau to open a branch there called George Chambers and Company. With offices located adjacent to Thompson, Rich and Company in Liverpool, William Bowman and

R. J. Tetley also set up a branch of Bowman, Tetley and Co. in Nassau. Commission merchants George Clark Bogert, Julian Moses Abrams, and Edmond Salomon of New Orleans moved to Nassau to start businesses.

William Boyd Sterrett, who would be dropped off by John Maffitt near Wilmington in 1865, was in the city with his wife by the summer of 1863. One observer noted about Nassau at the time, "Most of those who have flocked there since the commencement of the war, went with the purpose of taking the shortest road to wealth, regardless of the means employed to reach the desired goal. Blockade-runners, and all others having dealings with them, will do well to keep a sharp lookout, and even then they may be thankful if they are not very deeply gouged. The best plan is to trust none, and watch all. The mania for money making is similar to the California gold fever of some years past."

In addition to all the merchants, a number of Heyliger's friends from New Orleans fled that city when it came under Union control and came to Nassau to ride out the war. These included newspaper editor E. C. Hancock, businessmen Myer M. Simpson, attorney Pierre Soulé, and physician Thomas Hunt.

These men and many more competed for business with each other and the original Nassau-based merchants who had been in the game from the beginning. But from the middle of 1863 to the fall of 1864 there was enough to go around. After the war, the value of imports to Nassau were estimated in British pounds:

1860: £92,800
1861: £136,002
1862: £352,520
1863: £2,932,945
1864: £3,772,389

The values of exports from Nassau to Canada in these years are also revealing:

1860: £1,401
1861: £43,901
1862: £304,733
1863: £978,681
1864: £889,470

These large numbers are listed as Canadian exports because they cleared Nassau customs for Saint John, but were actually headed to Charleston and Wilmington. In 1860 four ships cleared Nassau for Saint John but 323 did so in 1863–64. As we shall see, the Great Carnival began to wind down in the second half of 1864, accounting for that year's total being slightly less than the previous year.

To help facilitate the large amount of quartermaster's supplies (i.e. most everything that was not a weapon or ammunition), Major Richard Parham Waller received orders in late July to proceed to Nassau and arrived there on August 10, 1863. Waller was a clothing merchant in Richmond before the war. He had been appointed captain in the Quartermaster Department in July 1861 and promoted to major in October 1862. Before coming to Nassau he was in charge of the Richmond Clothing Depot. Waller dealt with all the most prominent longstanding merchants as well as with most of the newcomers to secure clothing materials and shoes for the soldiers. He paid for these goods with funds Heyliger was obtaining from Fraser, Trenholm and Co. from cotton sales in England.

Nassau harbor was teeming with life and adjustments were being made. The government needed more help in processing all the ships, as the port had only three tidewaiters and each boat that arrived ideally should have its own. A tidewaiter is a customs officer who checks goods upon a vessel's landing in order to secure the payment of duties. In addition to this need, Receiver-General Fletcher Whitley died in October 1862 (though apparently from old age and not yellow fever) and needed to be replaced by someone who could handle the chaotic situation on the water. That man appointed to take Whitley's place had the melodic name John D'Auvergne Dumaresq, and he arrived on the new mail steamer *Corsica* from New York in mid-July. The new receiver-general would prove to be less accommodating to the blockade-running business than was his predecessor.

After nearly a year of the smaller *British Queen* taking the place of the *Karnak*, the *Corsica* provided roughly the same passenger and cargo capacity as the ship that wrecked in 1862. Captain Le Messurier continued to be the captain of this third ship, but on the first trip down in May 1863 he feared that her draft was too deep to cross the bar. He sailed all the way out to Cochrane's Anchorage to let the passengers be brought in from there by smaller boats. He then proceeded all the way to Southwest Bay, twelve miles from Nassau, to unload the cargo, which then had to be taken by bad roads in wagons back to the city.

The House of Assembly made a formal complaint that this inconvenience was not what they had bargained for in their Cunard contract, and on his way back from Havana two weeks later, Le Messurier anchored a bit closer, off of Hog Island. Finally, on his next voyage from New York in June, he got up his courage and brought the *Corsica* inside the bar. Passengers were ferried to land on the steam tug *Quick*, owned by Sawyer and Menendez.

As business exploded, residents of the city found creative ways to make money. At his store, Charles Perpall began selling charts of the South Carolina and North Carolina coasts. This seems a suspicious offering since three-quarters of the ships leaving Nassau during the war cleared for Saint John, New Brunswick. With the price of cotton skyrocketing, John Rahming had seeds sent to Long Island, Bahamas, about two hundred miles southeast of Nassau, in hopes of starting a homegrown crop.

Americans John Howell and Epes Sargent, as loyal to the Union as they were, could not help but take a piece of the action. On May 9, 1863, they opened their dry dock facility on Hog Island. Several hundred guests came across in small boats and gathered under canopies for the dedication. The first boat to be hauled up the 800-foot-long marine railway for an overhaul was Governor Bayley's yacht the *Georgina*. Sargent ran the operation from offices on Hog Island while Howell continued to oversee the Royal Victoria. The dry dock stayed busy in the coming year as many of the blockade runners got repairs, a new paint job, or had their hulls cleaned. While boats were hoisted manually at the beginning, Howell and Sargent soon added a steam engine.

In early August Vice-Consul Thompson noted that Augustus Adderley's boat *Havelock* was having its hull cleaned in preparation for another run to Charleston. Augustus must have had great respect for British General Henry Havelock, who had died a hero in the India campaign in 1857 as he gave his racehorse that same name. The ship's name was later changed to the *General Beauregard* and ran aground off of Wilmington in December 1863. The wreck can still be seen from Carolina Beach at low tide.

The ineffectual Thompson could do little more than watch and comment on the swirling activity all around him. To make matters worse, the landlord of the building Sam Whiting had chosen for the consular office was George Harris of Adderley and Company. Every time Thompson tried to pay his rent, Harris made it a point not to be in his office, so by September Thompson was three months in arrears. Thompson did note one brief moment of truce in early September when the British and US flags were flown side by side at the wedding of Timothy Darling's daughter, but in general the vice-consul was treated as harshly as his predecessors.

As the money flowed in, the House of Assembly continued to allocate money for improvements, as did many of the merchants. In October the *Lucy Darling* arrived from New York with a cargo of thirty-four new streetlights and poles. Hope was expressed in the newspapers that lighting the downtown would reduce the number of robberies occurring. Along with the streetlights, Bay Street was finally widened to accommodate the heavy traffic and provided with granite curbstones to make the area look more elegant. The downtown theater received a new iron roof from England and new seats imported from New York. To improve sanitation, a new sewer line was being dug by a prison gang from the Royal Victoria down to the harbor.

Merchants put up new warehouses on both sides of Bay Street, and being flush with funds, they did not build ramshackle affairs but rather ornate stone buildings. Adderley and Company, Sawyer and Menendez, Saunders and Son, Robert Weech, and Alexander Johnson all expanded their facilities during 1863 and into 1864. A small boy was seriously injured by falling timber from the Adderley warehouse expansion, but that was likely seen as part of the cost of doing business.

Another negative aspect of the financial boom was rampant inflation. Everyone engaged in the business had lots of money, and prices on real estate and many goods tripled and quadrupled. The price of land downtown went up at least 300 to 400 percent over pre-war prices. John S. George sold a piece of land for £3,500 that he had bought in 1856 for £128. Thirty years later his son-in-law bought the land back for £90. Life became very difficult for those not making a killing. In the Confederacy, it took three Confederate dollars to get a dollar of gold in January 1863, but by January 1865 that same gold dollar required sixty Confederate dollars.

Despite the rollicking good times, there was a brief downturn in activity during August and early September 1863. As there were few Union ships in the area, this was probably due to yellow fever fears as during this period most of the traffic switched to Bermuda. The disease did not attack as it had done the previous summer, and by late September the traffic was picking back up. On the bright side, this temporary calm was probably beneficial for Richard Waller as it allowed him to adjust to his new surroundings.

Lingering tensions between the largely African soldiers of the 2nd West India Regiment and the Creole population resulted in a large-scale disturbance in July 1863. A Creole woman from Grant's Town got in an argument with the wife of one of the soldiers, and the soldier's wife threw a rock that broke the Creole woman's leg. A week later male residents of Grant's Town assaulted and seriously injured a soldier who was on duty in the town, and the next night more soldiers were attacked. On July 27 a group of soldiers retaliated by attacking and injuring quite a few Grant's Town residents, many of whom were probably not involved in the earlier attacks. The correspondent of the *New York Times* claimed that two or three people were killed on each side of the riot, but Governor Bayley's account only records one civilian and three soldiers were wounded.

✦ ✦ ✦

Toward the end of 1863 there was a bizarre international incident with a Nassau connection. The steamer *Chesapeake* was hijacked by Confederate sympathizers off of Cape Cod, resulting in several crew members being injured and one dying. The boat was taken toward Saint John, and from there the men hoped to take the boat to Wilmington to sell both the cargo and the vessel.

The mastermind of the plan went by the name of John Parker. Parker was already notorious in Nassau. He had arrived in early March as captain of the supposed Confederate privateer *Retribution*. The boat was built in 1856 as a New York tugboat but by 1861 had ended up in Charleston, now owned by Thomas B. Power. Power received a Letter of Marque that allowed *Retribution* to serve as a privateer, and by the time the boat arrived in Nassau, Parker had both the boat and the letter. On the back of the letter, the rights of the boat had been transferred from Power to Parker, but the circumstances surrounding this transfer were unclear.

On January 30, *Retribution*, flying a US flag, approached the commercial schooner *Hanover* off the coast of Haiti. As she got close to the *Hanover*, Parker took down the flag and hoisted that of the Confederate States. He informed the master of the *Hanover*, Washington Case, that the ship was now his prize. Case argued that he was closer than three miles to Haiti, but Parker insisted they were four miles off and put a prize crew on board. After letting Case and his crew off on shore, Parker sailed both ships to Long Cay, about 250 miles from Nassau.

At Long Cay, Parker sailed the *Hanover* in to port and announced himself as Washington Case. He sold the cargo off the boat and then bought a load of salt to send to Charleston. After carrying out this deception, he left the *Hanover* and brought the *Retribution* to Nassau. On the way, he took the *Emily Fisher* as prize and announced himself to the master of that boat as John Priestly. The *Retribution* was about worn out, and in Nassau Parker sold it to Henry Adderley and Company who immediately sold it to Charles Perpall.

Charles Jackson got word of what had happened at Long Cay from Thomas Sampson, a detective hired by the Board of Underwriters to investigate the blockade runners in Nassau. According to Sampson, Captain Parker had at one time been a clerk for Adderley and Company. Jackson wrote a letter to Governor Bayley informing him of the situation and that Parker had misrepresented himself as Case. Parker was soon arrested but freed on bail. During his time in Nassau, Parker took up residence at the Royal Victoria and became good friends with John Howell.

By July the *Retribution* changed hands again and was owned by Gustave Renouard and Byron Bode of Nassau. The boat was renamed the *Etta*, and when it was later captured on a perfectly legal trip to New York, the two Bahamian businessmen filed suit. Unfortunately the New Jersey District Court ruled that they should have known the boat's history since Adderley advertised it as the "Confederate schooner *Retribution*" and dismissed their claim to the boat.

When it came time for Parker's trial, he had jumped bail and was in Saint John plotting his next adventure. In Saint John he reconnected with John Clibbon Braine, a young man he had met earlier that year. It seems that Parker and Braine were made for each other.

Born in England, Braine's family settled in Ohio, and by his early twenties he had a reputation as "an unmitigated scoundrel and swindler." Parker assigned Braine with the task of setting up meetings for him with potential recruits for his proposed mission of taking a Northern steamer. The meetings took place in the Lower Cove area of Saint John, the lower-class section next to the wharves. Parker showed the men his Letter of Marque for the *Retribution* and promised them each $500 in gold once the boat and cargo were sold. He also convinced the men that once they captured the *Chesapeake* and renamed her *Retribution*, his letter would protect them from charges of piracy.

Braine recruited a crew of fourteen men and left with them for New York on December 3 while Parker remained in Saint John. Braine and his men arrived in New York on December 5 and left that afternoon on the *Chesapeake*. About 1:00 a.m. on December 7, as the boat was just off Cape Cod, Braine and his men overpowered the crew of the *Chesapeake*. In the struggle, one of the Chesapeake's crew was shot dead and two others wounded. Near Grand Manan Island, south of Saint John, Parker met the *Chesapeake* in a pilot boat and the passengers and most of the crew were put off into the pilot boat.

Braine and Parker took their ship close to Saint John, where they obtained a small amount of coal. Not long after, the original crew of the *Chesapeake* reached Saint John and immediately alerted the US consul there. The chase was on. Braine and Parker took the ship across the Bay of Fundy to Nova Scotia in hopes of obtaining more coal. Here they sold most of the cargo and obtained a little more coal, but it was too late. Two US warships cornered them.

In a strange twist, one of the ships was USS *Dacotah*, which had such trouble obtaining coal in Nassau the year before. Three of the men were captured and charged with piracy, but Braine and Parker escaped. The prisoners were aided in their defense by one of Henry Adderley's Canadian allies, businessman Benjamin Wier of Halifax. One of the key parts of the trial was determining whether Parker actually had a letter allowing him to operate as a privateer. Local sea captain Ebeneezer Locke stepped forward and testified that Parker, alias Washington Case, alias John Priestly, was his brother Vernon Guyon Locke, and this actually does appear to be the man's given name. His brother had seen both the man and the letter when he was on a trip to Nassau earlier that year. As if the world was not confusing enough, Ebeneezer had a son in 1864 and named him Vernon Guyon Locke. The real John Parker was a sea captain who died in Richmond just before Locke took over the *Retribution* and assumed his name.

Locke resurfaced in Nassau late in the war when, as we shall see, the con man's luck finally ran out. The next word from Braine was in August 1864 when he presented himself to Charles Helm in Havana with orders supposedly from

Secretary of the Navy Stephen Mallory and told Helm that he had received $3,000 from Mallory but needed $1,500 more to carry out a new mission. He also told Helm that he had been to speak in person with Jefferson Davis about this mission. Mallory apparently did give Braine a temporary commission before the *Chesapeake* affair, but he was now on his own.

Helm declined to help Braine on the grounds that aiding him in Havana would violate neutrality, but his gut instincts must have told him something was wrong. He soon got a letter from Judah Benjamin informing him that the entire story was a fabrication. Braine tried to raise money in Havana on the credit of Colin McRae but without success. He managed to recruit a new crew of men and recreated the *Chesapeake* mission by taking over the steamer *Roanoke*, and this time the captain of the ship was complicit in the takeover. Braine and his men sailed the ship to Bermuda where they confiscated about $70,000 in cash before burning the vessel and heading back to Wilmington on John Maffitt's blockade runner *Owl*.

Braine's next adventure was capturing the schooner *St. Mary's* in the Chesapeake Bay on April 1, 1865, and sailing it to Nassau before leaving the ship in Jamaica. Braine fled to Liverpool but was eventually captured in 1866 and held in the Brooklyn jail until 1869. When he was released, he spent the next three decades giving speeches about his wartime exploits. Before he died destitute in Tampa, Florida, in 1906 he claimed to have inherited four million dollars, promised $500,000 as a prenuptial gift to a beautiful young woman, and was accused of selling subscriptions to books that did not exist.

✦ ✦ ✦

As 1863 turned into 1864, everything seemed to be humming along in Nassau. On Christmas, fireworks and rockets were set off from the dry dock and from several of the steamers, and the "usual number of firecrackers were let off by the boys." But some signs of weakness were beginning to show in the Great Carnival. The Union captured Morris Island outside of Charleston, taking away the main channel for blockade runners and decreasing the amount of shipping to and from that city for the rest of the war. Smaller ships would now need to use Maffitt's Channel near Sullivan's Island.

In 1862, there were fifty-nine arrivals in Nassau from Charleston compared to sixteen from Wilmington, but by 1864 things had reversed with only twenty-nine from Charleston and seventy-six from Wilmington. In Nassau, John Dumaresq, the new receiver-general, was not bound by old friendships, and during the fall he began seizing items that had been coming in from Charleston and Wilmington but for which proper duties had not been paid.

But this was an annoyance compared to the problems the Confederates were inflicting on themselves. In 1861 no one could foresee how active the port of Nassau would be and how many jobs Lewis Heyliger would be asked to carry out. The addition of Richard Waller helped some, but Heyliger was still trying to balance the needs of all the various Confederate departments requesting supplies. At various times he was trying to provide for the Navy, Commissary, Ordnance, Quartermaster, Nitre and Mining, Medical, and Treasury Departments. There were a lot of mouths to feed.

Complicating matters were orders he received in the summer of 1863 to include twenty tons of lead and saltpeter in every boat coming out of Nassau. The merchants were not pleased with this turn of events as transporting the heavy lead meant carrying fewer of the more profitable items like brandy, silk, linens, and quinine. The lead was shipped in bars about thirty inches long, six inches wide, and three inches high, each weighing about 220 pounds. Over the next year almost 1,500,000 pounds of lead came through the blockade.

Meanwhile, the Commissary Department was clamoring for meat and the Quartermaster Department for winter clothing and shoes. In addition to all the shipping logistics, Heyliger had a number of other obligations that took up valuable time. Judah Benjamin relied on Heyliger for shipment of foreign papers, office supplies, and even law books from New York. In August of 1863 he was also given duties similar to a consul, and all those wishing to enter Charleston from Nassau now needed to see Heyliger for a passport.

Money was an issue as well as time. In late November 1863, Alexander Lawton (who replaced Abraham Myers as Quartermaster General) received a letter from Fraser, Trenholm and Company informing him that they could not handle both James Ferguson in England and Heyliger in Nassau drawing on their cotton funds for supplies. Richard Waller was doing such a good job filling orders for clothing supplies and shoes that the money was running out. In fact, Waller wrote to Lawton expressing concern that he was already £20,000 in debt due to heavy shipments in the fall. This indebtedness became an ongoing and worsening issue.

In December 1863 the *Nassau Guardian* published an interesting story about Bahamian George Wolf, who had "a considerable amount of property illegally seized" from the *Corsica* by New York Custom House officials as contraband. The newspaper reported that the property had been restored through the intervention of Lord Lyons and that Wolf was initiating action against the United States government for damages. This brief story was the first hint of a major scandal involving the New York Custom House and Bahamian merchants. A large part of the blockade-running operation was about to come crumbling down.

11

Trouble in New York

In late November 1863, New York Custom House officers boarded the *Corsica* soon after its arrival from Nassau and seized papers held by British citizen George Garcia Wolf. Wolf was outraged, and by the time he made his way back to Nassau on the steamer *Governor Bayley* on Christmas Eve he was filing for damages. The *Bahama Herald* called for war against the United States for this insult against the empire. The papers the officers confiscated from Wolf helped lift the lid off the blockade-running activity in Nassau and elsewhere. The ensuing congressional investigation would make it clear to everyone that many people in the North, including those in the New York Custom House, were involved in the Great Carnival.

Wolf was carrying papers that included an invoice for cargo held on the *Margaret and Jessie*, the same ship fired on by USS *Rhode Island* six months earlier. *Margaret and Jessie* was captured near Wilmington on November 5, 1863, and brought to prize court in New York. Wolf's invoice not only matched the cargo found on *Margaret and Jessie* but also that of *A. V. Goodhue*, a vessel that had cleared from New York to Bermuda three weeks before *Margaret and Jessie* was captured. Obviously, the clearance to Bermuda was a ruse as the goods were sent to Nassau, transshipped onto the *Margaret and Jessie*, and then sent toward Wilmington. The cargo on *A. V. Goodhue* had been sent to Nassau by Lewis Benjamin and Abraham Hoffnung, George Wolf's brother-in-law.

George Wolf and his older brother Aaron Wolf were English but lived in Montreal and then New York in the 1850s and sold a variety of goods as A. Wolf and Company. Shortly after the war broke out, the Wolf brothers moved to Nassau to begin running the blockade, setting up Hoffnung and Benjamin as their New York connection. The Wolf brothers were in their late twenties, and one observer described Aaron as "a diminutive dark little man of Jewish aspect, . . . who had made a fortune on a cargo of shoddy, landed in the dark of a conspiring moon and sold to the rebels."

Aaron Wolf told authorities with no shame that his agents Hoffnung and Benjamin paid the equivalent of £500 at the custom house to have the goods on the *A. V. Goodhue* cleared. He told people in Nassau that he had "facilities" for getting goods through the custom house, and he told officials in New York that he was a British subject and would do what he pleased regarding the blockade. In addition to partially explaining how the blockade-running scheme was working, these revelations clearly implicated people residing in New York and the rest of the North with involvement in the business.

Corsica was part of the racket, as had been her predecessors *Karnak* and *British Queen*. In addition to taking contraband cargoes, Nassau merchants sent communications to their partners in New York by way of *Corsica*'s purser instead of through the usual mail. The purser, for a fee, then delivered them to the offices of the Cunard offices where they were distributed to the intended recipients. One observer said that the crew members on these Cunard mail steamers were so pro-Confederate that they would hide suspicious characters behind the coal so New York harbor police would not find them.

When people think of blockade running, they often think of goods arriving in the Confederacy from England, but much of what kept the South afloat for four years actually came from north of the Mason-Dixon Line. War profiteering was rampant in the Union from the beginning of the war, and the mass production inherent in the industrial revolution allowed the scale of fraud to far surpass anything seen before. Woolen mills sprouted in dozens of locations, and many produced uniforms of such inferior materials that the new word "shoddy" was created to describe them, and "shoddy millionaires" was the phrase used to describe their manufacturers. Shoes made of wood chips fell apart after a short march.

For men whose desire for money was stronger than their desire to do the right thing, finding a way to also supply needs in the South was a natural extension of their business. The strong pre-war commercial connections between New York and Nassau continued through the conflict. Both Augustus Adderley and Pembroke Saunders traveled to New York during the war, presumably to work on deals. As one Confederate buyer stated, "In New York I could purchase almost as readily from a Union man as from a 'sympathizer.' No questions were asked. They had the goods and I had the money." Large quantities of beef and pork for rebel armies came from the North, and since it was often spoiled, it was jokingly suggested that the Confederate government should have their own meat inspector in New York.

The most obvious way to send goods from the North was to ship directly to the Confederacy, and once the Union captured Beaufort, Port Royal, and New Orleans and reopened them on June 1, 1862, some clever traders found accomplices who would take care of business on the southern end. Admiral David Farragut said he never approved of taking Mobile "unless we had an overwhelming force to hold it, as the whole of Rebeldom would be supplied through it by our own people."

Another trick was to clear for Beaufort or Port Royal but sail to nearby Wilmington or Charleston. Some also shipped to Washington but made a stop at Aquia Creek near the mouth of the Potomac to unload contraband. An interesting incident along these lines occurred in the spring of 1863 when David Risley of Georgetown, South Carolina, teamed up with Samuel Griffin Miles of Baltimore.

Risley was originally from Philadelphia but had been in South Carolina running lumber mills since the 1850s. Miles was a slave owner and notorious in Baltimore for his southern sympathies and his dealings with the Confederates. When the Confederates abandoned Fredericksburg in April 1862, two of the supply boats they burned to keep out of Union hands belonged to Miles. In Baltimore he was known as "the prince of the contraband traders."

Miles bought the schooner *Secretary* and partnered with Risley to buy $13,000 worth of cargo in Philadelphia. The cargo came off the *Princess Royal*, a Trenholm-owned blockade runner that had been caught near Charleston and brought to the Philadelphia prize court. How they obtained the cargo, which consisted of cannons, small arms, and ammunition, is unclear. In May, Risley had *Secretary* cleared for Port Royal and told Master Benjamin Naylor that he would pay him $500 to take the boat to any Confederate port. The boat tried to run into Wilmington but was intercepted by USS *De Soto* and made to continue to Port Royal. The provost marshal would not let the cargo be landed, and so the boat cleared for New Orleans but instead headed to Nassau. There Risley made a deal with Henry and Pembroke Saunders to take the cargo off his hands. Saunders and Son had the vital equipment delivered to Charleston on their boat the *Lizzie*.

This event shows that instead of shipping direct from the Union to the South, a safer and more efficient way to move large cargoes was to ship to a neutral foreign port and then transship the cargo to the Confederacy. Matamoras, Mexico, had been a mostly forgotten port before the war, but in March 1863 eighty-two vessels sat in that harbor, many from New York and Boston. In 1861 one ship cleared from New York to Matamoras; in 1863 the total was seventy-one. Goods taken in at Matamoras were then transshipped by land into Texas and helped keep the western half of the Confederacy going long after the Union severed the new country by taking the Mississippi River. Havana also saw some activity through Mobile but nothing approaching the connection between Nassau and Bermuda with Wilmington and Charleston.

Merchants at Nassau and Bermuda both had access to the newest vessels being developed in England to circumvent the blockade. In one of the earliest versions of stealth technology, these boats were low, fast, and painted a light gray to blend in with the sea and sky. Many of the boats running from Nassau had their hulls painted this color on John Howell's dry dock. Nassau had the advantage over Bermuda of a more thriving merchant scene and proximity to Charleston (and equal distance to Wilmington) but the distinct disadvantage that the New York Custom House seemed to be more vigilant about the bonds required for shipping there. It was in overcoming this system of bonds that the Nassau and New York merchants showed the height of their creative powers, and some of the officials at the custom house showed the depths of their corruption.

Although Treasury Secretary Salmon Chase had been asking custom officials to deny the export of any cargoes that appeared headed to the Confederacy since May 1861, it was not until the spring of 1862 that Congress officially authorized the requirement of bonds for goods being exported to Nassau. The New York Custom House was divided into ten divisions. A merchant clearing cargo for Nassau would first go to George Embree, the deputy collector of the fourth division. Embree compared the merchant's manifest with the manifest verified by officials who had observed the ship being loaded. If he felt that there was a chance that the cargo might end up in the Confederacy, he would require a bond. This was issued by the ninth division. Once the cargo had been landed in Nassau and the consul was satisfied that it would not be sent to the rebels, he signed a certificate, and the merchant would have the bond amount refunded. A large series of bonded warehouses that held goods waiting to be verified grew along the water in Nassau.

One way to attempt to bypass the system was to hide contraband cargo so it did not show up on the manifest. For example, George Wolf shipped 105 bales of blankets filled with swords from New York to Nassau on *Governor Bayley*. This same cargo included bales of hay that enclosed coils of telegraph wire. That blankets were cleared for a tropical port like Nassau must have raised some eyebrows, and the same might be said of shipments of railroad iron since the Bahamas had no railroads. Apparently eight or nine cannons were boxed as hardware and made their way to Nassau from New York on the *Indus*. In another incident with *Indus*, a small boat met the ship after it left the harbor and a large crate allegedly containing a torpedo was transferred over.

These known examples are likely a small percentage of the total number of these kinds of deceptions. A similar method was to "hide" contraband in plain sight. This technique made use of the fact that customs officials only checked about one case out of ten in the cargo. Shippers would make some sort of intentional error on the duty for a case they knew to match their invoice, requiring that case to be opened and many fraudulent ones to pass through.

An additional method of deception was to ship to another British port and then to Nassau. This could be to an accomplice like Benjamin Wier in Halifax or more often to one of the outer Bahamian islands such as Green Turtle Cay, Harbour Island, or Rum Cay Island. There the cargo could be transshipped, and since it was moving from one British port to another, it did not require bonding or approval by the consul. As mentioned earlier, the consul and Bahamian custom house could be "fooled" by designating ports like Saint John as the intended destination. Everyone knew it was a lie. Finally, ships would sometimes clear for ports that did not require bonds but then arrive in Nassau in "distress" with some supposed repair needed.

A creative method to attempt to avoid seizure was to carry official British mail on board. Henry Adderley and Company, Sawyer and Menendez, and other larger commission merchants also added to their treasure chests by acting as forwarding agents for mail going back and forth from the Confederacy to the North or to Europe. Before the war, the average number of letters mailed from Nassau was fewer than 7,000 per year, but by 1864 almost 44,000 letters were mailed. By placing outgoing Confederate mail under British covers and postage, the mail gained a bit of legitimacy. Letters headed to the Confederacy would not have gone through the post office but would be placed on the appropriate blockade runner.

When the steamer *Adela* was seized off Abaco in July 1862 and taken to prize court in Key West, she was carrying two large sacks of British mail from the postmasters at Liverpool addressed to Stephen Dillet, the postmaster at Nassau. This caused quite a stir up to the upper levels of government. There was little doubt that the ship had contraband on board, but seizing British mail was seen as going a bit too far. Union officials claimed all documents on a prize were potential evidence, and that after they had read them all they would be happy to return those that were not incriminating. This did not please the British at all, but the ship and mail remained in custody.

The bond certificates themselves could be tampered with. A consul's signature might be forged. In another instance, a Nassau merchant (likely Timothy Darling) claimed in a letter to Collector of the Port Hiram Barney that on four separate occasions the Wolf brothers had cargoes sent to him from New York. When the cargoes arrived in Nassau, the Wolfs went to William Thompson and claimed to be acting as agents for Darling because he was off the island. Since Darling was the only merchant trusted by the consul's office, Thompson issued the Wolfs a signed bond certificate for the cargoes that they then claimed.

Even more sinister in the eyes of Union officials than all these creative methods was the implication that the whole process could be circumvented within the custom house itself. Based on information received after Aaron Wolf's papers were seized, Lewis Benjamin and former Nassau residents John C. Rahming and Joseph Eneas were arrested in New York on December 31, 1863, and imprisoned in Fort Lafayette. Benjamin's friend and partner Abraham Hoffnung was lucky enough to be in Halifax at this time and did not return to New York.

In January 1864, the US Congressional Committee on Public Expenditures began to call witnesses and investigate what was happening at the custom house and between New York and Nassau. What they unearthed would be described in detail in a report released June 15, 1864.

It turned out that the easiest way to beat the bond system was through bribery and by having men on the inside. In late summer 1863 word reached Hiram Barney that people in Nassau were claiming that bonds could be "bought up" in New York. In other words, for a fee much smaller than the value of the bond, the certificates could be cancelled or destroyed. In other cases, the bonds could be intentionally made out for an amount far less than that on the manifest. Barney started a Treasury Department investigation and found "atrocious malfeasance" in the ninth division of the custom house. The deputy collector in charge of that division, Henry Stanton, and his twenty-two-year-old son Daniel Stanton were removed from their positions in October 1863. The younger Stanton admitted to cancelling bonds worth huge amounts for very small payoffs.

It was a very public disgrace for Henry Stanton, who had been a well-known abolitionist orator before the war and was married to women's rights pioneer Elizabeth Cady Stanton. It appears that their son carried out his treachery without the father's knowledge, and while his son was indeed a crook, there are some indications that Henry Stanton might have been set up by political enemies. While Henry Stanton might not have been devious, he was not a good supervisor. One observer said of the ninth division that "the whole office was rotten" and that this was not a new thing. For years custom officials were known to open cases of goods and remove free samples. One customs broker said that he had been paying the clerks at the custom house bribes of $10 a month for fifteen years in order to get work on his cargoes processed faster.

A month after dismissing the Stantons, Barney received the letter that was most likely from Timothy Darling outlining Aaron and George Wolf's operation. Darling also pointed out that on the latest trip of the *Corsica*, almost forty cases of goods had been shipped to local merchant James de Jongh and immediately handed over to John Lafitte. Darling's letter implicated Hoffnung and Benjamin as being heavily involved with buying up bonds for the Wolfs and found that a customs officer named William Smalley had been their contact on almost all of these bonds and that Joseph Eneas had been shipping much of their material.

In addition to helping clean up the custom house, the testimony from the congressional investigation provided a fascinating look at the inner workings of the blockade-running business. Some interesting schemes were uncovered. Hiram Barney received a letter on October 25, 1863, from someone named James Haggerty staying at the Royal Victoria. The man, whom Barney assumed was writing under an assumed name, made "fearful revelations" but offered to provide tips leading to captures for an upfront sum of $18,000 and 60 percent of the proceeds from all the captures. Barney wrote, "Humbug!" on the letter and ignored it.

In revealing testimony before the congressional committee, Samuel Myers, a commission merchant in New York since 1850, claimed that he had acted as an agent for blockade runners but had been cheated out of $70,000. He had made an offer to custom-house officials to get his money back and some measure of revenge by going to Nassau and placing orders that could then be seized, with Myers getting a share of the proceeds. Myers said, "I know a great many people from Nassau by reputation and a great many of them are here."

According to Myers, he had shipped many times to his son-in-law Israel Wolf in Nassau (no relation to Aaron and George Wolf), and his son-in-law had already made $2 million on the war. If there is any truth to this statement, we can only wonder what kind of profits Adderley and Company and the other major merchants were pulling in. Even with more boats being captured or destroyed, business was good. Myers, however, felt that the "blockade business was played out" and wanted to make a big score before the fun ended. He said that because there were so many Union spies in Nassau, he wanted an official letter that he could show the consulate so these spies would not hinder him. He also asked for a $1,000 advance as the cost of living was so high in Nassau, and he would have to be drinking a lot of champagne with the blockade runners. Custom-house officials turned him away, one saying that he regarded him as a swindler.

On March 19, 1864, Joseph Eneas was interrogated. A boat in which he had an interest, the *Jose*, had been captured on October 6, 1863. It seems that several custom-house agents convinced Myers, who must have been a frequent visitor to the building, to act as an intermediary and go to Eneas to offer him a deal. For $25,000 (to be split between Myers and the agents), *Jose* would be released. Believing he had a case to be made without assistance, Eneas declined the offer.

The committee asked Eneas questions about tampering with bonds, with allegations that he had shipped a wagon for Confederate use on *Jose*, and about the incident with the torpedo on *Indus*, and Eneas denied everything. When asked how much business he had done with Nassau since the beginning of the war, he astonished the members by saying he could not estimate it within $100,000. Eneas was never tried for a crime but sat in Fort Lafayette until July 2, 1864, when he was released on bail. He might have been held so long because Lewis Benjamin had also been released on bail in the spring and ran off to Canada. While most merchants in Nassau were merely opportunistic, Eneas was a true flim-flam man. We will see from his post war adventures that his Civil War exploits were just one phase of a life of deceit.

✦ ✦ ✦

Adderley's old friend Francis Montell was not arrested but did testify to the committee on March 17. The committee accused him of being someone who should know something about the buying up of bonds, but he denied it. He said he had been doing business with Nassau for thirty years, and all that had happened in recent years was that his business had doubled. He had had about forty bonds cancelled and had one hundred sitting in the custom house waiting to be cancelled.

The committee questioned John Rahming on the same day they saw Eneas. Rahming told the committee he was a Nassau native but had come to New York in June 1861. He claimed that he had a liver ailment, and coming north was just following doctor's orders. Given the timing of his arrival, it is unlikely that the committee bought it. He claimed he had never shipped any contraband and was mystified as to why he had been arrested. His only thought was that he must have enemies. Rahming pointed out the times he had helped Sam Whiting with coal and loans and said that because of this, his firm had been "spotted" in Nassau, and that he and his brother "got the black look of most of the people of the country."

Though his brother lived in Nassau, he claimed to have no knowledge of anyone shipping from New York for the purpose of sending contraband to the Confederacy. He claimed that his business had increased so much since the start of the war because he and he brother were the only ones looking out for the residents of New Providence while everyone else was running stuff to Charleston and Wilmington. It did not help his case when on January 15, a boat loaded with contraband consigned from John Rahming to Alexander Rahming and Brothers in Nassau was refused clearance.

The conditions at Fort Lafayette were bad enough that a number of prisoners, including Eneas and Lewis Benjamin, were asked to testify in February

1864 about the conditions. The prison was crowded (ten men to a cell) and dirty. Like Eneas, John Rahming was released on July 2, 1864, after having spent six months in confinement. Because of the six months he had spent at Fort Lafayette, Rahming claimed damages of $580,800 plus interest, providing some indication of the amount of business he was doing. He was later awarded $38,500. Eneas claimed $720,000 and was awarded $1,540.

While most of the testimony to the committee focused on how the Bahamas trade caused or increased corruption within the custom house, two Americans who had spent time in Nassau were questioned at length about what was happening in that city.

First up on April 12, 1864, was Ezra Cuyler, a self-described gentleman of leisure, who spent April to early October of 1863 in Nassau waiting to get his wife out of Charleston. During his short stay he seems to have observed the Great Carnival in some detail. He first noted the shipping of goods to the out islands before sending them to Nassau to prevent consular inspection and then told the committee about a man named George Hayning who made forged consular certificates. He said every "barn and rookery" on the island was now a bonded warehouse for contraband goods and that Vice-Consul Thompson could see all the action from his office window but did nothing.

He did not care much for Thompson, declaring, "He does not make any acquaintance with anybody, and he has a morose and sour disposition, and I consider him a very unfit person for the position he occupies." He told the committee about Lafitte and Heyliger and mentioned that one of the boats that delivered goods to them from New York was the schooner *J. C. Rahming*, owned by John Rahming and his brother. He described other vessels involved in the New York trade that were owned by Sawyer and Menendez, Alexander Johnson, and Saunders and Son. On the New York end he implicated Rahming, Eneas, and Montell and said all these arrangements were common knowledge in Nassau. He claimed to have seen every conceivable sort of contraband on the docks there.

Cuyler gave detailed testimony about the arrangements between the Wolf brothers and Hoffnung and Benjamin, all of whom he had gotten to know well. George Wolf told him that he could ship ten locomotives from New York to the Confederacy if he could get the order. He also claimed that Eugene Thompson, who managed the Royal Victoria for John Howell, was heavily involved by getting things shipped under the pretense that they were for the hotel.

The most detailed expose of what was happening in Nassau came on April 23, when John Howell's dry dock partner Epes Sargent testified for the committee. Sargent left Nassau on March 12 to come to New York to give his testimony. He mentioned that he had talked with George Wolf, who had boasted about his ability to pay off the custom house in New York. He then revealed to the world the names of the major players in the Great Carnival, including Henry Adderley and Company, Alexander Johnson, William Albury, the Wolf brothers, Sawyer and Menendez, John J. Turtle, Gustave Renouard, Charles Perpall, Julian Abrams, James de Jongh, Abraham Holmes, Manuel Menendez, Michael Knowles, Charles Kemp, John Rahming, George Bogert, Sylvain Haymann, the Weech family, John S. George, Henry and Pemroke Saunders, Jervey and Mueller, and Samuel Johnson. Sargent said he could give many more names of lesser importance, but this list should give the committee some idea of the extent of the trade going on in Nassau. Despite his revealing testimony, which soon filled newspapers across the country, Sargent might have been playing both sides of the game a bit. Just before he left Nassau, one of Henry Adderley's newest blockade runners, the *Will of the Wisp*, was up on his dry dock being repaired.

❖ ❖ ❖

Meanwhile, in Nassau, the first half of 1864 was much like most of 1863, with the ships rolling in and out of the harbor with great frequency. There was cotton everywhere, and in January Adderley's boat *Nonesuch* caught fire in the harbor. As the white gold burned and threatened to catch neighboring ships on fire, Adderley reluctantly had the boat sunk. Losing the cotton that was tucked on ships and in every available space in Nassau was another impetus behind the construction of the new stone warehouses along Bay Street. There was some big local news in May when John Howell sold his interest in the Royal Victoria to George Johnson. The dry dock business must have been good. To celebrate, Howell took a group of friends on a cruise to Harbor Island.

The newspapers continued to apologize to their readers about the condensed state of their news reporting due to so many ads. There was a new bowling alley and new restaurants, and an equestrian show in March drew two thousand spectators. In mid-April USS *Galena* made its way into Nassau harbor low on coal, and mainly through the work of Charles Jackson, was allowed by Governor Bayley to obtain a small amount. During the three-day stay, the commander of the boat noted that he and his officers were taunted by the lower classes on shore and said he was told they were paid by the rebels to do so. He provided a detailed list of fifteen blockade runners in port at that time to Gideon Welles, many of them flying both the British and Confederate flags.

The streets as well as the waters were full to capacity. The boom in Nassau did not extend to the other Bahamian islands, so many residents of those desolate places came to the city. The men worked as stevedores and draymen on the docks while the women found menial work around town. Serious crime, so rare before the war, was now reported in almost every issue of the papers. Burglaries seemed to happen at least once a week, and a policeman was stabbed at a liquor store. Even the once genteel Sunday concerts at Fleeming Square turned violent as people fought to get closer to the band and soldiers had to break up the ensuing brawl. After this the concerts were moved to the grounds of Fort Charlotte.

Much of the crime was caused by the hordes of sailors and out islanders roaming the town. Many of the sailors were those the British called "run sailors," those who ship from port to port and "a more reckless and desperate set do not exist." An editorial in the *Nassau Guardian* lamented, "What are we to do for the amusement of the masses of sailors daily and nightly thronging our streets? Jack cannot exist without amusement." On another occasion editor Mosely of the *Guardian* mused that "there is scarcely a night but adds sorrow to the dawn, by disclosing the fatal consequences of the orgies which are unblushingly engaged in at the dens of iniquity skirting our otherwise fair city.... Let any one pass from the Cathedral to the officers' quarters and he will there find enough to shock him in broad daylight." Although printed recollections and contemporary crime statistics do not mention it, there must have been a fair amount of prostitution in the city. In opening the legislature session, Bayley talked about the influx of strangers and crime and recommended more and better policemen. The swollen city treasury would allow a new larger prison to open on top of the ridge in 1865, just in time for most of the potential occupants to be leaving the island.

While out islanders looking for work likely stayed with relatives, the sailors slept in the streets or if they were lucky in some decrepit flophouse. Even the Royal Victoria was suffering from overcrowding. Again the *Guardian* described the situation, stating that the hotel was "inundated by a heterogeneous crowd, many of whom were better and more profitable to the hotel than agreeable and acceptable to their fellow boarders." Vice-consul Thompson was "at his wit's end" in finding ways to deal with all the sailors asking him for assistance. He wrote that it cost twenty-five dollars to send each man home on a steamer and that he had been boarding two men from a wreck for six weeks. Thompson seemed to be overwhelmed, as witnesses claimed that he was cancelling New York certificates on the flimsiest of oaths. He was still unable to find George Harris to pay his rent, and it became obvious that Harris was looking for an excuse to break his lease and deprive the consul of his prime view of the harbor. Overall, Thompson seemed unprepared for the task Seth Hawley had given him.

By late 1863, Seward accepted that Hawley was not going to return and began once again to search for a new consul. He first turned to his Auburn, New York, neighbor, Thomas Kirkpatrick. Kirkpatrick was a loyal Republican, had worked with the penal system for many years, and was currently warden of the state prison at Auburn. Kirkpatrick was in his early fifties and had been born in England. Seward hoped his British heritage and law-enforcement background would overcome his lack of maritime experience in carrying out the consular duties.

Kirkpatrick declined the offer for the familiar reason that the pay was too low. On May 5 Seward was able to get John G. Hinckley, a judge from Westfield, New York, to accept the position, but before the month was over Hinckley too changed his mind. Finally, Seward turned to Kirkpatrick again. Seward had his political mentor and ally Thurlow Weed convince Kirkpatrick that legislation to raise the salary was finally going to come through. With this prodding, Kirkpatrick finally gave in and accepted the position. When he finally got to Nassau he would find that William Thompson had sunk to depths unknown even to Sam Whiting.

There were also problems on the Confederate side as Richard Waller's money issues continued. In February he wrote to Alexander Lawton that he was almost £6,000 in debt and that Heyliger had informed him that he could not advance him any more money for purchases. Colin McRae in Paris wrote to Secretary of War Seddon about Waller's overdrafts. He also wrote to Waller and chastised him for the position in which he had placed them. McRae was out of funds, but to decline Waller's drafts would destroy his credibility in Nassau. He told Waller to not purchase anything else without clearing it through him first. Lawton wrote to Waller that despite his growing debt, he needed to find a way to keep purchasing as shoes would be especially needed for the summer campaigns.

As if Waller did not have enough worries, in March Lawton asked him to help an agent of the Quartermaster's Department named Thomas Sharp, whom Lawton was sending to Nova Scotia by way of Nassau. Sharp was a plow and farm-implement maker from Nashville, Tennessee, whose mechanical skills came to the attention of Lawton. Sharp was to head to Halifax to purchase machinery with which the Confederacy could manufacture their own shoes, and to that end Waller was to provide him with £3,500. Lawton told Waller to make this his top priority. To Lawton's regret, Waller could only scrape up £500 to assist Sharp. Waller told Sharp he could purchase some of what he needed with that money in Nassau.

Originally intending to fulfill his mission in Nova Scotia, by June Sharp was seeking shoemaking machinery in Manchester, England. He let Lawton know that he had asked Waller to forward any unused money to him because he could make better use of it in England than Waller could in Nassau. His short time in Nassau also left him with a bitter taste regarding Confederate operations there. He claimed that he was privy to a sale of mediocre cloth that

James Ferguson in England had rejected in England but was subsequently sold at a much higher price by "Israelites" to the Confederate agent in Nassau.

According to Sharp, "The agent at Nassau who made this clever sale and whose business qualifications are so highly appreciated here is named Louis Heyliger, and is reported here among the uninitiated to have the ears and exercise no small influence on government officials at Nassau. He can make sales when no other man can, since the consignees feather his own nest at same time." He also insinuated that it would be foolish to think this particular sale was an isolated case.

As spring turned into summer, the bloody battles in Virginia at Spotsylvania and the Wilderness segued into a stalemate between Lee and Ulysses S. Grant at Petersburg. Unlike the two prior years, Lee did not vanquish the Union army and take the fight to the North. He lost Stonewall Jackson in 1863, and in May 1864 he lost J. E. B. Stuart. Just as Nassau had taken an ugly turn, the war itself seemed different. The days of chivalry and gallant charges were over, and the precursors of World War I–style trench warfare were beginning. Farther south, Chattanooga was in Union hands, and by summer's end William Sherman would take Atlanta and begin preparations for his march of total warfare to the sea.

On June 8, 1864, Henry Adderley appears to have traveled to Grenock, Scotland, on the *Fannie*, possibly to personally oversee something regarding the new Clyde steamers being built there. Two days before that, Governor Bayley and his wife left Nassau for the last time, boarding *Corsica* for New York and then traveling from there to England. His Confederate sympathies had finally led to his recall. As before, Charles Nesbitt was sworn in by Judge Lees as acting governor until Bayley's replacement arrived. Due to his leave in England in 1861, Bayley had missed the beginning of the Great Carnival, and now he would also be absent as the curtain came down.

Henry Adderley

Augustus Adderley

John J. Turtle with family and servant

Timothy Darling

John Lafitte

Euphrosine Lafitte

William J. Weech

John S. George

Lewis Heyliger's monogrammed stationery

Men standing in Nassau navy yard

Charles John Bayley

George Anderson

Major James Mends

Seth Hawley

John Maffitt

"Florie" Maffitt

Sidney Root

George Bogert

The Curtain Falls

12

"It is rather sickly here"

Thomas Kirkpatrick and his wife Anna took *Corsica* from New York on July 16 and arrived in Nassau on the morning of July 21, 1864. He already knew that he would find the state of the consulate as bad as or worse than when Seth Hawley had taken over for Sam Whiting. Before Kirkpatrick's departure, Charles Jackson informed the New York Underwriters (who informed Seward) that the Nassau consulate was closed and that William Thompson had been arrested for embezzlement. Thompson had been released on bail paid by Jackson.

Kirkpatrick entered the consulate on July 25, but like Hawley he found the office in a chaotic state, and Thompson was nowhere to be found. It turned out that he had been placed into custody again as a flight risk in light of two suits filed against him. He owed a year's rent on the office, as he had never been able to pay George Harris. The other suit involved $600 owed to Timothy Darling. Thompson had used this money to help sailors in trouble but had kept no record of the transactions. In fact, he had kept little record of anything. The consular post record book that had almost daily entries by Whiting and Hawley had only five entries by Thompson for the entire six months before Kirkpatrick's arrival. Kirkpatrick was finally able to meet with Thompson on July 29, and they officially transferred the duties of the position, but Kirkpatrick told Seward that no information of any use could be had from Thompson as "his mind is diseased." As he had predicted in the spring, Thompson had reached his wit's end.

However the two law suits worked out, it was obvious that the consular office needed to be moved out of George Harris's building. Robert Murray, the US Marshal for New York City, mailed Kirkpatrick a letter that he had received from John Howell. Murray's cover letter introduced Howell as a true friend of the Union cause, who had provided much information on blockade runners. While this was true, Murray must not have known about Howell's involvement with the dry dock or his many jocular conversations at the Royal Victoria with captains running into Wilmington and Charleston. Howell had taken a quick trip to New York after selling the hotel and had sent the letter to Murray from there. When he returned to Nassau, he and Kirkpatrick connected. Perhaps Howell's trip back to New York had rekindled his patriotic spirit or he felt guilty about the dry dock, because he rented out a whole building (instead of just the typical second-story space) on Bay Street in which to house the consulate. As Kirkpatrick told Seward, Howell was doing this as a favor to the Union cause and would be taking a large financial loss.

In preparation for the move, Kirkpatrick was able to sit down with George Harris and discuss resolution of the back-rent issue and other debts incurred by the office dating back to the repair of the windows Sam Whiting had broken out. Howell also informed Kirkpatrick that he had a new idea that would help the Union: he wanted to establish a coal depot for US merchant ships on Hog Island near the dry dock. The towering coal depots of Henry Adderley and the other merchants on the Nassau shore and Hog Island were dedicated to fueling blockade runners at the expense of other vessels. A side benefit of Howell's proposed coal yard would be that coal could be loaded onto barges and taken to US Navy warships at Bahamian out islands without violating the governor's proclamation. Not having to head all the way to Florida for coal would make another dedicated cruising squadron more viable.

Strangely, one of the things Kirkpatrick did not need to worry about in his first months on the job was blockade running. From the time he got to Nassau until late September the amount of contraband shipping to Nassau took a huge dip. Part of this came as a result of the New York Custom House scandal. The procedures for securing and cancelling the bonds were tightened up so that most of the kinds of contraband that had previously come from New York would no longer make it through to Nassau. In addition, Kirkpatrick published a notice in the Nassau newspapers in late summer declaring that henceforth he would have the right to approve all passengers heading from Nassau to the United States.

The main reason for the downturn in activity was the same as the summer of 1862: the return of yellow fever. In 1864 Yellow Jack came back with a vengeance. On July 23, two days after Kirkpatrick's arrival, Heyliger wrote to Benjamin that "it is rather sickly here." This was a tremendous understatement. He wrote to Benjamin in August stating again, "It has been rather sickly here for the last month," but he added that the disease seemed to be abating due to lack of nourishment. In other words, "Scarcely anyone here has escaped attack." About four hundred people had contracted the disease in 1862, and almost twice that many were smitten this time around.

In his memoirs, Captain Tom Taylor claimed to have seen seventeen funerals passing his house in one day and had himself attended the funerals of three close friends. John Howell's letter that Thomas Kirkpatrick received in early August contained the phrase "trusting that you and your lady are enjoying good health." Howell had no way of knowing that Anna Kirkpatrick would die of yellow fever that same week, only two weeks after arriving in Nassau. Well known Bay Street Boy and House of Assembly member Thomas K. Moore died at age forty-six in late June, though his death was apparently from tuberculosis and not yellow fever. Eventually 141 residents of Nassau fell victim to the disease. Local authorities tried to deal with the epidemic by quarantining incoming vessels at Athol Island and by hiring men to act as scavengers to keep the streets clean. The *Nassau Guardian* complimented their work in August, claiming that Bay Street was finally completely free of orange peels and banana skins.

Ships sailing from Nassau had to be quarantined for at least fifteen days at Wilmington, so most shipping diverted to Bermuda as in previous summers. The Confederates were in desperate need of lead, and the raging disease caused Ordnance Bureau chief Josiah Gorgas to divert five hundred incoming tons of the metal from Nassau to Bermuda.

However, this August even Bermuda suffered from the disease, and a similar quarantine in Wilmington was instituted for ships originating from there. Major Norman Walker, who had filled a role similar to Heyliger's in Bermuda since February 1863, decided to move his base of operations because of the disease. In late June he made a quick trip from Bermuda to Richmond (through Wilmington) while his wife and children left Bermuda for England. When Walker returned to Bermuda in late July, yellow fever had hit and had already killed one of his clerks. He decided to relocate his work temporarily to Halifax. Halifax had major disadvantages of longer distances and the rougher seas of the North Atlantic, but yellow fever was a rare visitor at that high latitude.

US Consul Mortimer Jackson in Halifax wrote in August that "owing to the prevalence of yellow fever at Bermuda and Nassau this port has become the headquarters of those engaged in running the blockade." In early September there were seven blockade runners in Halifax harbor, but by the second half of September the fever had dissipated and Nassau and Bermuda were back in business. Before leaving Bermuda, Walker did his best to get plenty of cotton to Liverpool to keep the Confederate coffers full. In late summer 1864, about 45 percent of the cotton arriving in Liverpool was from Bermuda and only about 16 percent from Nassau. Most of the rest was coming from Matamoras. This port had become more important after the fall of Vicksburg, Mississippi, cut the Confederacy in two in July 1863. For the Confederates west of the river, Matamoras was now the main entry point for supplies.

After spending ten days setting things up in Halifax, Walker joined his family for a short time in England before they all returned to Halifax in mid-October.

By the time Walker and family finally returned to Bermuda in January 1865, blockade running was near its end. In his journal Tom Taylor mentions an interesting and somewhat disturbing offshoot of the yellow fever epidemic. An eminent Confederate military doctor proposed that clothing infected with yellow fever should be collected at Nassau and Bermuda and sent to Northern cities to start an epidemic. Taylor was appalled at the idea: "This was too much, and I shouted at him, not in the choicest language, to leave the office. It is difficult to conceive of such a diabolical idea, not only to spread havoc among combatants, but among innocent women and children, being present in an educated man's mind."

Taylor's tirade did not dissuade the doctor from making one of the first attempts at biological warfare, as testimony presented just after the war ended implicated Dr. Luke Blackburn of Kentucky in a plot to infect the North with yellow fever. Blackburn traveled to Bermuda in 1864 to help deal with the outbreak there and hatched the idea that he shared with Taylor. He packed trunks of new clothing with bedding and clothing from infected patients and took them to Halifax. From there he paid a man named Godfrey Hyams to take the trunks and sell the contents. Hyams sold some of the trunks in Washington, DC, and the others in Union-occupied New Bern, North Carolina.

What Blackburn and others did not know at the time was that yellow fever is spread by mosquito bites and not by contact, so his treacherous scheme did not have the desired effect. In Halifax, a truly evil character helped Blackburn with the logistics of his plan. Alexander "Sandy" Keith, a Halifax native, was a sort of informal Confederate consul during the war, helping for a fee on all sorts of issues, including blockade running. But he did not value human life nearly as much as he valued money. He was suspected of using a bomb to sink the blockade runner *Marie Victoria* in order to collect the insurance. The lost ship carried down Patrick Martin, a transplanted Confederate living in Montreal and a business partner of Nehemiah Clements and Benjamin Wier. Years later in a similar scheme, Keith planted a bomb on a ship in Bremen, Germany, that exploded while still at the dock, killing eighty people and injuring fifty more. Rather than be caught, Keith committed suicide.

✦ ✦ ✦

While the death of his wife was a horrible blow for Kirkpatrick, he threw himself into his work. For the first time, the State Department seemed to recognize the importance of the consul's position in Nassau, and the consular salary was doubled to four thousand dollars. While this was still only two-thirds of what

Charles Jackson was making, it would allow Kirkpatrick the ability to have some status in the local society.

Up to this point, the consuls had always been at a distinct disadvantage in battling against Heyliger and Lafitte. Those men seemed to get whatever they needed from the Confederacy and they fit well into the local scene. Tom Taylor noted that Lafitte was richer than the governor and in a town where money ruled that was high praise. As rich as Lafitte might have been, his employers George Trenholm, Charles Priloeau, and Theodore Wagner were doing even better. Seward also provided money to take care of the various local needs. One of these was taking care of the black pilots who had been helping the US fleet under Whiting and Hawley. Some of these pilots were still in jail because they could not pay their fine, and their families were suffering. Some of the pilots still had unpaid prize tickets for ships they had helped catch. Kirkpatrick started to help these men out, explaining to Seward how important it was to do this, as aside from a few Americans like Jackson, Howell, and Sargent, "nearly all the known friends we have here are of this class."

Kirkpatrick was able to recruit a couple of spies within the blockade-running companies. Up to this point, Union spies were sometimes unknowingly hired as stewards on blockade runners, but having people on the inside of the firms was a coup. One spy was Henry G. Root, a young American (apparently no relation to Sidney Root) working as a clerk for Adderley. Root traveled to New York from Nassau in February 1864, so was likely a trusted go-between for Adderley and Francis Montell.

Another spy was a sea captain named Richard Squires. Squires had been hired as a deputy marshal by Robert Murray, the same US marshal who introduced Kirkpatrick to John Howell. Murray sent Squires to Bermuda to infiltrate a blockade-running operation there. Squires managed to become temporary master of an Alexander Collie ship sailing to Nassau, and on arrival he was hired as a shipping agent at the Collie and Company branch in Nassau. He presented himself to Kirkpatrick and proved to be a useful source of info in the coming months, as no one suspected such a man of being a spy. He could go on board any ship in the harbor and gain access to most shipping information.

John Howell and Eugene Thompson of the Royal Victoria had been valuable sources of information for previous consuls, and new owner George Johnson also aided Kirkpatrick. The new consul also recruited Edward Chapman, a porter at the hotel, as an informant. The twenty-eight-year-old Irishman must have provided quite a bit of useful information to Kirkpatrick as after the war Chapman headed for New York, and Kirkpatrick gave him a glowing letter of introduction to hand to powerful political boss Thurlow Weed.

✦ ✦ ✦

On the warfront, things were turning decidedly against the Confederacy as Atlanta fell to Sherman in the first week of September. Still the race to make more money continued. From late August to mid-October, the number of boats arriving and departing Nassau surged one final time. The new low-profile and extremely fast boats designed for running the blockade were arriving from England on a regular basis, being painted at the dry dock and heading off on their runs. Before the war, fewer than ten boats per year entered Nassau from Great Britain but in 1864, 233 ships came across the Atlantic to Nassau.

Kirkpatrick received reports from England about ships being launched in Liverpool, and during the late summer he watched them appear in Nassau. Between August 24 and September 24 Kirkpatrick noted twenty-eight arrivals and departures. Despite the occasional lapses, Nassau remained by far the most important port for keeping the war going. In the two-year period 1863–1864, estimates show that 24,522,900 pounds of cotton made it to England from Nassau, compared to 6,431,100 pounds from Bermuda and 5,910,400 pounds from Havana.

One notorious new ship was the *Colonel Lamb*, with Tom Lockwood as master. The boat was named for the commander of Fort Fisher at Wilmington, William Lamb, who was a great friend to the blockade runners. The boat was two hundred eighty feet long, with four watertight bulkheads and with a blazing speed of seventeen knots. She was registered to John Lafitte. Lockwood ran the boat into Wilmington and back out to Bermuda with almost 1,800 bales of cotton, arriving there on Christmas Eve 1864. He then headed to Halifax to pick up a cargo of ammunition and boots, and from there back to Nassau. We will explore his frustrating attempts to unload his cargo in the next chapter.

Around the time of the loss of Atlanta, a group of Confederate expatriates in Nassau published a plea in the papers requesting money for wounded Southern soldiers. Addressed to "Friends of the Cause of the Confederate States," it was signed by eleven men including John Lafitte, merchants Julian Abrams, George Bogert and Lewis Jervey, John Tuomey (who was in Nassau securing clothing for the army in Charleston), and two friends of Heyliger from New Orleans, E. C. Hancock and Myer M. Simpson. Also signing was Samuel Boyd, a former Mississippi judge notorious for the ill treatment of his slaves.

As the shipping surged once more, the Great Carnival continued as if oblivious to impending doom. The Nassau Races were held again in September, and the ladies enjoyed the broader Bay Street for their shopping and carriage rides. An observer at the time noted, "The females of Nassau are principally the wives and daughters of the merchants and other tradesmen, and are neat looking and intelligent. They dress fashionably, when they go out, and appear very lady-like. They may be seen every evening, when the weather is fair, riding out with their husbands, brothers or beaux."

Another schooner, this one belonging to Sawyer and Menendez, was destroyed when its cotton cargo caught fire. This accelerated the construction of additional ornate warehouses along the waterfront. George Harris put up a stone front warehouse on the south side of Bay Street. John S. George erected a "new and extensive" facility at the corner of Bay St. and East St. with red brick arched entrances and windows and a "handsome balcony" imported from England. Aaron Wolf had his offices in this building. Saunders and Son put up a new warehouse at the corner of Bay Street and Union Street. The previously empty lots on the north side of Bay Street were being filled with buildings. The *Nassau Guardian* opined that "when all the new warehouses on the north side of Bay Street are completed if we could remove the impediment of the bar our commercial relations would be complete." Unfortunately the treacherous sand bar would not be removed until the harbor was dredged for cruise ships a hundred years later. In any case, most of the new warehouses would soon be empty as the Great Carnival shut down.

Some of the Bay Street Boys lived on that street, but a few lived in elaborate mansions elsewhere. Timothy Darling lived at the Hermitage on the eastern end of the island, while Robert Sawyer lived at Greycliffe on West Hill Street just west of the city center.

The King Conch, Henry Adderley, was happy to spend some of his riches making his living and working spaces commensurate with his prominence. Though he owned land throughout the island and several houses in town that he rented out, he concentrated his efforts on the Adderley mansion on Bay Street across from Parliament Square. A large warehouse and wharf were on the water behind the house along with kitchens and servant's quarters.

The mansion itself was formed from two houses on land first granted to Henry's grandfather Abraham Adderley. Henry had the two houses connected and wide verandahs built on both floors on three sides of the structure. His large and exquisitely appointed drawing room measured eight hundred square feet with fifteen-foot ceilings, mahogany furniture, and a grand piano. Decorative plaster in the house was done by French specialists brought in for the job. His office was on the first floor facing Bay Street. Also included were a nursery for Henry's children and grandchildren and a billiard room where Heyliger and Lafitte most likely spent time relaxing with Adderley. Bathrooms included tubs enclosed in mahogany and flush toilets (even though there was no running water).

An amusing assessment of Henry Adderley's wealth came from a local pilot working with blockade runner John Wilkinson. According to Wilkinson, this man "had the profoundest respect for the head of the firm of Adderley and Company in Nassau, the 'King Conch' as he was irreverently styled by us outside barbarians. Speaking of the firm on one occasion he assured me the members were as wealthy as the *Roth's children*." Of course by the mid-nineteenth century, the Rothschild family was already a worldwide symbol for incomprehensible wealth.

A new prison was built on East Street on the ridge up above the Royal Victoria to replace the smaller jail (which became a library) behind Parliament Square, and it appeared to be needed. Numerous burglaries continued to be reported, and a large depot for stolen goods was discovered to the west of the city. Another reason for the new warehouses was that people were attempting to steal the cotton on the docks. In late September two men tried to steal cotton off the Saunders and Son wharf but were seen by a night watchman. One dove into the harbor and the other was discovered the next morning hiding in the bales of cotton.

✦ ✦ ✦

By late October 1864, the last surge of shipping in and out of Nassau was dying off. Part of this was due to Thomas Kirkpatrick's call for a new flying squadron to come to the Bahamas and reactivate Charles Wilkes's idea of nipping blockade runners off at the source. USS *Shenandoah* and USS *Isonomia* began prowling around Nassau as summer turned to fall.

A second and bigger factor was that Wilmington was getting increasingly difficult for blockade runners to enter. With Lee's army hunkered down around Petersburg, Wilmington had become the logical destination for all supplies and equipment coming from Nassau. Some steamers continued to run in and out of Charleston, but that city was far away from Lee and would soon be threatened by Sherman. Realizing all this, Union forces were preparing to finally take out Fort Fisher and capture Wilmington. In preparation for the assault, a slow and steady buildup of Yankee ships began outside of that port. Quite a few of the ships hovering around the port were captured blockade runners.

An example of the tightening cordon around Wilmington is shown in the continued efforts of Richard Waller and Thomas Sharp to get shoemaking tools and equipment to the Confederacy. In November, Waller successfully shipped the tools he had bought in Nassau into Wilmington on the *Armstrong*, but that ship was captured on her way back to the Bahamas. Sharp purchased three sets of shoemaking machinery in England and sent them on three separate ships to Wilmington.

The first set was on a new ship making her first voyage, the *Bat*. Attempting to enter Wilmington at about 3:00 a.m. on October 10, *Bat* was fired on by USS

Montgomery. The thirty-pound shot pierced the bow, taking off the right leg of Austrian sailor Match Madick, and *Bat* promptly surrendered. Madick, who had also been on the crew of *Alabama*, died from his wounds.

The second set of machinery was on the *Stag*, which delivered the machinery into North Carolina on December 5, but was herself captured the next month. There is no record of which ship the third set of machinery was on or if it made it through. It is possible that the machinery was delivered to Galveston by James Carlin on the *Imogene* in April 1865, far too late to do any good.

Bat and *Stag* were two of a series of the newest and most advanced blockade runners that Fraser, Trenholm and Company were building for the Confederacy. Two others, *Owl* (to be commanded by John Maffitt) and *Deer*, also made it across the Atlantic before hostilities ended. The boats were so fast that the Union navy immediately turned *Bat* into USS *Bat* and used it against the blockade runners in the closing months of the war. This continued a theme that began as early as 1862: as the ships created in the British Isles for the Confederacy became ever faster, the North took those that were captured and made them part of the blockade force. *Deer* was captured in February 1865 off of Charleston, but the elusive Maffitt never allowed *Owl* to fall into Union hands.

In mid-November Kirkpatrick was happy to report that arrivals from Charleston and Wilmington had decreased substantially, and by mid-December he reported that most ships from Nassau were turning back from Wilmington and Charleston.

For some Confederate needs, it did not matter. The Subsistence Department determined that eighty-one million pounds of meat would be required to sustain the armies through the winter and that it would need to come from abroad. The meat from Nassau was disdained by the soldiers, but it did not matter as Heyliger responded that there was none to buy in Nassau. By January, he had accumulated 2,500,000 pounds of meat, but it is not clear if any of it made its way into the Confederacy.

Over in Liverpool, Charles Prioleau was instrumental in organizing the Great Southern Bazaar, a festival in support of the Confederacy that ran for four days in St. George's Hall. He also spent the last part of 1864 and early 1865 attempting to funnel funds through New York to aid Confederate prisoners. But it was too late to do much good.

The Confederacy would not go down quietly, and there were continuing efforts to fight back against the increasing Union presence on the seas. Early makeshift raiders like *Sumter* and *Nashville* had given way to the more formidable *Alabama* and *Florida*. These latter ships had both been quite successful in disrupting Yankee shipping, but by October 1864 each had been put out of commission. *Alabama* met her end off Cherbourg, France, in June 1864 when she was sunk by USS *Kearsarge*. John Maffitt left command of *Florida* in late 1863 because of lingering effects of his bout with yellow fever, and that vessel was captured in Bahia, Brazil in October 1864 by Charles Wilke's old flagship *Wachusset*.

Despite these setbacks, a third generation of raiders was now on the water. CSS *Tallahassee*, a fast iron-hulled vessel outfitted with a variety of guns emerged from Wilmington in August 1864. She made a dazzling run up the Atlantic seaboard to Halifax, destroying twenty-six merchant ships and capturing seven more before returning to Wilmington in late August. She was then renamed *Olustee* and popped out of Wilmington again in late October. This time the ship ran up as far as Delaware, destroying six ships before coming back to Wilmington a week later. Renamed again *Chameleon*, she made her final exit from Wilmington on Christmas Eve 1864 and headed for Bermuda. Eventually finding herself unable to return to Wilmington, her commander John Wilkinson made a quick stop in Nassau and then took her to England where she remained as the war ended.

In early October 1864 *Sea King* slipped down the Thames from London and sailed for Madeira. The steamer *Laurel* left Liverpool around the same time and met *Sea King* in Madeira to transfer equipment and crew members. On October 19 *Sea King* raised the Confederate flag, and her name was changed to CSS *Shenandoah*. Over the next year *Shenandoah* circumnavigated the Earth and terrorized the United States whaling fleet, burning thirty-two ships and capturing thirty-eight. She continued her cruise of terror, her crew not knowing the war was over, finally surrendering in Liverpool in November 1865.

Her tender *Laurel* continued from Madeira to Nassau. To avoid neutrality problems in England, it was important to try to hide any connection between *Laurel* and *Shenandoah*. Arriving in Nassau, Commander John Ramsey met with Lewis Heyliger, and they determined to send her into Wilmington as a potential blockade runner and to have her name and registry changed there. In doing so they hoped to erase all traces of her having been the supplier of weaponry and ammunition to *Shenandoah*. The boat did reach Wilmington and was sold to Fraser, Trenholm and Company and renamed *Confederate States*.

While 1865 and the final months of the war would bring some other interesting new Confederate fighting ships to Nassau, 1864 ended with a controversy over a vessel that had been argued about for some time. The ship was built under the direction of Charles Prioleau in the Liverpool shipyard of William C. Miller and Sons, the same firm that produced *Florida*. She was named *Alexandra* in honor of the new wife of the Prince of Wales. The design was similar to *Florida* but about fifty feet shorter.

After the issues with *Florida*, the US consul in Liverpool and his spies were on top of *Alexandra* from the beginning, and when she was launched in

March 1863, they successfully had the boat seized and brought to trial by the British government. The defense attested that despite her sturdy and somewhat suspicious construction, the vessel was meant to be a yacht. The trial, in which the vessel and her manufacturers were finally acquitted, lasted until mid-1864.

Alexandra left England for Bermuda and from there to Halifax where she was refitted in order to increase her speed. By November 30, 1864, *Alexandra* had been renamed *Mary* and was in Nassau harbor consigned to Henry Adderley and Company. One look at the ship convinced Kirkpatrick that she was going to be outfitted just as *Florida* had been. He made a request to Receiver-General Dumaresq for information on her cargo but received no reply.

He then went to the custom house to try to get the manifest of the ship but saw only the same generic list used for most ships in Nassau, nothing but "casks" and "cases" with no indication of the contents. Adding to Kirkpatrick's suspicions was the arrival of *Confederate States* from Charleston with an unusually large load of coal instead of the normal blockade runner's cargo of cotton. He wondered if the boat that had acted as tender to *Shenandoah* might serve the same purpose for *Mary*. Due to his suspicions, when *Confederate States* left Nassau HMS *Fawn* headed to Green Cay to see if there might another transfer of supplies as with *Florida*, but *Confederate States* instead was headed to Liverpool.

Kirkpatrick sent a strongly worded message to Charles Nesbitt that *Mary* had guns aboard and must be seized. In what looked to be a reenactment of the *Florida* story, Nesbitt had the boat searched by the receiver-general and reported that nothing amiss had been found.

Kirkpatrick did not give up. Using his skills in recruiting informants, Kirkpatrick was able to secure the services of George Wilson, a black man working for a repair crew on *Mary*. Wilson reported seeing guns and enough hammocks to berth a large crew. Kirkpatrick made another plea to Government House, insisting that allowing *Mary* to go to sea would cause a huge diplomatic controversy. Finally at long last the entreaties of a US consul in Nassau did not fall on deaf ears.

Kirkpatrick's timing was good as the new Bahamian governor, Rawson William Rawson, arrived on *Corsica* on December 9. He relieved Nesbitt, who once again had been filling in as governor since Bayley left in June. Rawson had most recently been colonial secretary in Capetown, South Africa and had seen the results of neutrality violations there when *Alabama* had shown up and tried to dispose of her prizes. Rawson wasted no time in having *Mary* searched again and officially seized for violating the Foreign Enlistment Act and ordered held for trial.

Kirkpatrick wrote exultantly to Seward on December 13 about the seizure. Heyliger wrote to Benjamin a week later of his shock that a vessel absolved by the highest British courts would be seized in the Bahamas. He let Benjamin know that the defense case was in the hands of Bruce L. Burnside "who so ably defended us in the trial of the *Oreto*. He is shrewd, intelligent and industrious and will neglect nothing to ensure a favorable issue for the defense."

Heyliger then lamented that he wanted to watch the case carefully as it would add to the record of the numerous instances where British neutrality worked to the disadvantage of the Confederate States. This was of course a ludicrous statement given what Heyliger, Lafitte, and Adderley had accomplished in the previous three years. Henry Adderley and Company attempted to buy George Wilson's silence for $300 but Wilson did not give in. Lewis Heyliger's optimism that *Mary* would be freed in a timely fashion like *Oreto* proved to be in error. The trail dragged on and the ship was not released until June 1865 when she was no longer of any use for military purposes.

In mid-December Charles Prioleau wrote John Lafitte that they would not be buying any more steamers. They had spent nearly £300,000 on steamers in late 1864 and none of them had brought the company any income. He instructed Lafitte to begin selling off their ships. Clearly the end was in sight. Trenholm and his partners had been the first into the game and were going to do their best to unload their liabilities before the conflict ended.

13

"Blockade-running from this port has ceased"

In the fall of 1864, there was still money to be made running the blockade if you had a fast enough ship and there were a few notable successes in the final days. In one example, Tom Taylor got the *Banshee II* into Wilmington from Nassau in late December with enough meat to feed Lee's men for a month. He bought the meat in Nassau for $6,000 and sold it in Wilmington for $27,000. But by mid-January 1865 the game was about over.

In the first week of the year, the ships *Banshee*, *Night Hawk*, *Hansa*, and *Virginia* entered Nassau from Wilmington and *Confederate States* and *Chicora* arrived from Charleston, collectively bringing in cotton valued at over $3 million. On January 15, Fort Fisher fell and with it the most important port left to the Confederacy. While Charleston would not be evacuated for another month, there was little hope of getting supplies from there to Lee's army. Between January 12 and January 16, eight ships left Nassau for Wilmington, but none succeeded in getting through.

While blockade running, even to Nassau, continued for a bit longer, the Great Carnival was coming to a close. Post-war estimates claim that while the rate of captures of blockade runners was only one in seven in 1862 and one in four in 1863, by 1864 one in three vessels was captured, and in early 1865 there was a capture for every boat that made it through. Ships continued to come to Nassau, but with Wilmington closed they had nowhere to go.

On January 21, Kirkpatrick wrote to Seward that a large number of blockade runners were accumulating at the port and that there were thirty-five there that day. For the first time in years the shipping news in the local newspapers contained no departures to Wilmington or Charleston.

Some merchants reacted to the news of Fort Fisher's fall immediately, while others tried to squeeze out a bit more gold before the fighting stopped. John S. George and Robert Weech placed ads asking all customers to settle debts immediately, and other merchants soon followed this path. Weech's ad also noted a new branch of his company in London, a destination to which he and others would soon be moving. Tatum and Company continued to proudly offer merchandise to "their Southern friends." James G. Bailie, of the Augusta Importing Company, advertised that he was open for business from room 65 of the Royal Victoria. He had been filling orders for Governor Joe Brown of Georgia from there since 1864. It is unlikely that he got many takers at this late date.

In the last few trips into Wilmington, even the pilots who helped navigate the ships into the Cape Fear River tried to cash in. While pilots were normally paid on the order of $500 to guide a ship into port, in late December pilot Julius Dozier informed Joseph Fry, the commander of *Agnes E. Fry* (named for Fry's wife) that he wanted $3,500 to travel back from Nassau to Wilmington with the boat. Fry went to Heyliger, who grudgingly gave Dozier the money as the armies were in desperate need of the cargo. On December 27 Dozier ended up running the boat ashore on the approach to Wilmington and was promptly arrested by Confederate authorities for his extortion of the government.

On January 20, 1865, Heyliger wrote that the going rate for pilots was now $4,000 payable in advance, but even at that rate he was having trouble finding anyone. When pilots for Wilmington were caught, they were held for the duration of the war and not exchanged for Northern prisoners, so the supply was dwindling. Henry Adderley and Company milked the system for money even in the worst circumstances. When *Caroline* returned to Nassau on February 7 after an unsuccessful attempt to pierce the blockade, Adderley charged the Importing and Exporting Company of South Carolina £5,000 for failure to deliver the cargo.

The last ship sent out by Lafitte and Heyliger was likely *Syren*, which left Nassau on February 15 for Charleston loaded with beef and other provisions. Heyliger had no way of knowing that Charleston was being evacuated that day and *Syren* was captured there three days later. Ironically, in the letter Heyliger sent to inform Confederate officials of *Syren*'s departure, he stressed how important it was that he be kept fully informed of current events. It must have been frustrating for him to send these valuable cargoes into the unknown.

On January 20 new policemen arrived from London in the schooner *Hannah*, but they were on the scene too late to do much good as many members of the "floating population" (as the newspapers called it) were now looking for a way off the island instead of ways to get into trouble. The crews of the blockade runners began to book passages to new lives. In late winter and spring, a number of vessels like *Georgianna* and *Drover* made their way from Nassau to Port Royal, which had been under Union control for some time. They carried sailors, machinists, stevedores, blacksmiths, pilots, and carpenters from a huge variety of nations. While most were from England and Ireland, others came from Denmark, Switzerland, Germany, Scotland, Poland, Greece, and Portugal.

The lure of blockade-running money had ranged across the world. One observer in Nassau said, "To listen to all the different languages one hears on the streets in a few hours is sufficient to remind him of the confusion of the tongues of Babel." Almost all of these men indicated that they intended to make the United States their new home.

Other English sailors, and most of the blockade-running crews were English, headed to New York on their way home. The number of passengers on *Corsica* swelled far beyond that in the same months in other years, as the tourists ending their vacation a bit early were joined by British mariners. The *New York Times* reported in March that *Corsica* was already fully booked for her next three trips. While most people were leaving, Thomas Kirkpatrick noted one odd influx of passengers to the city. In January a number of Union prisoners of war who had escaped popped out of a blockade runner on which they had stowed away.

The Royal Victoria placed an ad for staff help, a first during the war years, likely because Bahamians from the out islands were also headed back home. George Johnson, who bought the hotel from John Howell the year before, held a dinner for the government commissioners of the hotel (including Henry Adderley and Timothy Darling) in an effort to show them that he was improving the quality of the place.

When Eugene Thompson left to run a hostelry in St. Louis, Johnson hired a new manager, James Carroll, who arrived from New York at the beginning of the tourist season in November.

Carroll had been employed at some of the most lavish hotels in the United States, including the McClure House in Wheeling and the St. Nicholas in New York. He had good connections as the dinner included fresh oysters from the Fulton Fish Market in New York, venison shot days earlier in the Adirondacks, and canvasback ducks from the shores of the Chesapeake. It was all washed down with champagne from the celebrated French house of G. H. Mumm. Around this same time Thomas Kirkpatrick wrote to Seward letting him know that George Johnson had also been a source of much valuable information regarding blockade runners. He had taken up where Howell left off in terms of ingratiating himself with his guests but keeping his ears open for news that might be of use to the consul.

This was not the only partying going on as things began to wind down. John Laffite hosted a large party at the Royal Victoria in February, where according to Kirkpatrick "nobody with Northern sympathies" was invited. This was most likely a farewell party by Lafitte and Heyliger for their Bahamian friends and colleagues.

One of the last guests to leave the party around 4:00 a.m. was none other than the new governor, Rawson W. Rawson. Despite his quick action on *Mary*, he liked a good party. Only two weeks after his arrival, Mrs. Rawson held her first formal social gathering at Government House. Since then, Nassau residents had been delighted to find that their new governor was more personable than John Bayley. His personal motto was "Suum Cique" or "to each his own." The *Nassau Guardian* praised his frequent social appearances and stated that "Nassau has at last resumed its wanted gaiety. For upwards of three years we have heard of scarcely anything but business-business-business."

The editor then went on to compare the two governors. Bayley had been sedentary and businesslike and very seldom accepted the hospitality of others. This put a certain restraint upon the citizens of Nassau that the present governor had taken off. Rawson had taken them by surprise, as he was more approachable and spent time going among the citizens, judging them on personal observation rather than hearsay. Rawson also gave a speech at the reopened Bahama Institute on "The Bahamas." This seems a strange topic for a newcomer to the islands, but the paper claimed that a large audience listened "with astonishment" at the facts about the islands that the governor revealed.

Confederate Brigadier General William Preston was in Nassau for a few weeks during this period, to the disgust of Thomas Kirkpatrick. After serving on the battlefield for three years, Jefferson Davis had given Preston the difficult task of securing recognition for the Confederacy from Mexico. Kirkpatrick said of Preston, "He has been here for some time, though he has made one or two attempts to reach the confederacy, but without success. He has been quite a lion here, having been an attendant at governor's parties and balls; has been called up in person by the governor at the hotel." Preston took *Corsica* to Havana in February, making his way from there to Texas via Matamoras after it was clear the Confederacy was done.

This was not the only annoyance for Kirkpatrick in early 1865. On January 1, USS *San Jacinto* wrecked at No Name Key, and the wreckers descended on it. USS *Honduras* was sent immediately from Key West to assist. When the wreckers demanded money to return what they had salvaged, *Honduras* came to Nassau to obtain the money. Kirkpatrick asked Rawson for permission to have *Honduras* enter the harbor, but his request was denied, supposedly because she had not followed quarantine protocol. To add to Kirkpatrick's ire, John Wilkinson brought the former raider CSS *Tallahassee*, now named *Chameleon* and stripped of her armaments, into Nassau harbor for coal with no restrictions.

A familiar face appeared in Nassau in February. John Maffitt, after convalescing in England from his yellow fever, had gotten back into the blockade-running game in 1864. In May he took passage to Bermuda on a new ship, *Lillian*, and once there was offered the chance to take command of the ship and run her into Wilmington. After taking *Lillian* to North Carolina in early June, he received orders to take command of CSS *Albemarle*.

This interesting ship was built to protect the sounds of North Carolina from Union men-of-war. The ironclad ram was built far up the Roanoke River and then brought down to Plymouth in May where it had cleared out the Union forces holding that place. Maffitt and the *Albemarle* continued to hold the area under Confederate control through the summer. To his relief, as guarding a river entrance was a bit tame for his taste, on September 9, 1864, he was placed in command of the new government-owned steamer *Owl*.

On October 3 he made his first trip in *Owl* from Wilmington to Bermuda with a load of cotton, having nine shots fired at the ship on his way out. He left Wilmington again just before Christmas and headed to Bermuda with 780 bales of cotton. Because of the Union capturing *Bat*, sister ship of *Owl*, and turning her against the blockade runners, Stephen Mallory wrote Maffitt and told him to make plans to abandon and destroy *Owl* rather than let her be captured.

In Bermuda, he sold the cotton and received a cargo of clothing shipped from England. He also bought an interesting supply of less urgently needed items including hairbrushes, perfumes and powders, corks and green tea. On his return trip, he also brought back seventeen crew members of *Florida* who had made their way from South America to Bermuda. Nearing Wilmington, he was surprised to find that all was quiet on his approach to Fort Fisher but quickly realized the awful truth that the Yankees had taken the fort. With one Union ship in pursuit he made a quick reversal and decided to try Charleston.

Approaching Rattlesnake Shoals off of Charleston, *Owl* nearly collided with an anchored blockade runner. They were close enough that they could hear the enemies order to "heave to, or I'll sink you!" Ignoring the command, Maffitt pulled the boat away only to have a full broadside tear into the ship, injuring twelve men. A couple of days later he made it to Nassau. According to an observer, *Owl* had "a shot hole through her funnel, several more in her hull, standing rigging in rags, and other indications of a hot time."

Once on shore, Maffitt reported that both Wilmington and Charleston were in the hands of the Union. A letter from Secretary of the Navy Mallory was waiting for Maffitt in Nassau. The letter was infused with a fatalistic tone. Mallory began by stating that the fall of Charleston and Wilmington made it critical that Maffitt attempt to find some other useful purpose for *Owl*. He suggested that Maffitt might try running the boat into Georgetown, South

Carolina, if her draft would allow it. Failing that, he should consider heading all the way to Galveston if practical. If neither of those choices looked promising, his best bet was to turn the boat over to John Laffitte as property of Fraser, Trenholm and Company.

When Maffitt left in late February for Georgetown, he made a quick diversion to drop off William Sterrett and Thomas Connolly as close to Wilmington as he could get them. Connolly had attempted to get into the Confederacy earlier in the month, but had been turned back to the Bahamas when the ship he was on, *Florence*, collided with another ship.

During his time in Nassau, Connolly stayed with John and Euphrosine Lafitte. He witnessed the opening of the legislature where he said Governor Rawson gave "a fiery speech chiefly about yellow fever and sewers." Charles Prioleau wrote Lafitte about Connolly in less than glowing terms: "The Honorable MP Tom Connolly is a good fellow to have with you but a considerable humbug and quite ignorant of business matters. I would not negotiate any bills for him unless on confirmed bank credit." Connolly had originally tried to get into the blockade-running business with Robert McDowell, formerly of New Orleans and a good friend of Lewis Heyliger. When that venture fell through, Connolly decided to sightsee through the dying embers of the Confederacy.

Finding himself unable to get into Georgetown, Maffitt headed for Cuba and then Galveston, ending up in that port by late April. General Kirby Smith would not surrender Confederate forces west of the Mississippi until early June so the blockade was still in force at Galveston. Maffitt made one last inbound run through the blockade and got his vessel and cargo safely into the port. His stay in Galveston coincided with that of *Imogene* under James Carlin, who was in port from April 16 to May 3. Maffitt later got *Owl* back out through the blockade to Havana, Halifax and finally to Liverpool where he turned her over to Charles Prioleau.

Mallory's February 1865 letter to Maffitt also asked him to oversee the use of another boat that was soon expected in Nassau. *Ajax* was one of a series of shallow draft boats being built in Scotland for service in the Cape Fear River with the hope of defending Wilmington. John Low, the same Confederate navy officer who brought *Oreto* to Nassau in 1862, shepherded *Ajax* from Scotland to Nassau. As with *Oreto*, Low nominally acted as supercargo until the boat arrived in Nassau. Low's orders assumed that it was unlikely Maffitt would be in Nassau when Low got there, so he was to meet with Lewis Heyliger to obtain funds with which he would pay off and discharge the crew of *Ajax* and then recruit a new crew. At that point he should attempt to get into Wilmington and have the boat armed for harbor defense. If that port was closed, he should try Charleston and if that was also closed off he should get a letter of introduction from Heyliger and proceed to Havana to consult with Charles Helm. Perhaps the boat might aid in keeping Galveston open.

On January 13, *Ajax* left Glasgow and arrived in Dublin, Ireland, five days later. The U.S consul there alerted British customs officers to the suspicious nature of the vessel. While not looking like a warship, she had the low profile of a blockade runner and berths to accommodate sixty-four crewmen. The boat was inspected twice, and during that time fifteen of the twenty-one crewmen deserted. The nominal captain, George Adams, accused the men of mutiny, but when they were apprehended the men explained to police that they were convinced that the boat would become a Confederate gunboat. They mentioned the presence of Low, who they knew to be a Southern man and associated with *Fingal* and *Florida*. Customs officials claimed there was insufficient evidence to hold the boat, and on January 22 *Ajax* left Dublin. Charles Adams, ambassador to England, made a request to Earl Russell that British officials in Nassau, Bermuda, and Halifax be on the lookout for the vessel and that construction on her sister ship, *Hercules*, be halted.

Attempting to conserve precious coal, *Ajax* crossed the Atlantic mainly under sail, arriving in Nassau harbor on March 11 after a fifty-day voyage. Maffitt was long gone at this point and Mallory's request that he supervise the use of *Ajax* was irrelevant. Within hours Governor Rawson had Receiver-General Dumaresq searching the boat from bow to stern. Low met with Heyliger and obtained the funds to pay off the crew. The two men sold the boat to George Harris who then had it registered in his name.

Low hired a new crew and headed for Bermuda on April 8 since Wilmington was now closed. Rawson sent a letter to Governor William G. Hamley of Bermuda indicating that he found nothing suspicious about the vessel and that she was most likely to be used as a tugboat. Her arrival and departure were mentioned by Kirkpatrick to Seward but with little drama as the war was obviously in its final days. On arrival in Bermuda, Low attempted to outfit the ship with guns, but Hamley refused as he feared Low might turn her into a privateer. But when word reached Bermuda that Lee and Johnston had surrendered their Confederate armies Hamley told Low he could do whatever he wanted with *Ajax*. With just enough men to make the voyage, Low took the boat back to Liverpool, arriving there on June 9.

Colonel Lamb, one of the best blockade runners ever built, made it out of Wilmington to Bermuda right at the end of 1864, and then to Halifax. US Consul Mortimer Jackson reported on January 18, 1865, that *Colonel Lamb* was loaded with ammunition and boots and headed for Wilmington. He did not know that Wilmington had just fallen into Union hands. Also unaware of the news, Captain Tom Lockwood took the boat to Nassau in preparation for running into Wilmington. There he found out that Wilmington was no longer an option and that Charleston was about to be evacuated.

This left him no option but Galveston so he headed from Nassau to Havana and then to Galveston, but found the water was too low to enter the harbor. With nowhere to go, he headed back to Halifax, touching at Havana, Nassau, and Bermuda on the way. At Halifax, Lockwood received word of Lee's surrender and Lincoln's assassination and decided to head to Liverpool. Leaving Halifax on May 5, 1865, the vessel traveled through stormy seas and arrived in England on June 1. Lockwood turned the boat over to Charles Prioleau and after a few days of rest he and his men returned to Halifax on the Cunard ship *China*. The tense situation regarding the transshipment of British goods on *China* was only three years earlier, but must have seemed a lifetime ago to these men. Fraser, Trenholm and Company sold *Colonel Lamb* to a Greek shipping company that renamed her *Bouboulina*. In late 1867 the boat was destroyed in a massive explosion in Liverpool, as either steam from the boilers or a spark ignited the munitions on board.

✦ ✦ ✦

When Maffitt made his brief stop in Nassau in February, he brought with him a notorious passenger. Vernon Locke, who had skipped bail in the *Retribution* case and then been involved in the affair of the *Chesapeake*, was arrested on Monday February 20 on the *Owl* and thrown into the new prison. Attorney General George Campbell asked Charles Jackson to try to get officers of *Hanover* (the ship captured by *Retribution*) back to Nassau by April to testify for the prosecution. As soon as word got to Seward that Locke had been apprehended, he sent a request that Locke be put in US custody for piracy and murder on *Chesapeake*.

By the middle of May the saga reached London, where Earl Russell opined that if the United States would present sufficient evidence for the more serious charges against Locke, they would waive their charge of impersonation and extradite Locke to the United States. But Locke's good fortune continued. His trial in Nassau was on May 1, and he was acquitted for lack of evidence. With Lincoln assassinated and Seward gravely injured, no one from the United States made apprehending Locke a priority, and he headed to Havana and disappeared once again. He seems to have stayed out of trouble until 1890, when he died as captain of a yacht out of Boston that sank after striking a rock. An interesting tidbit from the Nassau trial was one witness's testimony that the only time he had ever seen Locke before was in Henry Adderley's office. Henry Adderley seemed to have his hand in every conceivable bit of mischief.

Maffitt's stop in Nassau almost got him arrested too. Kirkpatrick sent a letter to Governor Rawson on February 23 pointing out that Maffitt was in port and asking the governor and attorney general to have him arrested for illegally recruiting men for *Oreto* in Nassau in the summer of 1862. He said (incorrectly) that this was the first time Maffitt had been back to Nassau since then and they should jump on this chance to apprehend him. He also pointed out that at least two of that crew were in the city, that Charles Jackson could identify them, and that they could be made to testify against Maffitt.

The next day Kirkpatrick received a response from Charles Nesbitt. According to Nesbitt, Rawson had received Kirkpatrick's letter late on the 23rd and wasted no time in getting it into the hands of Attorney General Anderson the next morning. Maffitt, perhaps tipped off, left Nassau on the evening of the 23rd. Kirkpatrick wrote back in somewhat scathing language about how much he regretted the inability of the British to act on this in a timely manner. He added that he also had some new information that Confederates were preparing ships in Havana that would sail as privateers but under US colors and attack British merchant vessels in order to provoke a war.

These testy exchanges made their way upward and were finally put to rest when Earl Russell responded to US ambassador to England Charles Adams on May 3, 1865. Russell stated first that the rumors of privateers fitting out in Havana appeared to be false but that the consuls of the United States and England were working with Spanish authorities there to make sure nothing happened.

He then communicated Rawson's take on Kirkpatrick's letter. First, he said that Maffitt had in fact been in Nassau since the enlistment events of which he was accused (during *Florida*'s visit to Nassau in January 1863). Since US authorities had done nothing at that time it had not occurred to Rawson that there were any problems with Maffitt being in port. He also threw blame back on Kirkpatrick and wondered why he waited until the day Maffitt was leaving to make his request for action. He also said Kirkpatrick should have brought forth evidence of the crime of which he was accusing Maffitt and insinuated that Kirkpatrick did not understand the legal issues involving the case.

Finally, he took umbrage at the tone of Kirkpatrick's letter and also implied that Kirkpatrick had been speaking less than kind words about the colonial government to others on the island. The end of the war within a few weeks of this letter made the arguments something of a moot point and Kirkpatrick and Rawson appear to have eventually mended fences as each stayed in their respective positions until the end of the 1860s.

On February 24, the day after Maffitt left Nassau, Kirkpatrick wrote Seward, "I have the honor to inform you that blockade-running from this port has ceased." This was not quite true but for all practical purposes Nassau was at the end of its run as a blockade-running hub. *G. T. Watson* (formerly *Kate*) arrived in Nassau from Charleston with 520 bales of cotton and 200 boxes of tobacco on February 12 and the newspapers reported that she was the last blockade runner from that port and "probably the last vessel we shall have from the Confederacy for some time."

The last-ditch efforts to supply the Confederacy were switching to Havana, Galveston, and Matamoras. Charles Prioleau wrote to John Lafitte on February 10, 1865, to keep at it until Charleston was no longer available, but that it would not pay to set up a new operation in Havana. In mid-March, Norman Walker came from Bermuda to visit Heyliger to see if he could be of any use in Havana, but Heyliger told him it was too late. Walker returned to Bermuda a week later and began preparations to take his family back to England.

During February and March the major Nassau merchants sent shipments to Havana and Matamoras. *Banshee* left Nassau for Galveston in late February and returned to Nassau on March 31 with a thousand bales of cotton, but it was too late to do any good. By the time the cotton reached England, Lee's army had surrendered at Appomattox. The last shipment into Nassau from a blockaded port appears to have been on *Imogene* arriving with cotton from Galveston on May 10. Saunders and Son sent two vessels to Matamoras in the second half of March, and Sawyer and Menendez sent two more in early to mid-April, and that seems to be the end of outgoing supplies from Nassau to the Confederacy.

More merchants began to place newspaper ads asking all customers to settle debts. Perhaps the symbolic end of the Great Carnival came in mid-March when Henry Adderley and Company placed their ad asking everyone to settle up. Around this same time Augustus Adderley returned to Nassau from England. He arrived on the schooner *Surprise* by way of St. Thomas and Turks and Caicos. Subsequent events would indicate that he was in England arranging a landing spot there for the Adderleys. On April 12, Henry Adderley advertised a carriage and horses for auction at the Vendue House. These were probably his own.

The number of boats in and out shrank as winter turned to spring. In the week ending March 11, Henry Adderley and Company had one boat to Havana and one to Halifax, and Sawyer and Menendez had one to Halifax. Feisty Cornelius Lightbourne placed an ad inviting customers to his Market Street store: "Come before the war is over!" By the first week of April, the classified ads that filled most of the newspapers since 1862 were dropping off drastically, and the Bay Street stores that had been such a hot commodity were beginning to empty out. In early March Alexander Johnson advertised two offices and a large bonded warehouse on Bay Street for rent, and Henry Adderley advertised a couple more. John S. George advertised the space in his building occupied by Aaron Wolf as being available when the lease ended on July 1, 1865.

Wolf placed an ad on April 22 requesting everyone to settle their claims with him. Ramon Menendez of Sawyer and Menendez placed an ad offering his household furnishings for sale, and his brother Manuel offered up his house for sale a month later. A couple of merchants held out a bit longer. At the end of May Alexander Johnson offered up his entire stock of goods and his schooner *Adelaide*. Finally, at the end of June George Chambers placed an ad for all to settle their debts with him.

As the boats backed up in the harbor, the most prominent merchants including Saunders and Son, Sawyer and Menendez, and Henry Adderley and Company began to dump products back to New York. In one example, *Sarah Flagg* arrived in New York from Nassau on March 13. Forty-six of the forty-nine passengers were laborers, mostly Irish, fleeing Nassau to make a new start in New York. The cargo was made up of supplies worth more than $40,000 that had been on *Emily* when she got turned around at Charleston. The cargo belonged to the Importing and Exporting Company of South Carolina by way of Jervey and Mueller but was being handled by Adderley and now consigned to Montell and Bartow. All of this information was provided to Thomas Kirkpatrick by Henry Root.

In another example provided to Kirkpatrick by Root, *Mary Harris* arrived in New York with another group of Irish laborers and drugs from Saunders and Son. Kirkpatrick alerted the collector at New York and told him that he could get the information from Root himself, who had left Nassau and was now working for a bank in New York. Kirkpatrick said that Henry Ansell, who had supervised Adderley's warehouses but left the firm on bad terms, was also in New York and might provide information.

When the cargo from *Sarah Flagg* was seized, an indignant George Harris arrived in Kirkpatrick's office offering to give an affidavit asserting the innocence of the cargo. Kirkpatrick told him to make his statement to a notary public and bring it back after having it signed. Harris never returned. Trying another tactic, in early August the Adderleys had Charles Passailaigue naturalized as a British citizen and sent him to be a witness in the New York prize court trial for the goods.

Lewis Heyliger began sending supplies back to James Ferguson in England. Sidney Root of Beach and Root arrived in Nassau from Europe and spent about two months that spring trying to settle accounts and sell what he could. Root had traveled through Nassau in December on his way to Europe and published a memoir of his journey called *Exotic Leaves Collected by a Wanderer*.

The end was near, and everyone in the city knew it. As John Wilkinson put it,

> The speculators in Nassau saw that the "bottom had fallen out," and all of them were in the depths of despair. Some of them, it is true, had risen from the

desperately hazardous game with large gains, but the majority had staked their all and lost it; and even the fortunate ones had contracted a thirst for rash ventures, which eventually led to the pecuniary and social ruin of some of them. Even the negro stevedores and laborers bewailed our misfortunes, for they knew that the glory of Nassau had departed forever.

Another observer commented that while some would make off with their millions, "others acquired a taste for wild speculations and lived to illustrate the truth of the saying 'wealth gotten by vanity shall be diminished." In February, the legislature sent a formal message to their new governor that included their observation that "we are grateful for the flourishing financial condition of the city but not unmindful that this has arisen from fortuitous circumstances and can only be temporary." Three months later Rawson gave a speech that summed up their current situation: "The extraordinary channels of trade during the last three years have been closed and the colony will be thrown upon its ordinary resources."

On April 26, *Corsica* left Nassau for Havana with John Laffitte, his wife Euphrosine and niece Virginia Fourgeaud on board. Lewis Heyliger and Richard Waller were most likely passengers on this voyage also. The farewell parties were over and there was no longer any work for them to do in Nassau, so it was time to move on. From Havana, all three men would find their way to England. In Havana the Lafittes met up again with Douglas French Forrest, their visitor from 1863, who was on his way from England to Texas to try to fight what was left of the war.

Richard Waller found that escape to England did not get him out of financial troubles. George Trenholm was now secretary of the treasury of the Confederacy and as might be expected his interests in the cessation of blockade running were financial. He pointed out to Secretary of the Navy Stephen Mallory that Waller was over £200,000 in debt and wondered how this would be paid off. This debt led to a huge fiasco after the war as Waller would be personally sued for it.

Before leaving Nassau, Lafitte presented some of his own books to the public library. The books showed evidence of his fine education and wide interests. He was a lover of French literature as shown by *The Works of Alexandre Dumas* (twenty-five volumes), *The Works of Francois-Rene Chateaubriand* (twenty volumes), *The Works of Alphonse de Lamartine* (twelve volumes), *The Works of Adolphe Thiers* (thirty volumes), and *The Works of Henri Martin* (seventeen volumes).

He had an interest in science and technology as well, donating *Botany for Beginners* and Ure's *A Dictionary of Arts, Manufactures and Mines*. This latter book, by Scottish chemist Andrew Ure, was devoted to all aspects of the growing industrial revolution. Finally, he donated his six volumes of the *Rebellion Record*, the fascinating series of books put out by Frank Moore during the war that included up-to-date reports on every skirmish and battle. While the volumes donated by Lafitte contained information up to just before the battle of Chancellorsville in May 1863, there is little mention of all the activity in Nassau that was keeping the Confederates fighting.

As soon as *Corsica* departed, Henry Adderley and Company was auctioning off the furniture from Heyliger's residence on Bay Street and from Lafitte's office, which was across Bay Street from George Harris's residence. Lafitte's office included an upright desk with a stool, book shelves, three office desks, a copy press (for making duplicates of letters), a walnut stand for the copy press, another large stand with drawers and a marble top, a small iron chest, an iron safe, and a "choice selection of stationary and office fixtures." A couple of weeks later Adderley auctioned off the furniture from James Crenshaw's office, and John G. Meadows put Crenshaw's large residence on Charlotte Street up for rent. Henry Adderley stayed busy until the time came for him too to depart, continuing to act as booking agent for *Corsica* into June.

In early May a formidable warship, consigned to Adderley, entered Nassau's harbor. CSS *Stonewall* had been started in France and completed in Denmark. Heavily armored, the ship had a 300-pounder cannon aft, two 70-pounder guns mounted in a revolving turret, and a steel ram. She was probably the most dangerous ship afloat. After commissioning, Captain Thomas Page took her from Denmark down the coast of Spain and Portugal and then across to Nassau. Thomas Kirkpatrick noted the arrival of the ship on May 6 and that she had taken in 120 tons of coal before leaving on May 8. He also noted Page spending time with George Harris. A passenger on *Corsica* claimed that smaller boats off the mail ship had aided in coaling *Stonewall*, but Captain Le Messurier retorted that the boats were merely moving buoys back into place. When Page got the news that the war was over, he headed off to Havana. He sold the ship for $16,000 to the Spanish government, paid off his crew, and headed off to start a new life in Argentina.

After possibly helping to coal *Stonewall*, *Corsica* left Nassau for New York, arriving on May 12, 1865. On board and headed to England were women and children of the Adderley clan. Knowing that they would not be welcome in New York, Henry Adderley, Augustus Adderley, and George Harris made their way to England by other routes. All three men were now so wealthy that they would never be able to spend their riches in the now less attractive, mosquito-infested islands of the Bahamas.

It was frustrating for Kirkpatrick to see these men get away with their loot. He wrote to Seward, "Now why have not these Adderleys been indicted and punished will be best explained by stating the positions they hold and their connections with the government of the Bahamas." He claimed with disgust that having George Harris on the Executive Council was as good as giving the position to Jefferson Davis.

During the last week of May 1865, the once bustling harbor recorded two arrivals and one departure. During that same week James Welsman, businessman to the end, wrote from South Carolina to Charles Prioleau in Liverpool regarding drugs that Fraser, Trenholm and Company had delivered to the Confederacy for which they had not yet received payment. On June 20, a jeweler named H. Stricker placed an ad offering his entire stock of watches and jewelry at cost and said he would be leaving on the next trip out on *Corsica*. At the end of June the British officially allowed US Navy ships back in the harbor without restriction, and on July 1 George Johnson announced that he was putting his interest in the Royal Victoria Hotel up for auction. In mid-July Thomas Kirkpatrick reported to Seward that Henry Adderley was now in England. The Great Carnival was over.

14

Like a Town Sacked and Burned by the Enemy

As Rawson and the legislature predicted, it did not take long for Nassau to resume its normal state as a forgotten and destitute outpost. While the effects of the Civil War are still being felt in the United States, the cessation of blockade running immediately took with it the financial windfall of 1862–1864. All that remained of those days were a few ships and the ornate warehouses that were now almost empty. As one observer commented, "Our trade since the capture of the Southern ports has collapsed. The merchants who made so much money in the blockade business have left the colony, and we have not now even the legitimate trade that we had in former years."

The evening of Sunday, September 30, 1866, was unusually warm and calm, and there was a peculiar red tinge to the clouds. The people of Nassau spent their time as they did on most Sunday evenings, lounging by the water or on their verandahs, perhaps attending a church service. But at about 8:00 p.m. the wind started to blow. Communications of the day were too slow to alert the residents of the city to what was coming as the wind picked up and began to howl around the eaves of the buildings. Except for an hour-long lull on Monday evening when the eye of the storm passed over, the wind would blow at speeds of up to 140 miles per hour until finally dying down early Tuesday morning.

During those thirty-six terrible hours, hundreds of homes and businesses were completely destroyed. The top floor of the elegant warehouse John S. George had built in 1864 was blown off. On Bay Street alone twenty-seven buildings were a total loss, forty-six were badly damaged, and all the new streetlights were destroyed or damaged. The new Methodist church on Frederick Street that had been completed in 1864 was leveled. Government House was so mutilated that Governor Rawson was forced to live in a private residence until it could be repaired. The American consulate was lucky, losing only both flag staffs and suffering some minor interior damage. The ocean raged over top of Hog Island into the harbor and onto Bay Street with surges as high as the sixty-foot lighthouse. Over two hundred boats were in the harbor, and ninety-three were totally destroyed and ninety-seven severely damaged.

When it was over many thought it was God's retribution for the sins of the Great Carnival. Many in the Union had probably wished for something to take Nassau out of the blockade-running game, and this storm answered their prayers, even if a bit late. According to one eyewitness, "In twenty-four hours, the city was like a town sacked and burned by the enemy." For some time afterwards, New Providence was thrown back to a reliance on wrecking, the only industry that had not been decimated. Of course, while men like Henry Adderley still had property in Nassau and much of it was destroyed, most of their riches were with them in England now. The city and the islands would slowly rebuild, but they would never again see the likes of the crazy years during the Civil War.

Some memories of that time were triggered three years after the hurricane when notorious blockade-running captain James Carlin appeared in the harbor. Carlin was now master of the *Salvador* and was carrying forty-two Cuban men. The people of Cuba had just started their first attempt to gain their independence from Spain, and Nassau became a staging area for the revolutionaries. Carlin arrived on May 7, 1869, and *Salvador* was searched the next day, but other than a few rifles Receiver-General Dumaresq found nothing that could implicate the ship. Carlin cleared for St. Thomas on May 10 and left the harbor, but anchored just east of the city opposite Fort Montague.

At sunrise the next morning, eighty more Cubans came on board the ship from Nassau, clearly a violation of the Foreign Enlistment Act. HMS *Royalist* came out of the harbor and fired a shot over the bow of *Salvador* but Carlin weighed anchor and took off for Cuba. After arriving three days later, Carlin discharged his passengers who went ashore and immediately began building a fortification in order to begin fighting the Spanish. Carlin had the audacity to then return to Nassau where *Salvador* was, not surprisingly, seized. The admiralty court upheld the seizure later that summer and the boat was sold.

The closest thing to the blockade-running frenzy came years later when the United States passed the Eighteenth Amendment and began twelve years of Prohibition in 1920. Once again the people of Nassau invoked their opportunistic spirit to defy the United States as boats began to run from the city and Bahamian out islands like Bimini to Florida and Northern ports. Instead of military contraband, the small fast ships now avoiding Coast Guard cutters were carrying rum, Scotch whiskey, English gin, and Champagne. Gangsters like Al Capone made their way to Nassau, and many spent time at the Lucerne

Hotel on Frederick Street. The Lucerne would be the unofficial meeting spot for the rum runners just as the Royal Victoria had served for the blockade runners. The Bahamian government invested in building the original version of Prince George Wharf (where cruise ships now dock) to accommodate the increased shipping activity and used the influx of money to make numerous improvements including modern electrical and sewage systems. Normally tranquil Bay Street was again filled with all sorts of shady characters, and there were many parallels with the blockade-running era.

Along with the Lucerne Hotel, the premier hotel in Nassau by the time of the rum runners was the British Colonial Hotel. It was built on top of Fleeming Square and the old army barracks, just a bit west of the Vendue House. The hotel was built by Henry Flagler, a cofounder of Standard Oil and the man responsible for much of the early development on the Atlantic coast of Florida. In 1898, Flagler bought the Royal Victoria Hotel from the Bahamian Government but immediately started construction on the Colonial Hotel that would take its place as the choice for wealthy tourists. The Colonial was finished in 1901. In addition to building railways and plush hotels in Florida, Flagler operated a steamship line that brought tourists from his Palm Beach hotels to Nassau.

Over time the Royal Victoria became dated and finally closed down in 1971. Part of the abandoned building later caught fire and the remaining structure was finally demolished. All that remains today of the lively center of blockade-running life is a small part of the hotel's gardens. After the rum runners, Nassau got a bit of international attention during World War II when the Duke of Windsor, who abdicated as king to marry Wallis Simpson, was exiled there to be governor. He was probably not a beloved leader as he referred to the Bahamas as a "third class British colony."

✦ ✦ ✦

Those involved with the activity in Nassau during the Civil War followed widely varying paths after the war ended. The US consulate was the center of opposition to blockade-running efforts during the war and the four men who occupied that office had different degrees of success in their attempts to stop the shipping of contraband. Sam Whiting was a high-spirited patriot and master mariner who helped the cause but was undone by drink. Seth Hawley was a good fit for the job but was not in the position long enough to accomplish much. Vice-consul William Thompson seems to have been ineffectual and to have come completely unraveled by the hostile environment in which he found himself. Thomas Kirkpatrick was competent and gets credit for having blockade running come to an end on his watch, but in reality it was probably dying when he arrived in Nassau.

After leaving Nassau in March 1863, Sam Whiting headed back to Winona, Minnesota, but also took to the road to talk about his experiences. In September 1864 he presented a paper at a county meeting in Hempstead, Long Island, titled "Experience in Charleston, South Carolina in the Earlier Part of the Rebellion, and as United States Consul at the Bahamas during the First Two Years of the War." It is too bad that a copy of the paper did not survive, as it must have been fascinating. A few years later, he published a brochure titled "Capt. Sam Whiting's Popular Lectures," which stated, "Thirty years of travel through the most interesting portions of the habitable globe, have enabled me to draw from my daily journals several interesting lectures, which I propose to deliver through the Western States this winter."

In addition to talking about his Nassau experiences, he had a speech on the Kane expedition, a speech on his third voyage around the world and another on his experience in the Gold Rush of California. He would deliver one lecture for $50.00, two for $85.00 or three for $100.00. He moved to Illinois and then later to Tallahassee, Florida, where he was editor of a newspaper. By 1880 he was a widower living in a home for old sailors called Sailors Snug Harbor on Staten Island. On July 30, 1882, at age sixty-eight, Captain Sam was found dead in his bed with his throat cut from ear to ear by a razor that was by his side. His death was ruled a suicide.

After his short tenure as consul, Seth Hawley returned to the New York City Police Department and it does not seem that his decision to bail out of the consul's job affected his long friendships with William Seward or Thurlow Weed. One of his new duties was the interrogation of prisoners at Fort Lafayette, so he may have spent time talking to John Rahming and Joseph Eneas during their confinement in 1864. He was Chief Clerk of the NYPD when he died from pneumonia at age seventy-four on November 10, 1884.

Thomas Kirkpatrick stayed on as US consul in Nassau through 1869. During that year he was charged by the Department of State with interviewing many of the Nassau residents who had been involved with the blockade-running frenzy earlier in the decade. He was especially interested in those men who had taken part in the saga of the *Oreto/Florida*. The US government was seeking damages against the British for the havoc wreaked on merchant shipping by *Florida*, *Alabama*, and other commerce raiders to which the British had turned a blind eye. The so-called Alabama Claims were eventually settled by international arbitration in 1872, when the British agreed to pay $15,500,000 to the United States. Leaving Nassau, Kirkpatrick made his way back to Albany, where he was again elected state prison inspector, holding that position until 1874. He died in Brooklyn on April 9, 1892, when he was about eighty-two years old.

Three Americans gave significant aid to the consul's office during the war. Charles Jackson, the underwriter's agent, continued in that role after the war until returning to Boston, where he became a successful merchant. He died of a brain hemorrhage in New Haven, Connecticut, on March 6, 1887, at age sixty-one. John Howell, proprietor of the Royal Victoria and Nassau Dry Dock, friend and confidant to people on both sides of the conflict, stayed in Nassau after the war. Howell brought his younger brother Alexander into the dry dock business, but they might not have been on the best of terms. When John Howell died in Nassau of fever on December 15, 1872, at the age of forty-seven, his brother successfully sued his estate for money John owed him. Epes Sargent was a doctor, boarding house proprietor, Howell's partner in the dry dock, and Timothy Darling's brother-in-law. He stayed on in Nassau directing the dry dock facility into the 1870s. The dry dock was destroyed by fire in 1889. Sargent returned to the United States in 1880 and worked as a clerk in the Bureau of Clothing and Provisions for the US Navy. He died in New York on April 3, 1902, at age seventy-four.

Former US consul Timothy Darling was the only prominent merchant to be an ardent supporter of the Union cause. Like his brother-in-law Epes Sargent, Darling was a true New Englander living in the tropics and was in strong opposition to the slave-holding Confederacy. Still, he served on powerful legislative bodies with blockade runners like Henry Adderley and the same men spent time together as Freemasons.

Despite his opposition to blockade-running, he continued to be well accepted in the Nassau community. He remained as a member of the legislature and senior member of the Executive Council until poor health and advancing years forced him to step down. When he died on October 28, 1880, at age seventy, the *Nassau Guardian* obituary showed how much the city cared for him: "His death was not unexpected, yet the news of it was received by the whole community with unaffected grief and a profound sense of the loss which the Colony has sustained by his removal. For nearly forty years he was one of our most prominent and honoured citizens, and the large concourse which assembled yesterday to attend his remains to their last resting-place, composed of representatives of every class and creed, from the highest officials to the weeping descendants on his bounty, proved the respect in which he was held, and the high and special esteem with which he was universally regarded."

The three British officials who caused so much consternation for the US consuls and Navy commanders were Governor John Bayley, Colonial Secretary and often Acting-Governor Charles Nesbitt, and Attorney General George

Anderson. John Bayley returned to England in 1864, but having angered his superiors he did not find another diplomatic position. He died in London on July 6, 1873, at age fifty-six.

Charles Nesbitt might have been the most influential man in the political life of the Bahamas in the nineteenth century. He held public office for over fifty years and guided policy more influentially than most of the governors he served. He finally resigned his position as colonial secretary in 1867 at age sixty-eight and was succeeded in the position by John Dumaresq. After traveling to England and spending some time in Macon, Georgia, Nesbitt returned to Nassau and served as Justice of the Peace until his death on December 15, 1876.

George Anderson continued as attorney general of the colony and Speaker of the House of Assembly until becoming chief justice in 1875. He was knighted in 1874. He moved to Ceylon to become chief justice there before returning to Nassau, where he died on March 1, 1883, at age seventy-eight.

Out islanders had seized the blockade-running opportunity as eagerly, albeit on a lower financial level, as the merchants. In the summer of 1865 they trickled back to their islands and their families, some with a little gold still in their pocket. Except for those who made enough to head for Europe, the native Nassau merchants resumed the quiet lives they had before the war.

John Turtle, who provided provisions for *Florida*, took an unusual path by moving to Maryland and becoming a US citizen. He served as US consul to Brazil and Mauritius before returning to live in Delaware, where his second wife was from and where he died in 1885.

The three Bahamian merchants who had served as connections in New York did not return to Nassau. Francis Montell continued as a commission merchant in New York with his two sons Frank and John. He died from pneumonia on May 11, 1883, and was buried in Baltimore. John Rahming stayed in the commission business in New York, mainly dealing in sponges from Nassau. He went bankrupt twice but still found resources to attempt investment in the fledgling Dominican Republic. He died at his home in New York on September 28, 1895. Joseph Eneas also stayed in New York and continued his shady dealings. A newspaper reported in March 1877 that Eneas had disappeared and left over $60,000 in debt. He was also accused of forging his wife's name on a mortgage. He fled to Panama, leaving his wife to live with her father in Brooklyn. In Panama, he was arrested for passing counterfeit US dollars. Eneas died in Panama in 1898 with an estate of only $800.

John Maffitt, probably the most popular of the ship captains frequenting Nassau, remained in England after bringing *Owl* back to Liverpool. Like many others, he was not ready to beg for pardon. In September 1865 he wrote, "My stomach is as yet too delicate to take the nauseous dose, or "pardon-asking pill.'" He took the board test to become a certified English captain and began running the steamer *Widgeon* between Liverpool and South America. Missing his home and children, in March 1867 he resigned his commission and returned through New York to Wilmington, North Carolina. There he purchased a 212-acre farm near the shore and named his home "The Moorings." He passed away in Wilmington on May 15, 1886.

After the war ended, there was still a significant stock of contraband in Nassau. In March 1866 Thomas Kirkpatrick wrote to Freeman Morse, the US consul in London, to be on the lookout for goods being sent there by Henry Adderley and Company. Though the senior members of the firm were in England, the company was still operating in Nassau under the charge of Charles Passailaigue and a year after the war Passailaigue was still negotiating settlements with firms like the Importing and Exporting Company of South Carolina.

According to Kirkpatrick, goods had been transshipped from *Mary* to the *Alert* with the blessing of local customs officials. He said that when *Alert* arrived in England, they would find goods marked "L. Heyliger" and "L.H.," along with boxes and two cedar chests containing Heyliger's financial records and papers. There is no evidence that Morse or anyone else was able to secure these items and they appear to be lost to history.

In September 1865, Kirkpatrick informed Adderley and Company that the company's remaining Confederate supplies were now considered US property. Passailaigue stated that the firm was still owed over £2,000 by the Confederates for these materials. Never missing a trick, Passailaigue indicated that in addition to the value of the materials, Adderley also wanted the US government to pay them for having stored their property for them! Kirkpatrick went with Epes Sargent to look at a large group of carbines held by Adderley and Company, but said only one in six was still any good due to damage from the hurricane. The US and Henry Adderley and Company finally reached a settlement on the property in March 1869.

Despite his long service to the Adderleys, Charles Passailaigue eventually decided to provide information to Kirkpatrick as the latter gathered evidence for the Alabama Claims. Despite the somewhat acrimonious negotiations for Confederate property, the information he provided on *Oreto* and *Mary* helped him receive a recommendation and high praise from Kirkpatrick when Passalaigue applied in late 1869 to be the official US commercial agent in the Dominican Republic.

According to Kirkpatrick, Passailaigue was "thoroughly competent, honest and in every way reliable" and had provided "valuable and reliable information regarding the fitting, manning and equipping of the '*Oreto*, alias *Florida*' at Green Cay in the Bahamas." Kirkpatrick asked Secretary of State Hamilton

Fish to give a positive reponse on Passalaigue's application as he would be leaving Adderley's service at the end of the year and would "no longer have access to the books and papers of Henry Adderley and Company." Shortly thereafter, Passailaigue left Nassau for the Dominican Republic with his wife Florence. His grandson, Charles Clarence Passailaigue, was a well-known athlete playing cricket in Jamaica in the 1930s.

The government also went after George Trenholm and his companies. Trenholm himself was incarcerated in Fort Pulaski near Savannah for several months after the war before being pardoned. But the lawsuits filed against his companies and falling cotton prices eventually forced the once dominant conglomerate to file for bankruptcy in November 1867. It was a devastating finish for a company that had made so many millions from blockade running. Still, the people of the South never forgot what George Trenholm had done for the Confederacy, and when he died in 1876 the Charleston Chamber of Commerce published "A Tribute of Affection and Respect" for him.

Fraser, Trenholm and Company was involved in another lawsuit just after the war, this with a fellow Confederate. Richard Waller, who ran up large debts in his attempts to supply the Quartermaster's Department from Nassau, had a major misunderstanding with the Liverpool depositaries of the Confederacy. According to Waller, George Trenholm (in his role as secretary of the treasury) promised him in early 1865 that Fraser, Trenholm and Company would cover £60,000 in liabilities that he had incurred with Aaron Wolf, Jervey and Mueller, Benjamin Woolley Hart, and William Sterrett.

The funds were to have come to Fraser, Trenholm and Company from the sale of Confederate ships by James Bulloch and Colin McRae. Charles Mueller sailed from Nassau around April 1, 1865, and arrived in Liverpool on April 25, demanding from Charles Prioeau the money owed Jervey and Mueller. Prioleau claimed to know nothing of the obligation and refused to pay. According to Waller, Bulloch knew of the debt but never handed over the money. As a result, in May 1866 Waller sued everyone involved for restitution of the money: Trenholm, Prioleau, Bulloch, McRae, Theodore Wagner, James Welsman, and William Trenholm.

The partners of Fraser, Trenholm and Company (excluding George Trenholm, who had given up his partnership to take on his Treasury role) countersued Waller. Not only did they say they were under no obligation to pay the debt, but they accused Waller of treachery. Their account stated that just before the war ended Lewis Heyliger returned a large amount of supplies to James Ferguson, the Quartermaster Department purchasing agent in England. Ferguson and Waller had then arranged to have these goods shipped to South America to be sold and had then pocketed the proceeds. Not only would this have been dishonest, but the amount received would have easily satisfied Waller's debts in Nassau.

It is not clear how the lawsuits were resolved or who was telling the truth, but by the middle of 1867 Waller was back in Richmond and received his pardon that October. In his petition to be pardoned he indicated that lawsuits were still in progress in England, but he did receive a letter from the US government releasing him from all pecuniary demands he incurred during the war. Waller died in Richmond at age forty-eight on December 6, 1868.

✦ ✦ ✦

It was the great fortune of the Confederacy to have a man like Lewis Heyliger in Nassau. He was a critical conduit between all the various Confederate departments, the cotton brokers, and the shipments coming in from Europe. He served well as a businessman and also as a well-respected representative of the Confederate government in one of the war's most important and politically charged locations.

Years after the war Bulloch wrote high praise for Heyliger and his colleagues in Havana and Bermuda:

> In all great wars there are men who contribute to the general objects of the contest, and yet must be content with such reward as comes from the consciousness of duty faithfully performed. The Confederate agents at Nassau, Bermuda and Havana were of that class. Their services were well known and appreciated by those who had official correspondence with them during the war, but a brilliant dash at the head of a troop of cavalry, or participation in a successful sortie from beleaguered Richmond, would have made their names current where they are not likely mentioned now. Active service at the front wins the 'bauble reputation.' The men who work in the rear are not despised or even undervalued, but they must have the nerve to stifle their ambition. They may expect fair and just commendation, but then they must not aspire to stand side by side with those who wear the "myrtle crown."

Like many others, Heyliger headed to England as the war was ending and took up residence at 17 Lower Seymour Street on Portman Square in London. It was a ritzy area and home to several dukes and earls. He was likely in touch with Norman Walker and Richard Waller, who settled in Leamington, a town northwest of London that became a popular landing spot for ex-Confederates. In a letter dated February 1, 1866, and sent from New Orleans, Heyliger petitioned President Andrew Johnson for amnesty under Johnson's May 29, 1865, amnesty proclamation. The handwriting on the letter does not match Heyliger's so it was likely written on his behalf by someone else in New Orleans at that time.

Johnson's proclamation excluded automatic amnesty for a number of people, including those who had a net worth exceeding $20,000. Heyliger's letter indicated that his worth exceeded this amount, and while the pardon was granted on February 21, 1866, Heyliger was never able to enjoy having his rights restored. After a painful illness lasting several months, he died on August 18, 1866, at Tainfield House in Somerset, the home of lawyer William Edward Surtees. He was buried at St. Mary's Cemetery in Taunton on August 22. His obituary in the *New Orleans Times-Picayune* said that "he displayed much ability and tact. He was much liked by all who knew personally from unfailing courtesy and affability."

Heyliger's personal life is something of an enigma and it is not clear if he ever had a wife and family. His will sheds a bit of light as he left his estate (valued at over $40,000, a very large amount at the time) to three people. First, he left about $100 to William Norris, the Confederacy's Chief Signal Officer and the man responsible for transmitting documents to agents in foreign countries. Whether this small amount was a debt, a wager or something else is not known.

He left about half of his estate to "my friend Mrs. Martha Stanard." Mrs. Stanard, whose husband Robert C. Stanard died in 1857, was considered the premier socialite in Richmond before and during the war. She was good friends with the wives of Jefferson Davis and Robert E. Lee and famed diarist Mary Chestnut. Her mansion at the corner of Grace and Sixth Streets in that city was visited for frequent dinners and parties by everyone who was anyone in Richmond. This included Heyliger's friends Judah Benjamin and Pierre Soulé. Described as beautiful, gracious, and witty, she and Soulé almost married before she called it off. Although she was under his spell when in his company, when alone she apparently realized she had no future with a sixty-year-old man.

After her house was burned when the Union forces entered Richmond, she went to England for a time. It is possible that she first met Lewis Heyliger there, but Pierre Soulé said he had known her for thirty years so Heyliger may have been an old friend as well. Given his generosity to her in the will, Heyliger must have thought very highly of her.

He gave the rest of his estate to a teenager named Emile Le Mesnil by way of the Central National Bank in New York. There are records of Emile being in a school for boys in New Orleans in 1859. Was he Heyliger's child or just a favored relative?

Although he was working for a private company, Heyliger's friend and colleague John Lafitte was probably just as important to the cause due to the close connection between Trenholm's companies and the Confederate government. Like Heyliger, his intelligence and breeding served him well in Nassau.

Tom Taylor said Lafitte was "a charming man in every respect." John Lafitte, Euphrosine, Virginia Fourgeaud, and son James Lafitte traveled Europe after the war before returning to Charleston in June 1866. He applied for a presidential pardon from Berne, Switzerland, and his request was approved on May 2, 1866.

Like Heyliger, he admitted to having a net worth in excess of $20,000. He also stated that he would do "all in his power to repair the injuries of the past." He got back into the cotton business in Charleston and was also president of the People's Bank of Charleston. He remained a devout Catholic as he and Edward gave large donations to support St. Mary's Church. Virginia Fourgeaud married Frank Dawson on May 1, 1867. They were happily married until she was struck down by illness on December 6, 1872, at the young age of twenty-eight.

In 1870 John and Euphrosine moved to New Orleans, where he opened up another cotton firm with son James. As his business thrived after the war, he managed to stay in touch with prominent Confederates. In January 1867 he received a letter from Robert E. Lee thanking Lafitte for the telescope that he had sent to Lee. About ten years later he received another letter of thanks, this from Jefferson Davis. Lafitte had sent Davis a copy of the obituary of their mutual friend George Trenholm. He and James closed their firm in 1885, and John became president of the National Cotton Exchange of America. James's son and John's grandson Edward Lafitte was born in 1886 and became a major league baseball pitcher from 1909–1915.

John and Euphrosine lived at 319 Bourbon Street, where John Lafitte died on May 21, 1887, at age sixty-five. His obituary lauded Lafitte as "a gentleman of rare ability." The paper asserted that his financial abilities were recognized everywhere and that he was also very popular and eminent for his social qualities. Euphrosine moved back to Charleston, where she passed away in 1900. She was remembered as full of life and "sprightly in conversation and full of joyous humor, no word ever fell from her lips intended to wound." It is little wonder that the Lafittes were the center of social activity in Nassau.

✦ ✦ ✦

The three men who most epitomized the success of the opportunism surrounding the Great Carnival were Henry Adderley, his son Augustus, and their business partner and Henry's son-in-law George David Harris. In his 1862 report to London, Governor Bayley lamented the prospects for the colony ever becoming thriving, partly due to a "white population wedded to the most petty form of commerce."

The Adderleys and Harris certainly made a mockery of Bayley's words with the millions they raked in during the Civil War. Napoleon Bonaparte supposedly derided the British as a "nation of shopkeepers," but these three men took shopkeeping to a new level. They all moved their riches and their families to England, where they could finally live in the high society they had emulated in Nassau. They lived in mansions in the Paddington area of London, where George Harris had grown up and not far from former Nassau neighbors like Robert Weech, who also fled to England with his riches. The two younger men became involved in London politics, and both were eventually knighted for their service. Augustus Adderley died in London in 1905 at age seventy. George Harris also died in London in 1902 at age seventy-five.

Henry Adderley, the "King Conch" and probably the most notorious of all men associated with blockade running, enjoyed his riches for a decade after the war. He maintained control of the company in Nassau and continued to spend some time there until his death in 1875, when his nephew George Butler Adderley took it over. The Adderley mansion remained on Bay Street as a reminder of those glorious times until it was demolished in the 1960s. When Henry died he left an estate in excess of $1 million. Like son Augustus and George Harris, Henry was buried in Kensal Green Cemetery about a mile northwest of Paddington.

✦ ✦ ✦

Since the days of the Civil War, Nassau has expanded, and its population is now about twenty times greater than it was then. Nothing remains of the Adderley House or the Royal Victoria Hotel, but the sea and a spirit of opportunism still infuse Bahamian life. The deeper harbor now provides anchorage for more than a thousand cruise ships a year, providing a steady supply of customers for the shops on Bay Street. An international airport brings in many more people. The original idea to lure tourists that brought the Royal Victoria to life has become a reality far beyond the imaginations of John Bayley and Charles Nesbitt. Hog Island, home of John Howell's dry dock, is now Paradise Island and covered with resorts, casinos, and water parks. Still many of the visitors are interested in the history of the island. In their wanderings they begin to understand a bit about that brief moment in time when Nassau was transformed from what many viewed as an obscure tropical backwater into the frenzied center of commerce that captured the attention of the world.

Notes

Chapter 1: Two Arrivals

3 Anticipation of the prince's visit: *New York Times* March 26, 1861; April 24, 1861; June 16, 1861, hereinafter *NYT*.
3 Events for the prince: *War of the Rebellion: The Official Records of the Union and Confederate Navies* (Washington: Government Printing Office [hereinafter GPO], 1896), Ser. I, Vol. XII, 440, hereinafter listed as *ORN*, all series I unless otherwise noted.
3 Prince Alfred visit: Blue Curry, "Repairwork," accessed July 24, 2018, http://www.bluecurry.com/12.2.curry.pdf?id=9253218.
3 Enact a law: Assented to by the Bahamas General Assembly May 26, 1863, *Nassau Guardian*, December 4, 1867, hereinafter listed as *NG*.
3 Local newspaper: *Bahamas Herald*, December 11, 1861, hereinafter listed as *BH*.
4 Sterrett's journey: *Thomas Connolly, An Irishman in Dixie: Thomas Connolly's Diary of the Fall of the Confederacy*, ed. Nelson D. Lankford (Columbia: University of South Carolina Press, 1988).
4 Sterrett's profits: W. B. Sterrett in *Confederate Papers Relating to Citizens and or Business Firms, 1874–1899*, hereinafter *Confederate Citizen Papers*; James Stark, *Stark's History and Guide to the Bahama Islands* (Boston: James H. Stark, 1891), 94–95.
4 Connolly with dispatches: Royce Shingleton, *High Seas Confederate: The Life and Times of John Newland Maffitt* (Columbia: University of South Carolina Press, 1994), 96.
5 "Gold began to pour": G. J. H. Northcroft, *Sketches of Summerland, Giving Some Account of Nassau and the Bahama Islands* (Nassau: Nassau Guardian, 1900), 301.
6 1866 hurricane: Wayne Neely, *The Great Bahamas Hurricane of 1866* (Bloomington: IUniverse, Inc., 2011).
6 Nassau awoke: Charles Ives, *The Isles of Summer* (New Haven: Charles Ives, 1880), 271–272.
6 "The atmosphere of indolent acquiescence": Northcroft, *Sketches of Summerland*, 301.

Chapter 2: George Trenholm Sees the Future

9 Trenholm's resolution: "Resolution to Call the Election of Abraham Lincoln as U.S. President a Hostile Act and to Communicate to Other Southern States South Carolina's Desire to Secede from the Union," November 9, 1860, Resolutions of the

Notes

	General Assembly, 1779–1879. S165018 (Columbia, SC: South Carolina Department of Archives and History).
9	Edward Lafitte flag incident: *Charleston Mercury*, December 7, 1860.
10	Whiting and the flag incident 1860: *Despatches from US Consular Offices 1789–1906*, hereinafter *Despatches*, Roll 10; *NYT*, January 10, 1861; undated *New York Tribune* clipping from William Crozier.
10	Liverpool history and description: John Hussey, *Cruisers, Cotton and Confederates* (Merseyside: Countyvise, 2009), 3–7.
10	*Gondar* British registration: *ORN*, Vol. VI, 34.
10	Klingender: Thomas Sebrell II, *Persuading John Bull: Union and Confederate Propaganda in Britain, 1860–65* (Lanham, MD: Lexington Books, 2014), 130.
11	*Island Belle* registration: Records of District Courts of the United States, Admiralty Case Files, Philadelphia, February 19, 1864.
11	Prioleau gift: Samuel Crawford, *History of the Fall of Fort Sumpter* (New York: F. P. Harper, 1896), 397.
12	No cotton from Charleston in June 1861: Marcus Price, "Blockade Running as a Business in South Carolina during the War Between the States 1861–1865," *American Neptune* 9, no. 1 (1949), 53.
12	*Gondar* arrives September 2, 1861: *ONR*, Vol. VII, 282.
13	Charles Passailaigue and the *Savannah*: William Robinson, *The Confederate Privateers* (New Haven: Yale University Press, 1928), Chapters 4 and 12; John Scharf, *History of the Confederate Navy from its Organization to the Surrender of its Last Vessel* (New York: Rogers and Sherwood, 1887), 68–78.
15	Bulloch description: Thomas Dickinson, "Running the Blockade," *The Era Magazine* 13, no. 4 (April 1904), 250.
15	Bulloch's charge: James Bulloch, *The Secret Service of the Confederate States*. 2 volumes (New York: G. P. Putnam's Sons, 1885), 46.
16	Lincoln's breakfast with Grinnell: Leo Hershkowitz, *Tweed's New York: Another Look* (Garden City, NY: Anchor Press/Doubleday, 1978), 80.
16	Information on New York Board of Underwriters: *The United States Insurance Gazette and Magazine of Useful Knowledge* 14, no. 79 (New York: Gilbert Currie, 1862), 12.
17	Whiting and Lockwood: *Despatches*, Roll 10, January 19, 1862.
17	Whiting's New York lecture: *Brooklyn Daily Eagle*, February 1, 1861; *New York Tribune*, undated review from brochure "Capt. Sam's Popular Lectures" courtesy of William Crozier.

Chapter 3: Heyliger Arrives

19	Charles Jackson: *Correspondence Concerning Claims Against Great Britain*, Volume 6 (Washington: GPO, 1871), 336, hereinafter listed as *CCGB*; US Passport Applications, 1795–1905 (May 3, 1858, and July 6, 1869; Massachusetts Marriage Records 1840–1915.
19	Description of wreckers: *NYT*, Jan 17, 1865.
19	Epes Sargent: Emma Sargent, *Epes Sargent of Gloucester and His Descendents* (Boston, New York: Houghton-Mifflin, 1923), 383.
19	Sargent House: Charles Cory, *The Birds of the Bahamas Islands* (Boston: Estes and Lauriat, 1890), 17.

20   Summer of 1861 and *William H. Northrup: Despatches*, Roll 10, August 7, 1861. *Adaline: NYT* 8/30/61.
21   John Rahming's imprisonment: *Despatches*, Roll 10, September 30, 1861; *War of the Rebellion: The Official Records of the Union and Confederate Armies*, Ser. 2, Vol. 2 (Washington: GPO, 1880–1901), 627, hereinafter *ORA*.
22   Mason and Slidell: Stephen Wise, *Lifeline of the Confederacy: Blockade Running during the Civil War* (Columbia: University of South Carolina Press, 1991), 56–57.
22   Jackson's boat being chased: *Reports from Consuls of the United States* (Washington: GPO, 1862), Whiting to Seward, October 25, 1861.
23   Bulloch knows Low before the war: Warren Spencer, *The Confederate Navy in Europe* (Tuscaloosa: University of Alabama Press, 1997), 46.
23   Low travels to England with wife and Andrew Low: William Hoole, *Four Years in the Confederate Navy* (Athens: University of Georgia Press, 2012), 4.
23   *Fingal* voyage: Bulloch, *Secret Service*, Chapter III.
23   "If the Bahamas let you pass": Jonathan Nagel, "Heyday of King Cotton," *Confederate Veteran* 40, no. 6 (1932), 218.
24   For a detailed list of Wilmington pilots, see James Sprunt, *Chronicles of the Cape Fear River, 1660–1916* (Raleigh: Edwards and Broughton, 1916), 395.
24   As many as thirty ships, Fall 1861: *ORN*, Vol. XII, 441.
25   Francis Montell: *Baltimore Sun*, November 20, 1839; December 11, 1840; April 30, 1840; "Slave Registers of former British Colonial Dependencies, 1813–1834"; Peter Dalleo, "Montell and Co., the James Power and the Baltimore-Bahamas Packet Trade 1838–1845," *Journal of the Bahamas Historical Society* 30 (2008), 5–14; *NYT* May 13, 1883.
26   Wier flies Confederate flag: Barry Sheehy, *Montreal: City of Secrets* (Montreal: Baraka Books, 2017), 124.
26   William Stockman: *A. McElroy's Philadelphia City Directory*, 1855 and 1861 editions (Philadelphia: Isaac Ashmead and Co.); *Passenger Lists of Vessels Arriving at New York, New York, 1820–1897*, National Archives, hereinafter *NY Passenger Lists*; Samuel Blatchford, *Report of Cases in Prize Argued and Determined in the Circuit and District Courts of the United States for the Southern District of New York 1861–1865* (Washington: GPO, 1866), 294–296.
27   Foreign Enlistment Act: see for example Frederick Gibbs, *The Foreign Enlistment Act* (London: William Ridgway, 1863).
27   Letters from Nesbitt, Adderley, and Whitley: *The Counter Case of Great Britain as Laid before the Tribunal* (Washington: GPO, 1872), hereinafter *Counter Case*, 270.
27   Prince of Wales: John Bacot, *The Bahamas: A Sketch* (London: Longmans, Green, Reader, and Dyer, 1869), 48.
28   Whiting's poem: *BH*, December 4, 1861.
28   Heyliger's trip to Nassau: *ORN*, Vol. XII, 831; *Confederate Citizen Papers*; *ORA*, Ser. 4, Vol. 1, 781.
28   Heyliger's life before the war: *New Orleans Annual and Commercial Register for 1846* (New Orleans: E. A. Michel and Co., 1846); *Gardner's New Orleans Directory for 1861* (New Orleans: Charles Gardner, 1861); *New Orleans Times-Picayune* June 10, 1852; May 9, 1857; September 26, 1857; *About the New-Orleans Commercial Times* from *Chronicling America*, Library of Congress (LOC); US Naturalization Records, National Archives (hereinafter *NA*); *New Orleans Daily Crescent*, November 20, 1857; *NY Passenger Lists*.

29 Heyliger and the T. O. Moore Havana gun trip: *NA Confederate Citizens Papers*.
31 Heyliger and Helm December 1861: *ORA*, Ser. 4, Vol. 1, 784, 798, 799, 806; *Extracts from Letterbooks, 1861–1865*, Library of Congress (hereinafter *LOC*), Helm to William Browne, December 21, 1861, Image 20.
31 Benjamin writes to Moore about preserving Heyliger's position: *ORA*, Ser. 4, Vol. 1, 831.
32 D. T. Bisbie's letter: *ORN*, Vol. XXII, 835.
32 Whiting convinced skipper was bribed: *Reports from Consuls*, Whiting to Seward, December 23, 1861.

Chapter 4: "This Remote Western Maritime Colony"

35 Bahamas offer for steamship service: Paul Albury, *The Story of the Bahamas* (New York: St. Martin's Press, 1976), 220.
35 SS Jewess fire: Michael Craton, *A History of the Bahamas* (Waterloo, Ontario: San Salvador Press, 1986), 212.
36 "Everyone was poor": Thomas Taylor, *Running the Blockade* (London: John Murray, 1896), 23.
36 General description and history of the Bahamas: Albury, *Story of the Bahamas*; Charles Ives, *Isles of Summer*; Louis Diston Powles, *Land of the Pink Pearl* (London: Sampson Low, Marston, Searle and Rivington, 1888); Stark, *Stark's History and Guide to the Bahama Islands*; G. J. H. Northcroft, *Sketches of Summerland*; Frank I. Wilson, *Sketches of Nassau* (Raleigh: The Standard, 1864); J. Milton Mackie, *From Cape Cod to Dixie and the Tropics* (New York: G. P. Putnam, 1864); William Drysdale, *In Sunny Lands: Out-Door Life in Nassau and Cuba* (New York: Harper and Bros, 1881); James Wright, *History of the Bahamas with a Special Study of the Abolition of Slavery* (New York: Macmillan, 1905); Robert Douglas, *Island Heritage: Architecture of the Bahamas* (Trinidad: Darkstream, 1992).
38 Blacks not extended common courtesies by whites: *Colonial Office Files* 23/163/69–71, hereinafter *CO Files*, Bayley to Newcastle, August 15, 1860.
38 Shock at black postmaster: Henry Blun, *Reminiscences of My Blockade Running*. (Savannah: Braid and Hutton, 1910), 4.
38 Cunard wharf in Jersey City: ad in *New York Herald*, April 5, 1862.
39 Royal Victoria opening: *New York Herald*, March 7, 1861.
40 Being arrested for racial epithets: Wilson, *Sketches of Nassau*, 9.
39 Timothy Darling sells land for Royal Victoria: Gail Saunders and Michael Craton, *Islanders in the Stream* (Athens: University of Georgia Press, 1999 and 2000), vol 2, 75.
39 French's boarding house: Mary Moseley, *Nassau Guardian* Centenary Issue.
39 Description of Royal Victoria: Saunders and Craton, *Islanders in the Stream*, Vol. 2, 75; Ad for public auction of the Royal Victoria, *New York Daily Herald*, December 19, 1877.
41 Public hangings on Eastern Parade: William S. Lofquist, "Identifying the Condemned: Reconstructing and Analyzing the History of Executions in the Bahamas," *International Journal of Bahamian Studies* 16 (2010), 24.
41 Dogs: William J. Fielding, "Everybody in Nassau Has a Dog, and They Bark All Night: Potcakes, a History," *Journal of the Bahamas Historical Society* 28 (2006), 36–43.

42	Two-thirds of men involved in wrecking: Albury, *Story of the Bahamas*, 135.
42	"Idlers with maritime tastes": Mary Moseley, *Nassau Guardian* Centenary Issue, November 23, 1944.
42	Ice from Canada: Ronald G. Lightbourn, *Reminiscing II: Photographs of Old Nassau* (Nassau: Ronald G. Lightbourn, 2005), 28.
43	Fleeming Square and 2nd West India regiment: J. R. O'M. M'Lawler, "The Bahamas or Lucayos Islands," *Colburn's United Service Magazine and Naval and Military Journal* 14 (May 1861), 96–98.

Chapter 5: The Bay Street Boys

44	Stratification of Bahamian society: Gail Saunders, *Race and Class in the Colonial Bahamas, 1880–1960* (Gainesville: University Press of Florida, 2016), 34.
44	Stephen Dillet: Patrice Williams, "Personalities: Stephen Dillet, 1845–1930," *Journal of the Bahamas Historical Society* 7 (1985); James Johnson, *Along This Way: The Autobiography of James Weldon Johnson* (Boston: De Capo Press, 2000), 3–6; A. Talbot Bethell, *The Early Settlers of the Bahamas and Colonists of North America* (Westminster, Maryland: Heritage Books, 2008), 135.
45	White elite mimicking British upper classes: Saunders, *Race and Class*, 37.
45	Reserved for "the poor": Johnson, *Post-Emancipation Race Relations*, 11.
45	White elite looking down on tradesmen: Whittington Johnson, *Post- Emancipation Race Relations in the Bahamas* (Gainseville: University Press of Florida, 2006), 130.
46	2nd West India regiment backing up police: Howard Johnson, *Bahamas from Slavery to Servitude, 1783–1933* (Gainesville: University Press of Florida, 1997), 78.
46	Dillet and Kite Flying: Johnson, *Post-Emancipation Race Relations*, 104.
46	"No white man can go to prison": Saunders, *Race and Class*, 41.
46	Newspapers: Johnson, *Post-Emancipation Race Relations*, 101; Thelma Peters, "The Bahamas and Blockade-Running during the American Civil War" (master's thesis, Duke University, 1939), 25.
46	A good overview of Nesbitt's life: John M. Trainor, "The Ascendancy of Charles Rogers Nesbitt, Politician, Civil Servant, and Administrator," *Journal of the Bahamas Historical Society* 3 (1981), 3–12.
48	Information on Henry Adderley's early life from Ann Morley Carmel and from John Gorman, "The Adderley Family in the New World," *Journal of the Bahamas Historical Society* 22 (2000), 31–43.
50	Renouard and sponge industry: *Canandaigua Daily Messenger*, March 17, 1947.
50	Information on pre-war shipping patterns of the leading merchants in Nassau: *US Consular Records for Nassau, 1821–1935*, including Vessels Cleared and Consular Fees Paid, NA.
53	"In this mongrel port": *NYT* July 9, 1862.
53	Law of continuous voyage: Herbert W. Briggs, *The Doctrine of Continuous Voyage* (Baltimore: Johns Hopkins Press, 1926); Stuart L Bernath., *Squall across the Atlantic* (Berkeley: University of California Press, 1970).
54	Ships being bought at Key West prize court: *ORN*, Vol. XVII, 332.
54	Elliott's comments: Charles B. Elliott, "The Doctrine of Continuous Voyages," *American Journal of International Law* 1, no. 1 (January 1907), 76.

Chapter 6: Putting the Pieces in Place

60 Mountains of coal: *NG*, October 8, 1864.
60 Standoff makes it into newspapers: *NYT*, January 10, 1862; *Western Democrat*, Charlotte, NC, December 31, 1861.
60 Heyliger to Benjamin on transshipment: *ORA*, Ser. 4, Vol. 1, 815; *Papers Relating to the Treaty of Washington* (Washington: GPO, 1872) hereinafter *Treaty of Washington*, Vol. 1, 93.
60 Adderley to Nesbitt: *Counter Case*, 272.
61 Edwin Adderley: *NYT*, February 15, 1862; *ORN*, Vol XII, 628; *NYT*, April 25, 1862.
61 *Ella Warley*: *NYT*, August 2, 1863.
61 Trenholm to Benjamin, 12/30/1861: *ORA*, Ser. 4, Vol. 1, 819.
62 Harris and A. J. Adderley become partners with Henry: *BH*, February 1, 1862.
62 "Leading an active mind": *Despatches*, Roll 12, July 17, 1865.
62 A. J. Adderley in New York: *NY Passenger Lists*.
63 A. J. Adderley and the guard: Johnson, *Post-Emancipation Race Relations*, 124.
63 A. J. Adderley and Charles Jackson: *BH*, July 30, 1862.
63 Anderson mocking Union "victories": Whiting to Seward, August 1, 1862, *CCGB*, Vol. 6, 261.
64 Whiting's two drinking incidents: *Despatches*, Roll 10, January 19, 1862.
64 Buck Saunders: Samuel Preston, "In the Palmy Days of Wrecking," *Frank Leslie's Popular Monthly* 39, (1895), 49–53.
65 Whiting's feelings about Jackson: *Despatches*, Roll 10, January 19, 1862.
66 Others want Whiting's job: *Despatches*, Roll 10 April 13, 1862.
66 Kimball and Arnold: "Otis Kimball and Augustus Arnold v. the Steamship Dispatch and Benjamin Buck, Master," *Western Law Monthly* 4 (1863), 209.
66 Testimonial on Whiting's behalf: *Despatches*, Roll 10, January 19, 1862.
66 Fred Seward and the bond: *Despatches*, Roll 10, January 25, 1862.
67 John Powell: *NG*, February 25, 1863.
67 Bahama Institute: Virginia C. Balance, "A New Look at Old Books: The Collection of the Nassau Public Library in the Mid-19th Century," *International Journal of Bahamian Studies* 19 (2013), 42; Rawson W. Rawson, *Report on the Bahamas for the Year 1864* (London: Eyre and Spottiswoode, 1866), 78.
67 Thompson describes Whiting's lecture: *BH*, February 19, 1862.
68 Heyliger moves *Gladiator*: *ORN* Vol. 1, 281; *ORA*, Ser. 4, Vol. 1, 895.
68 Lockwood pleasure cruise: *ORN*, Vol. XII, 628.
68 *Kate's* cargo: *ORA* Ser 4, Vol. 1, 895.
68 Anderson reads circular to Temple: *ORN* Vol. 1, 85.
68 Heyliger gloats: *ORA* Ser. 4, Vol. 1, 895.
68 False bills of lading: *ORA* Ser. 4, Vol. 1, 896.
68 *Kate's* cargo landed safely: Wise, *Lifeline*, 260.
69 Maffitt background: Shingleton, *High Seas Confederate*.
69 Maffitt description: Emma Maffitt, *The Life and Services of John Newland Maffitt* (New York and Washington: The Neale Publishing Company, 1906), 351.

54 Bahamian governors being granted leave: Whittington Johnson, *Post-Emancipation Race Relations*, 11.

69	Trenholm suggests Maffitt be engaged in blockade running: *ORA*, Ser 4, Vol 1, 829.
69	Benjamin to Maffitt, January 27, 1862: *CCGB*, Vol. 6, 57.
70	Lafitte background: Frederick Ford, *Census of the City of Charleston, South Carolina for the Year 1861* (Charleston: Evans and Cogswell, 1861); *1860 US Federal Census Slave Schedule*; Obituary in *New Orleans Times-Picayune* May 22, 1887; *John B. Lafitte Papers*, South Caroliniana Library, University of South Carolina
70	Lafitte to England early 1862: *The Business Records of Fraser, Trenholm and Company of Liverpool and Charleston, South Carolina 1860-1877*, Merseyside Maritime Museum, hereinafter *Trenholm Records*, January 23, 1863.
70	Lafitte to Prioleau: *Trenholm Records*, January 23, 1863.
70	Lafitte's character: Carleton Hunt, "Fifty Years' Experience in Practice at the Bar," *Report of the Louisiana State Bar Association*, 1908, 49.
70	Lafitte and Vincent: *ORN*, Vol. VI, p.97; *ORA* Ser. 2, Vol. 2, 457; Scharf, *History of the Confederate Navy*, 441–442.
70	Lafitte selling iron from *Alliance*: *NA, Confederate Citizens Papers* for John B. Lafitte, September 4, 1861; September 14, 1861.
71	Bowie, Lafitte and Co.: *Abbeville Press*, November 16, 1860.
71	Mary Virginia called Virginia: her tombstone in St. Lawrence cemetery in Charleston reads "Our Virginia."
71	Miss Fourgeaud concert: *BH*, December 10, 1862.
71	Floyd: *Francis Warrington Dawson Family Papers, 1386-1963*, Duke University; *Official Register of the Officers and Acting Midshipmen of the United States Naval Academy* (Washington: William A. Harris, 1859), 14.
71	Alfred Trenholm travel: *Trenholm Records*, April 18, 1863.
72	Forrest on the *Trent*: Ethel Nepveux. *George A. Trenholm: Financial Genius of the Confederacy* (Charleston: Ethel Nepveux, 1998), 118.
72	Forrest's time in Nassau: Douglas French Forrest, *Odyssey in Gray: A Diary of Confederate Service, 1863-1865* (Richmond: Virginia State Library, 1979), 13–22.
72	Dawson background: *NYT*, March 20, 2012.
72	Mary Virginia description: Giselle Roberts, ed., *The Correspondence of Sarah Morgan and Francis Warrington Dawson* (Athens: University of Georgia Press, 2004), 6.
72	Lafitte at Royal Victoria: See for example *BH*, November 1, 1862.
72	Lafitte's office location: *NG*, April 29, 1865.
73	Heyliger, Lafitte, and Captain Bird: *CCGB*, Vol. 6, 60–66.
73	Passalaigue lives with Adderleys: *Despatches*, Roll 12, August 19, 1865.
73	Payments for *Gladiator*: *Papers Pertaining to Vessels of or Involved with the Confederate States of America*, hereinafter *Confederate Vessel Papers*, G-38
74	Adderley's charges: For example, invoice for cotton on the steamer *Caroline* in the *William C. Bee and Company Records, 1848-1912.*, South Carolina Historical Society, hereinafter *SCHS*.
74	Whiting on Lafitte and Heyliger: *Despatches*, Roll 10, April 30, 1862.
75	Heyliger impressed with Maffitt: *CCGB*, Vol. 6, 65.
75	Maffitt at the Royal Victoria: *CCGB*, Vol. 6, 317.
75	*Gladiator* leaves for Liverpool: *BH*, April 30, 1862.
75	Benjamin suggests Heyliger leave Nassau: *ORA*, Ser 4, Vol. 1, 985, 1018.
75	Maffitt letter from War Department: *ORA*, Ser. 4, Vol. 1, 1055–1056.
76	Ports sending cotton: "Ship News" column in *BH*, spring 1862; *NYT* April 25, 1862.

76	Heyliger comment on cotton: Dickinson, "Running the Blockade," 251.
76	Bayley returns: *BH*, March 12, 1862.
76	Bayley on black population: *Accounts and Papers of the House of Commons* 39 (1862), 8–9; Johnson, *Post-Emancipation Race Relations*, 131.
77	Pranks played on Whiting: James Sprunt, *Derelicts; An account of Ships Lost at Sea in General Commercial Traffic and a Brief History of Blockade Runners Stranded along the North Carolina Coast, 1861–1865* (Wilmington, NC: James Sprunt, 1920), 213–218.
77	*Karnak* wrecks: *NYT*, April 25, 1862; *BH*, April 16, 1862; April 19, 1862. Whiting tells Seward about Cooke rumors: *CCGB*. Vol. 6, 234.
78	*Karnak* statistics: *NY Passenger Lists*.
78	Pilot falls overboard: *NYT*, March 26, 1860.
78	Contraband on *Karnak*: *NYT*, April 25, 1862.
78	Sizes of Cunard ships: The Ships List, www.theshipslist.com, accessed July 29, 2018.

Chapter 7: The Lions of the Royal Victoria

79	Eliza and Andrew Low arrested: Hoole, *Four Years*, 15–19.
80	Bulloch and Low back to England: Bulloch, *Secret Service*, 149–151.
80	Dudley on *Oreto*: *ORN*, Vol. 6, 683–4.
81	*Oreto* cargo: *Treaty of Washington*, Vol. 5, 278.
81	*Oreto* arrives in Nassau: *BH*, April 30, 1862; *Despatches*, Roll 10, May 6, 1862.
81	Maffitt not in Nassau: *Despatches*, Roll 10, April 30, 1862.
81	Moving *Oreto* to Cochrane's: *CCGB*, Vol. 6, 234.
81	Heyliger's letter to the *Nassau Guardian*: *Confederate Vessel Papers*, B-120.
81	Heyliger's letter to Randolph: *CCGB*, Vol. 6, 73–74.
82	*Gladiator* to Bermuda: *CCGB*, Vol. 6, 76–77.
82	Saunders coal depot: *BH*, various issues May–June 1862.
82	Ships delayed for lack of coal: Kenneth Blume, "The Mid-Atlantic Arena: The United States, the Confederacy, and the British West Indies, 1861–1865" (PhD dissertation, SUNY Binghampton, 1984), 203; Maffitt to Mallory August 1, 1862, John Newland Maffitt Papers, University of South Carolina, hereinafter *Maffitt Papers*.
82	Heyliger to Bermuda: *CCGB*, Vol. 6, 76.
82	Lafitte covers Heyliger duties: *CCGB*, Vol. 6, 234.
82	Wilson arrives to help Heyliger: Frank E. Vandiver ed., *Confederate Blockade Running through Bermuda, 1861–1865; Letters and Cargo Manifests* (Austin: University of Texas Press, 1947), 18.
83	Heyliger arrives late June: *ORA*, Ser. 4 Vol. 1, 1174.
83	Bourne changes coal price: Vandiver, *Confederate Blockade Running*, 16.
83	Florie Maffitt singing at Royal Victoria: John Kell, *Recollections of a Naval Life : Including the Cruises of the Confederate States Steamers, "Sumter" and "Alabama"* (Washington: The Neale Company, 1900), 180.
83	Florie Maffitt story: Emma Maffitt, *Life and Services*, 240.
83	Low hands Maffitt letter from Bulloch: Emma Maffitt, *Life and Services*, 238.
84	Maffitt tells Adderley he will take command: Hoole, *Four Years*, 32.
84	Whiting calls Cochrane's Anchorage "rebel rendezvous": *Navy Department, 1861–1865, Log of Vessels in Bermuda and Nassau, LOC*, May 19, 1862, and June 9, 1862.

84	Whiting to Bayley: *CCGB*, 80–82.
84	*Bulldog* to Cochrane's: *Treaty of Washington*, 254.
84	Anderson on legality: *Counter Case*, 285.
84	*Oreto* can be loaded under supervision: *Counter Case*, 285.
84	George Harris offers bonus: *Counter Case*, 281.
84	Edward Jones writes Whiting: *Treaty of Washington*, 392.
84	Maffitt on Jones: Hoole, *Four Years*, 31.
84	Motley crew of sailors: Porter, David Dixon Porter, *The Naval History of the Civil War* (New York: Sherman Publishing Co., 1886), 624.
85	Maffitt to Mallory: *Maffitt Papers*, August 1, 1862.
85	George Anderson friends with members of firm: *Treaty of Washington*, 268.
85	Anderson is Adderley's attorney: *Treaty of Washington*, 268.
85	Hickley boards *Oreto*: *CCGB*, 245.
86	Whiting to Seward: *CCGB*, 241; *NG*, June 7, 1862.
86	Captain Allen and the flagpole: *Despatches*, Roll 10, June 8, 1862; *New York Daily Tribune*, May 20, 1862.
86	Whiting accuses McKillop: *Despatches*, Roll 10, June 8, 1862; *CCGB*, Vol. 6, 83. Whiting to Seward on Fort Sumter panorama: *Despatches*, Roll 10, May 6, 1862; May 15, 1862; *CCGB*, Vol. 6 78.
87	Kane expedition panorama: *BH*, May 21, 1862.
87	Adderley letter: Adderley to Bayley, May 12, 1862, *Accounts and Papers of the House of Commons* 72 (London: Harrison and Sons, 1863), hereinafter *Accounts and Papers*, 3.
87	Whiting gets Lafitte papers: *Despatches*, Roll 10, April 30, 1862.
87	Whiting and *Fanny Lewis*: *Treaty of Washington*, Vol. 4, 159.
87	Jackson and Lathrop: *Despatches*, Roll 10, April 29, 1862, May 24, 1862.
87	Custom officials require bond on the *Time*: *Accounts and Papers*, 8–9.
87	Adderley writes to Bayley to protest bond: *Accounts and Papers*, 3.
88	Chase gives Barney authority to require bonds: *Accounts and Papers*, 6.
88	Cunard Atlantic ship sizes and schedule: The Ships List and *NYT* ad November 4, 1863.
89	*William H. Clear*: *Accounts and Papers*, 16.
89	Whiting to Seward on *British Queen* arrival: *Despatches*, Roll 10, July 6, 1862.
89	Cargo on *China*: *Accounts and Papers*, 13–16.
89	British merchants protest: *Accounts and Papers*, 18–22.
90	Nassau merchants protest: *Accounts and Papers*, 26–27.
90	Edward Cunard writes to Adderley: *Accounts and Papers*, 7, 27.
90	Chase's presidential ambitions: Doris Kearns Goodwin, *Team of Rivals* (New York: Simon and Schuster, 2005).
90	Consular certificate: *Despatches*, Roll 10, no date.
90	Barney to Chase regarding Adderley: *Accounts and Papers*, 32–33.
90	Beach, Root, North, and Jorss: Frank Byrne, *Becoming Bourgeois: Merchant Culture in the South, 1820–1865* (Lexington: University Press of Kentucky, 2006), 176; *Accounts and Papers*, 34; *Confederate Citizens Papers*; Frank J. Byrne, "Rebellion and Retail: A Tale of Two Merchants in Confederate Atlanta," *Georgia Historical Quarterly* 79, no. 1 (1995), 30–56.
91	Adderley ships *Pacific* goods to Charleston: *BH*, May 23, 1862; Wise, *Lifeline*, 251.
91	Whiting to Barney: *Accounts and Papers*, 137.

Notes

91	Heyliger returns to Nassau: *Consular and Other Missions*, LOC, June 28, 1862.
91	George Anderson bent on securing *Oreto* release: *CCGB*, Vol. 6, 253.
92	"Wind blew prosperity to Nassau": Raphael Semmes, *Memoirs of Service Afloat during the War between the States* (Baltimore: Kelly, Piet, and Co.,1869), 350.
92	Maffitt, Semmes parties: *CCGB*, Vol. 6, 318.
92	"Lions of the Royal Victoria": *Despatches*, Roll 10, June 19, 1862.
92	Howell and Semmes: *CCGB*, Vol. 6, 318.
92	Semmes leaves July 13: *Consular and Other Missions*, Image 95, July 19, 1862.
93	Adderley travels on *Bahama*: *BH*, July 16, 1862.
93	Low travels on *Minna*: Hoole, *Four Years*, 34.

Chapter 8: Yellow Jack

94	Whiting spending money going to Cochrane's: *Despatches,* Roll 10, June 28, 1862.
94	Background on S. Isaac, Campbell and Company: Craig Barry and David Burt, *Supplier to the Confederacy II: S. Isaac Campbell and Co., London, Peter Tait and Co., Limerick,* Vol. 2 (Oslo: Stainless Banner, 2010).
94	B. W. Hart in New York: 1860 US Federal Census, 1855 New York State Census.
95	Hart would not talk to Heyliger: *CCGB*, Vol. 6, 90–91.
95	Horse races and mouse: *BH*, June 1, 1862.
95	Kimball and Arnold criticized: *BH*, July 19, 1862.
95	Same Whiting accused of holding up ice: *NG*, July 26, 1862.
96	Heyliger on positive effects of battles: *ORA*, Ser. 4, Vol. 2, 19.
96	Little girl and newspapers: *BH*, June 26, 1862.
96	*Oreto* trial was a farce: For example, Porter, *Naval History*, 624.
96	Edward Jones to NY: *Despatches*, Roll 11, August 22, 1862.
97	Letter for Grinnell: *Despatches*, Roll 10, June 29, 1862.
97	Rumor Whiting paid Jones not to testify: *NG*, July 26, 1862.
97	Blockade running captains testify as master mariners: *Treaty of Washington*, 281.
97	Lees, Anderson, and Bayley paid off: *Chicago Tribune* June 17, 1864; *CCGB*, Vol. 6 327; *Despatches*, Roll 12, July 17, 1865.
98	Gansevoort on Nassau: *CCGB*, Vol. 6, 260.
98	$10 million of goods: *NYT*, August 5, 1862.
98	"Nassau has done more . . .": *CCGB*, Vol. 6, 94.
98	Provisions from J. J. Turtle: *CCGB*, Vol. 6, 330.
99	*Cuyler* waits at Abaco: *ORN*, Vol. 1, 416.
99	Maffitt has only 22 men: Emma Maffitt, *Life and Services*, 246.
99	Three British sailors: *CCGB*, Vol. 6, 307.
99	Laffite purchases Prince Alfred from A. Johnson: *CCGB*, Vol. 6, 327.
99	Maffitt on yellow fever cases: *ORN*, Vol. 1, 764.
99	Lt. Brown dies: Emma Maffitt, "The Confederate Navy," *Confederate Veteran*, 25, no. 6 (1917), 264.
99	Henry Isaac dies: *Consular and Other Missions, LOC*, Image 100, August 1, 1862.
100	Caufield: *NG* Centenary Issue, November 23, 1944.
100	Whiting says five people dying per day: *Despatches*, Roll 11, September 6, 1862.
100	Yellow fever in Confederacy: *NYT*, November 19, 1862.

100	Maffitt and the *Oreto* at Green Cay: Emma Maffitt, *Life and Services*, 246.
100	Whiting makes charges against *Prince Alfred*: *Counter Case*, 113.
100	*Prince Alfred* as *Pocotaligo*: *Despatches*, Roll 12, July 17, 1865.
100	Helm welcomes *Oreto*: *Extracts from Letterbooks, 1861–1865*, LOC, Helm to Maffitt, June 6, 1862.
101	Maffitt to Florie: *Maffitt Papers*, September 8, 1862.
101	Butler accuses Whiting of writing pro-seccession poem: *Despatches*, Roll 11, August 4, 1862.
101	Whiting, August 22, 1863, letter: *Despatches*, Roll 11.
101	Whiting ad offering reward: *BH*, September 10, 1862.
102	Whiting gets to wreck on August 27, 1863: *ORN*, Vol. 1, 427.
103	Whiting says permission for coal will be granted: *ORN*, Vol. 1, 487.
103	Whiting on George Anderson: *CCGB*, Vol. 6, 98.
103	Anderson paid by American firms and consigns cargoes: *William C. Bee Records*, invoices July 13, 1864, September 11, 1865.
104	Shipments from Savannah, Port Royal, and Florida: *BH*, October 8, October 15, and November 29, 1862.
104	Sailors from *Ella Warley*: *NYT*, March 20, 1862.
104	Heyliger tells Benjamin about letter to Bayley: *Consular and Other Missions*, LOC, Image 122, October 13, 1862.
104	Nesbitt letter to Heyliger: *Consular and Other Missions*, LOC, Image 120, October 2, 1862.
105	Wilkes mission: *ORN*, Vol. 1, 470–471.
105	Loroda: Frank Tousley Edwards, "The American Consular Service in the Bahamas during the American Civil War" (PhD dissertation, Catholic University, 1968), 176.
105	*Herald* claims Nassau under blockade: *BH*, October 8, 1862.
106	Pilot Lloyd delivers proclamation: *NYT*, November 19, 1862.
106	Wilkes chases *Antonica*: Sprunt, *Derelicts*, 108.
106	Wilkes toys with boat: United States Department of State, *Message of the President of the United States, and Accompanying Documents, to the Two Houses of Congress, at the Commencement of the First Session of the Thirty-Eighth Congress* (Washington: GPO, 1863), 478.
106	Wilkes statement in newspapers: *BH*, November 22, 1862.
106	Heyliger says freight accumulating: *Consular and Other Missions*, LOC, Image 125, November 12, 1862.
107	Waller and Ferguson at Clothing Bureau: Harold S. Wilson, *Confederate Industry* (Jackson: University Press of Mississippi. 2002), 9.
107	E. Lafitte requests Mahoney: *Confederate Citizen Files*, NA, Edward Lafitte.
107	Mahoney background: US Federal Census 1850, 1870, 1880; "South Carolina's Centennial," *Rural Carolinian* 6, no. 14 (1875), 776; *Compiled Records Showing Service of Military Units in Confederate Organizations*, NA, hereinafter *Confederate Service Records*.
108	Mahoney dropped from roster: *Confederate Service Records*.
108	Collie supports statue: John Bennett, *The London Confederates: The Officials, Clergy, Businessmen and Journalists Who Backed the American South during the Civil War*. (Jefferson, NC: McFarland, 2008), 115.
108	Adderley returns: *BH*, November 26, 1862.

108 Sawyer and Menendez, Saunders and Son shipping: *BH*, "Arrived and Cleared Column" and "Ship News," 1862.
109 Confederate gun shipments: *ORA* Ser. 4 Vol. 1, 958; *ORA* Ser. 4 Vol. 2, 52.
109 Trenholm $20 million: Theodore D. Jervey. "Charleston during the Civil War" *Annual Report of the American Historical Association*, 1914, 167–176.
109 John Jones quote: John B. Jones, *A Rebel War Clerks Diary at the Confederate States Capital* (Philadelphia: J. B. Lippincott, 1866), Vol. 1, 223.

Chapter 9: A New Consul

110 Whiting "prim and stately": Albert Riddle, *Recollections of War Times* (New York: G. P. Putnam's Sons, 1895), 240.
110 Mrs Whiting on *British Queen*: *NY Passenger Lists*.
111 Whiting episode on British Queen: *Letters of Application during the Administration of Abraham Lincoln and Andrew Johnson 1861–1869*, Turley to Varree October 25, 1862, Varree to Seward November 4, 1862.
111 Whiting offers resignation: *Despatches*, Roll 11, October 27, 1862.
112 British officials 25 percent: Rawson, *Report on the Bahamas*, 67.
112 Doty background: A. O. Bunnell, *Dansville 1789–1902* (Dansville, NY: Instructor Publishing, 1902), 267.
112 Hawley background: Elias S. Hawley, *The Hawley Record* (Buffalo: E. H. Hutchinson and Company, 1890), 486–488.
112 Whiting told an American tourist: Riddle, *Recollections*, 240.
112 Whiting thanks unknown gentleman: *BH*, January 9, 1863.
113 Letters to Seward about salary: *Papers Relating to Foreign Affairs, 1863, Part II* (Washington: GPO, 1864), 1354.
114 Bayley on Whiting: Edwards, "American Consular Service," 236.
114 Hawley on blockade running profits: *ORN*, Vol. 9, 80.
114 Admiral Milne visits Bayley: *Consular and Other Missions, LOC*, Image 137, December 12, 1862.
114 "The town seems plentifully supplied . . .": *CCGB*, Vol. 6, 335.
114 Maffitt recruits sailors: *New York Sun*, February 21, 1863.
114 *Britannia*, *Georgiana*, and *Gertrude*: *ORN*, Vol. 13, 754.
114 *Emma Tuttle*: *ORN*, Vol. 8, 470; *Despatches*, Roll 11, December 29, 1862; *NY Daily Tribune* January 26, 1863.
115 *Harkaway*: *Consular and Other Missions, LOC*, Image 141, February 6, 1863; Milledge Bonham, *British Consuls in the Confederacy* (New York: Columbia University, 1911), 109–111.
115 Rise in salt prices: Hamilton Cochran, *Blockade Runners of the Confederacy* (Indianapolis: Bobbs-Merrill, 1958), 47.
115 Salt from Liverpool: Ella Lonn, *Salt as a Factor in the Confederacy* (New York: Walter Neale, 1933), 15.
115 Three photograph studios: Wilson, *Sketches of Nassau*, 48.
115 Photographers selling photos: Sprunt, *Chronicles of the Cape Fear*, 418.
115 "Money was almost as plentiful as dirt": E. Burton Milby, *The Siege of Charleston* (Columbia: University of South Carolina Press, 1982), 246.

116	"A stirring, colorful confusion of sailors, traders, agents and swindlers": Justus Schiebert, *Seven Months in the Rebel States during the North American War, 1863* (Tuscaloosa: Confederate Publishing Company, 1958), 22.
116	Nassau Races: *BH*, January 10, 1863, February 14, 1863.
116	Roads too narrow: *BH*, March 4, 1863.
116	"Miserable hovels": *BH*, May 28, 1864.
116	Boarding house rules: *BH*, March 25, 1863.
116	Spanish ads: *BH*, November 19, 1862
116	Royal Victoria sanitation committee: *BH*, April 8, 1863.
116	Police bribed with drinks to look other way: Wilson, *Sketches of Nassau*, 24.
116	Sailors drowning: For example *BH* December 24, 1862.
117	"Many a Dinah...": Bacot, *The Bahamas*, 51.
117	Dillet on lack of police: *NG*, April 1, 1863.
117	Crazy Mary: *BH*, August 6, 1862; December 6, 1862.
117	Whiting not at consulate for inventory: *Despatches*, Roll 11, March 13, 1863.
118	Anderson compares Whiting and Heyliger: *Treaty of Washington*, 268.
119	Bayley speech: *NG*, March 4, 1863.
120	House asks for higher tariffs: *NG*, March 7, 1863.
120	Duke of Newcastle to Bayley: *The Index*, April 7, 1864.
120	Steamers running like smoke: *Despatches*, Roll 11, George Gorham to N. H. Hall, March 17, 1863.
120	SH trouble communicating with navy: Despatches, Roll 11, March 13, 1863.
120	*New York Times* on Hawley: *NYT*, March 22, 1863.
121	Hawley at Bayley ball: *NG*, March 11, 1863.
121	Epes Sargent proposal: *Despatches*, Roll 11, March 20, 1863.
122	*Wild Pigeon* ownership: *American Vessels. Return of the Number and Tonnage of American (United States) Vessels Sold and Transferred to British Subjects in the Year 1863, with the Name of the Parties (Sellers and Purchasers)* (London: House of Commons, 1864); *The Commercial & Financial Chronicle*, May 30, 1868, 695.
122	Blockade runners caught spring 1863: *ORN*, Vol. 2, 120–121, 129, 133–134, 162–165, 175, 183, 199.
122	Heyliger on neutrality issues: *Consular and Other Missions, LOC*, Image 147, April 7, 1863.
122	No arrivals in a fortnight: *Consular and Other Missions, LOC*, Image 155, May 6, 1863.
123	Erlanger loan: For a detailed description of the loan, see Richard Todd, *Confederate Finance* (Athens: University of Georgia Press, 1954); Charles Davis, *Colin J. McRae: Confederate Financial Agent* (Tuscaloosa: Confederate Publishing, 1961).
123	Crenshaw on Huse and S. Isaac Campbell: *ORA* Ser. 4 Vol. 2, 543–547.
123	Huse on Ferguson and Crenshaw: *ORA*, Ser. 4 Vol. 2, 893.
123	Heyliger commission as depositary: *CCGB* Supplementary, 231.
124	Lewis Heyliger appoints Benjamin as attorney: *Consular and Other Missions, LOC*, Image 162, May 6, 1863. In this document and in his will, Heyliger writes his name as Lewis, though some sources refer to him as Louis.
124	Lewis Heyliger letter on *Margaret and Jessie*: *NG*, June 3, 1863.
125	148 ships captured or destroyed: Frederick Milnes Edge, *The Destruction of the American Carrying Trade, a Letter to Earl Russell* (London: William Ridgway, 1864), 13.
125	Seth Hawley leave of absence: *Despatches*, Roll 11, Hawley to Frederick Seward, April 2, 1863; May 5, 1863.

126 W. Thompson background: *Hunt's Merchant's Magazine and Commercial Review* 45 (1861), 517; *The United States Insurance Gazette and Magazine of Useful Knowledge* 14 (1862), 12; Edwards, "American Consular Service," 311.
126 Hawley describes Thompson: *Despatches*, Roll 11, May 7, 1863.
126 Bayley approves Thompson as vice-consul: *NG*, June 6, 1863.
126 Alternate routes: *ORN*, Vol. 2, 193.

Chapter 10: Living for the Hour

127 Trenholm write to Bayley: Mountague Bernard, *A Historical Account of the Neutrality of Great Britain during the American Civil War* (London: Longmans, Green, Reader and Dyer, 1870), 290.
127 For a good overview of the captains who ran the blockade, see Marcus Price, "Masters and Pilots Who Tested the Blockade of the Confederate Ports, 1861–1865," *American Neptune* 21, no. 2, (1961), 81–106.
127 There are many accounts of the dangers of blockade running trips, but one particularly entertaining one was written by James Ferguson's wife Emma Ferguson, "Running the Blockade: A Confederate Reminiscence," *Lippincott's Monthly Magazine* 52, (1893), 493–502.
127 Four British officers: *NYT*, January 8, 1893.
128 Hewett and *Condor*: *Papers Relating to Foreign Affairs*, 1862, part II, 719.
128 Hobart-Hampden anecdotes: Augustus C. Hobart-Hampden *Never Caught* (London: John Camden Hotten, 1867); "Hobart Pascha: A Modern Sea Rover," *New York Tribune*, December 29, 1886.
129 Murray-Aynsley description: Taylor, *Running the Blockade*, 92.
129 Nassau parties: Taylor, *Running the Blockade*, 87.
129 Second hand cattle boat: Taylor, *Running the Blockade*, 17.
129 Tom Taylor to New York: *NY Passenger Lists*.
130 *Banshee* causes sensation, financial success: Taylor, *Running the Blockade*. 40, 80.
130 "Coolness and daring": Taylor, *Running the Blockade*, 59.
130 Arthur Doering: Taylor, *Running the Blockade*, 89.
130 Santa Claus of the War: Taylor, *Running the Blockade*, 59.
130 Taylor and Heyliger: Taylor, *Running the Blockade*, 133.
130 In quarantine fifty days: Taylor, *Running the Blockade*, 97.
131 Enterprise of British merchants: Dean B. Mahin, *This Blessed Place of Freedom: Europeans in Civil War America* (Washington: Brassey's, Inc, 2002), 160.
131 Vizetelly description: G. Moxley Sorrel, *Recollections of a Confederate Staff Officer*. (New York and Washington: Neale Publishing Co., 1905), 123.
131 Vizetelly sketches through Nassau: *Theodore D. Wagner papers, 1853–1863, SCHS*, July 7, 1863.
131 Vizetelly and the frock coat: Taylor, *Running the Blockade*, 88.
131 Wigg in New Orleans: *Gardner's New Orleans Directory for 1861*, 455.
131 Wigg a friend of Heyliger: *Consular and Other Missions*, LOC, Image 128, December 12, 1862.
132 Lewis Grant Watson: Taylor, *Running Blockade*, 89.

Notes

132 Coffee prices: Andrea Mehrlander, *The Germans of Charleston, Richmond and New Orleans during the Civil War Period, 1850–1870: A Study and Research Compendium* (Berlin, New York: De Gruyter, 2011), 224.

132 Cotton prices: Neely, *Great Bahamas Hurricane*, 124.

132 For attitudes toward speculators, see for example the *Savannah Republican*, July 24, 1863, or attitudes toward Rhett Butler in Margaret Mitchell, *Gone with the Wind* (New York: Macmillan, 1936).

132 Stockholders of the Importing and Exporting Company of South Carolina.: Price, "Blockade Running as a Business," 36.

132 Bee sets reasonable prices: Price, "Blockade Running as a Business," 40.

132 Steamship Pet stock: Marcus Price, "Blockade Running as a Business" 34.

132 J. A. Enslow: *NG* April 8, 1863.

132 McLeod and Bell: *NG*, May 6, 1863.

132 Zachrisson: Vandiver, *Confederate Blockade Running*, 43; *US City Directories, 1822–1995* by ancestry.com for New York years 1840, 1848, 1860.

132 George Chambers: *The Liverpool Commercial List 1866* (London: Seyd and Co., 1866), 41.

133 Bowman, Tettley and Company: *ORA*, Ser. 4, Vol. 3, 157.

133 Sterrett in Nassau, summer 1863: Forrest, *Odyssey in Gray*, 21.

133 Lewis Heyliger friends in Nassau: *ORN* Ser. 2, Vol. 3, 805.

133 Import and export statistics: Rawson, *Report on the Bahamas*, 49–53.

133 Turpentine banned: *Despatches*, Roll 11, November 30, 1863.

134 Waller background: ORA Ser 4. Vol. 2, 658; *CCGB*, Vol. 6, 130.

134 Waller promoted: *Confederate Service Records*.

134 Waller merchants: *CCGB* Supplementary, 208–209.

134 Whitley death: Bahama death records, fourth quarter 1862, from Ann Carmel.

134 Dumaresq arrives: *NG*, July 22, 1863.

134 *Corsica*: *NG*, May 13, 1863; May 27, 1863; June 10, 1863; February 10, 1865.

134 Perpall selling charts: *NG*, May 20, 1863.

134 Three-quarters clearing for Saint John: Rawson, *Report on the Bahamas*, 54.

135 Rahming cotton seeds: *NG*, June 20, 1863.

135 Dry dock: *NG* May 16, 1863; Elmer Corthell, *The Atlantic & Pacific Ship-railway Across the Isthmus of Tehauntepec, in Mexico, Considered Commercially, Politically & Constructively* (New York: Bowne and Company, 1886), 54.

135 Dry dock adds steam: *NG*, October 17, 1863.

135 Bay Street improvements, land prices increase: Gail Saunders, "The Blockade Running Era in The Bahamas: Blessing or Curse?" *Journal of the Bahamas Historical Society* 10 (1998), 14–18; *NG Centenary Issue* November 23, 1944.

135 Theatre renovated: *NG*, October 17, 1863.

135 New RV sewer: *NG*, October 10, 1863.

136 New warehouses: *NG*, November 7, 1863.

136 Boy injured: *NG*, October 14, 1863.

136 CSA inflation: Colin Carlin, *Captain James Carlin, Anglo-American Blockade Runner* (Columbia: University of South Carolina Press, 2017), 179.

136 Inflation: Currency tables, *William C. Bee Records*, SCHS.

136 John S. George real estate: Keith Tinker, *The Bahamas in American History.* (Bloomington, IN: Xlibris, 2011), Chapter 4.

136	July Grant's Town incident:	Whittington Johnson, Post-Emancipation Race Relations, 133; *NYT* August 29, 1863; Bayley to Newcastle, September 15, 1863, *CO Files*.
136	Few Union ships:	*ORN*, Vol. 2, 432.
136	Traffic to Bermuda:	Vandiver, *Confederate Blockade Running*, 41; *Despatches*, Roll 11, August 10, 1863.
137	Thomas Power ownership:	*Counter Case*, 472–473.
137	Letter of Marques transferred to Parker:	Greg Marquis, *In Armageddon's Shadow: The Civil War and Canada's Maritime Provinces* (Montreal: McGill-Queen's University Press, 2000), 136.
137	Parker to Long Cay:	*Boston Traveller*, March 6, 1863.
137	John Priestly:	Marquis, *In Armageddon's Shadow*, 136.
137	Parker as clerk for Adderley:	*Treaty of Washington*, 474.
137	Parker and John Howell:	*Treaty of Washington*, 466.
138	"Unmitigated scoundrel":	*ORA*, Ser. 2, Vol. 2, 712.
138	Parker shows men Letter of Marque:	Edward, N. Valladigham, "Piracy or Privateering?" *Pearson's Magazine* 10, no. 1, 1903, 83.
138	Original John Parker had died:	Robin. Winks, *The Civil War Years: Canada and the United States* (Baltimore: The Johns Hopkins Press, 1998), 245.
139	Braine takes over *Roanoke*:	*ORN*, Vol.3, 239.
139	Braine's men on the *Owl*:	*New York Herald*, April 29, 1888.
139	Braine and *St. Mary's*:	*Despatches*, Roll 12, April 18, 1865; *CCGB*, General Appendix, 350.
139	Braine's later life:	*Atlanta Constitution* November 10, 1904; November 13, 1904; December 2, 1906; December 9, 1906; *NYT*, September 19, 1866.
139	Christmas fireworks:	*NG*, December 26, 1863.
140	Lewis Heyliger departments served:	*Trenholm Records*, July 8, 1867.
140	Lewis Heyliger must include lead and saltpeter:	*ORA*, Ser. 1, Vol. 28, Part 2, 243. Luxury items on blockade runners: For example, see the hundreds of items in the newspaper ads posted in the online discussion at Civil War Talk: https://civilwartalk.com/threads/notable-blockade-runner-captains.78616/page-2, accessed July 31, 2018.
140	Lead bars:	Sample in Mariner's Museum, Newport News.
140	Lead imports:	Todd, *Confederate Finance*, 193.
140	Lewis Heyliger ships books to Judah Benjamin:	*Consular and Other Missions*, LOC, Image 199, October 18, 1863.
140	Lewis Heyliger passports:	*ORA*, Ser. 1, Vol. 28, Part 2, 274.

Chapter 11: Trouble in New York

141	Wolf files for damages:	*NG*, December 26, 1863.
141	Hoffnung and Benjamin:	*NYT*, January 3, 1864.
141	Aaron Wolf description:	Riddle, *Reflections*, 240.
142	Wolf has "facilities":	*Reports of Committees of the House of Representatives Made during the First Session Thirty-Eight Congress, Report from the Committee on Public Expenditures on the New York Custom House* (Washington: GPO, 1864), hereinafter *NYCH*, 71.
142	Ease of purchasing in New York:	Lawrence Karson, *American Smuggling as White Collar Crime* (New York: Routledge, 2014), 68.

Notes

142 Purser as courier: *NYT*, January 3, 1864.
142 Adderley and Saunders to New York: *NY Passenger Lists* 1861, 1862, 1863, Coal stokers hiding suspicious characters: Schiebert, *Seven Months*, 21.
142 Shoddy millionaires: *NYT* May 9, 2011has a good overview.
142 Confederate meat inspector in New York: Richard Drysdale, "Blockade-running from Nassau," *History Today* 27, no. 5 (1977), 335.
143 Farragut on Mobile: Robert Means Thompson and Richard Wainwright, ed., *Confidential Correspondence of Gustavus Vasa Fox Assistant Secretary of the Navy, 1861–1865* (New York: The Naval History Press, 1918), 349.
143 Aquia Creek: Ludwell Johnson, "Commerce Between Northeastern Ports and the Confederacy, 1861–1865," *Journal of American History* 54, No. 1 (1967), 35.
143 Risley background: J. H. Easterby, ed., *The South Carolina Rice Plantation as Revealed in the Papers of Robert F. W. Allston* (Columbia: University of South Carolina Press, 1945), 118.
143 Miles as slave owner: John Thomas Scharf, *History of Baltimore City and County, from the Earliest Period to the Present Day* (Philadelphia: L. H. Everts, 1881), 149.
143 Miles and Confederates: Henry Bascom Smith, *Between the Lines: Secret Service Stories Told Fifty Years after* (New York: Booz Brothers, 1911), 152.
143 Miles boats burned: Hunnicutt, *The Conspiracy Unveiled* (Philadelphia: J. B. Lippincott, 1863), 317.
143 Risley sells to Saunders and Son: Johnson, "Commerce between Northeastern Ports," 37–38.
143 New York and Matamoras: *NYCH*, 7.
144 Ships painted at dry dock: *Despatches*, Roll 11, August 10, 1863.
144 Telegraph wire in hay: *NYCH*, 70.
144 *Indus* and torpedo: *NYCH*, 126.
145 Intentional errors: *NYCH*, 261–262.
145 Ship to outer islands: *NYCH*, 254.
145 Ships in distress: *Despatches*, Roll 12, October 31, 1864.
145 For an overview of Confederate mail, see "Civil War—Blockade of the Southern Coast," at http://www.rfrajola.com/NAB/NABpart3.pdf
145 Case of the *Adela*: *ORN*, Vol. 17, 280–286.
146 Wolfs and Darling: *NYT*, January 3, 1864.
146 Hoffnung in Halifax: *NYCH*, 165.
146 Whole office was rotten: *NYCH*, 110.
146 Removing free samples: *NYCH*, 83.
146 Paying clerks for fifteen years: *NYCH*, 247.
146 Blockade running good business: Bruce Hetherington and Peter Kower, "A Reexamination of Lebergott's Paradox about Blockade Running during the American Civil War," *Journal of Economic History* 69, no. 2, (2009), 528–532.
146 Stanton set up: Ann. D. Gordon, ed., *The Selected Papers of Elizabeth Cady Stanton and Susan B. Anthony. Vol. 1* (New Brunswick, NJ: Rutgers University Press, 1997), 529.
147 James Haggerty: *NYCH*, 52.
147 Myers wants to make big score, drinking champagne: *NYCH*, 176.
147 Eneas and *Jose*: *NYCH*, 231.
148 Eneas cannot estimate profits: *NYCH*, 129.
148 Benjamin jumps bail: Andrew W. Cohen, *Contraband* (New York: Norton and Company, 2015), 86.

212 Notes

148 Rahming and Whiting: *NYCH*, 268.
148 Alex. Rahming and Brothers: *Albany Argus*, Jan 16, 1864.
148 Fort Lafayette investigation: Samuel Negus, "A Notorious Nest of Offence: Neutrals, Belligerents, and Union Jails in Civil War Blockade Running," *Civil War History* 56, no. 4 (2010), 372.
149 Rahming and Eneas damages: *Treaty of Washington*, Vol. 6, 74.
149 Ezra Cuyler testimony: *NYCH*, 254.
149 Wolf brags about 10 locomotives: *NYCH*, 257.
150 *Will of the Wisp* on dry dock: *NG*, February 20, 1864.
150 *Nonesuch*: *NG*, January 1, 1864.
150 Howell sells Royal Victoria: *NG*, May 25, 1864.
150 Howell cruise: *NG*, June 15, 1864.
150 Newspapers apologize for lack of news: *NG*, April 30, 1864.
150 Equestrian show: *NG*, March 12, 1864.
150 *Galena* report: *ORN*, Vol. 21, 210–216.
150 Stevedores and Draymen: Gail Saunders, "The Blockade Running Era in the Bahamas: Blessing or Curse?" 14–18.
151 Burglaries, policeman stabbed: *NG*, January 9, 1864; January 23, 1864; January 30, 1864.
151 "Run sailors": P. D. Haywood, *The Cruise of the Alabama* (Boston and New York: Houghton, Mifflin and Co., 1886), 34.
151 "There is scarcely a night...": *NG*, December 24, 1864.
151 Concerts moved: *NG*, January 23, 1864.
151 Jack cannot exist without amusement: *NG*, July 2, 1864.
151 Royal Victoria description: *NG*, April 6, 1864.
151 Thompson at wit's end: *Despatches*, Roll 12, January 29, 1864, April 30, 1864.
151 Thompson cancelling certificates: *NYCH*, 57.
152 Hinckley and Kirkpatrick: *Despatches*, Roll 12, May 5, 1864; May 28, 1864; Edwards "American Consular Service," 374–377.
152 Waller to Lawton: *CCGB*, Vol. 6, 153.
152 McRae to Waller: *CCGB*, Vol. 6, 156–158.
152 Lawton to Waller: *ORA*, Ser. 4, Vol. 3, 288.
152 Lawton to Sharp: *ORA*, Ser. 4, Vol. 3, 210–211.
152 Sharp's background: *Confederate Amnesty Papers*, NA.
153 Waller only gives Sharp £500: *ORA*, Ser. 4, Vol. 3, 351.
153 Sharp on Heyliger: *Confederate Citizens Papers* for Sharp, June 8, 1864.
153 Adderley on *Fannie*, Bayley on *Corsica*: *NG*, June 8, 1864.

Chapter 12: "It is rather sickly here"

157 Charles Jackson on Thompson: *Despatches*, Roll 12, July 25, 1864; July 29, 1864.
157 Thompson's mind diseased: *Despatches*, Roll 12, September 23, 1864.
158 Kirkpatrick requires approval of passengers: *NG*, September 7, 1864.
158 "It is rather sickly here": *Consular and Other Missions*, LOC, Image 227, July 23, 1864.
158 "Scarcely anyone here has escaped attack": *Consular and Other Missions*, LOC, Image 229, August 20, 1864.
158 Taylor on Nassau funerals: Taylor, *Running the Blockade*, 96.

Notes

159   141 residents: Rawson, *Report on the Bahamas*, 20.
159   Howell letter to Kirkpatrick: *Despatches*, Roll 12, August 10, 1864.
159   Anna Kirkpatrick dies August 4, 1864: *NYT*, August 29, 1864.
159   Diverting to Bermuda: *Despatches*, Roll 12, July 25, 1864.
159   Gorgas sends lead to Bermuda: Frank E. Vandiver, *Ploughshares into Swords: Josiah Gorgas and Confederate Ordnance* (Austin: University of Texas Press, 1952), 177.
159   Cotton to Liverpool: *The Index*, October 13, 1864.
159   Norman Walker's travels: Georgianna Walker. *The Private Journal of Georgiana Gholson Walker: 1862–1865, with Selections from the Post-War Years, 1865–1876* (Tuscaloosa: Confederate Publishing, 1963).
159   Halifax temporarily replaces Nassau and Bermuda: *CCGB* Supplementary, 168; *NYT*, September 13, 1864.
160   Taylor on yellow fever plot: Taylor, *Running the Blockade*, 129–130.
160   Blackburn's yellow fever scheme: "The Yellow Fever Plot," *Medical and Surgical Reporter* 12, no. 35 (1865), 565–567; Nancy Baird, *Luke Pryor Blackburn: Physician, Governor, Reformer* (Lexington: University Press of Kentucky, 2009).
160   Alexander Keith: Ann Larabee, *The Dynamite Fiend: The Chilling Tale of a Confederate Spy, Con Artist, and Mass Murderer* (New York: Palgrave Macmillan, 2005); John Wilkinson, *The Narrative of a Blockade Runner* (New York: Sheldon and Company, 1877), 177–180.
160   Patrick Martin in business with Clements and Wier: *Papers Relating to Foreign Affairs, 1873*, Part II, Vol. 3 (Washington: GPO, 1874) 94.
161   Kirkpatrick's spies: *Despatches*, Roll 12, January 6, 1865; March 2, 1865; June 21, 1865; October 21, 1865; Edwards, "The American Consular Service," 388–392; *Thurlow Weed Papers*, University of Rochester, Kirkpatrick to Weed, December 15, 1865.
161   Lafitte richer than the governor: Taylor, *Running the Blockade*, 26.
161   Spies as stewards: Sprunt, *Derelicts*, 276.
161   Kirkpatrick on the class of his allies: *Despatches*, Roll 12, August 17, 1864.
162   Cotton statistics: Edwards, "The American Consular Service," 339.
162   Samuel Boyd: William Scarborough, *Masters of the Big House: Elite Slaveholders of the Mid-Nineteenth-Century South* (Baton Rouge: Louisiana State University Press, 2006), 213–216.
162   Ladies of Nassau: Wilson, *Sketches of Nassau*, 15.
163   Sawyer and Menendez schooner burns: *NG* June 25, 1864.
163   Harris warehouse: *NG*, October 29, 1864.
163   John S. George warehouse, *Nassau Guardian* on warehouses: *NG* August 27, 1864.
163   Darling, the Hermitage: Drysdale, *In Sunny Lands*, 15.
163   Adderley residence: Lightbourn, *Reminiscing II*,
164   Roth's Children: Wilkinson, *Narrative*, 141–142.
164   Stolen good depot: *NG*, September 17, 1864.
164   Men stealing cotton: *NG*, October 5, 1864.
164   Steamers continuing to run in and out of Charleston fall 1864: Stephen Wise, "Blockade Running 1861–1865," *South Carolina Encyclopedia*. http://www.scencyclopedia.org/sce/entries/blockade-running/ accessed August 2, 2018.
165   Match Madick: *ORN*, Vol. 10, 547–550.
165   Shoe machinery possibly on Imogene: Carlin, *Captain James Carlin*, 173.
165   Kirkpatrick says most ships turned back: *Despatches*, Roll 12, December 18, 1864.

165 81,000,000 pounds of meat: *ORA*, Ser. 4, Vol. 3, 784.
165 2,500,000 pounds: Scharf, *History of the Confederate Navy*, 489.
165 Meat disdained: J. C. Goolsby, "Crenshaw's Battery, Pegram's Battalion," *Southern Historical Society Papers* 28, (1900), 362.
165 Prioleau's efforts on behalf of prisoners: Trenholm Records, Reel 3.
166 Maffitt leaves *Florida*: Emma Maffitt, *Life and Services*, 327.
166 *Laurel*: *ORN*, Ser. 2, Vol. 2, 732–740, 779, 782.
167 Kirkpatrick looks for contents of *Mary*: *Despatches*, Reel 12, November 30, 1864.
167 *Mary* info to Kirkpatrick: *Despatches*, Roll 13, Kirkpatrick to Fish, November 20, 1869; *Despatches*, June 3, 1865.
167 Rawson arrives on December 9: *NG*, December 10, 1864.
167 Heyliger on seizure of the *Mary*: *Consular and Other Missions*, LOC, Image 240, December 19, 1864.
167 Confederate States: *Papers Relating to Foreign Affairs* (1865) Part 1, 249.
167 Prioleau says to sell ships: *Trenholm Records*, Prioleau to Lafitte, December 16, 1864.

Chapter 13: "Blockade-running from this port has ceased"

169 Tom Taylor and the meat delivery: Taylor, *Running the Blockade*, 137–140.
169 Three and half million in cotton: Scharf, *History of the Confederate Navy*, 489.
169 Eight ships leave Nassau: Sprunt, *Chronicles of the Cape Fear*, 475.
169 Rate of captures: Owsley, Frank Lawrence Owsley, *King Cotton Diplomacy* (Chicago: University of Chicago Press, 1931), 285.
170 Tatum and Company: *NG*, January 14, 1865.
170 James Bailie: *NG*, February 16, 1865; Letter from Bailie to Joe Brown, December 2, 1864, courtesy of Trish Kaufmann.
170 *Agnes E. Fry*: *ORA*, Ser. 1, Vol. 46, Part 3, 1011.
170 $4000 for pilots: J. D. Aiken letterpress copybook and letters, 1864–1865, SCHS, Heyliger to J. D. Aiken, January 30, 1865.
170 Adderley charges Importing and Exporting Company: Carlin, *Captain James Carlin*, 172.
170 *Syren* February 1865: J. D. Aiken letterpress copybook and letters, Heyliger to J. D. Aiken, February 12, 1865.
171 "Tongues of Babel": Wilson, *Sketches of Nassau*, 13.
171 *Corsica* booked next 3 trips: *NYT*, March 16, 1865.
171 Prisoners of war stowaways: *Despatches*, Roll 12, January 19, 1865.
171 Thompson leaves for St. Louis: Edwards, "American Consular Service," 384. Royal Victoria dinner: *NG*, January 14, 1865.
172 Rawson's social life and BI speech: *NG*, February 9, 1865; February 11, 1865.
172 Rawson's motto: *Governor Rawson Report on the Bahamas Hurricane of October 1866* (Nassau: 1868) in Neely, *Great Bahamas Hurricane*, 153.
172 Preston: *Despatches*, Roll 12, February 24, 1865; Peter J. Sehlinger, *Kentucky's Last Cavalier: General William Preston, 1816–1887* (Lexington: University Press of Kentucky, 2004), 188.
172 *San Jacinto* and *Honduras*: *Papers Relating to Foreign Affairs* (1865), Part 1, 185; *Despatches*, Roll 12, February 5, 1865.

172	*Chameleon* in Nassau: *Papers Relating to Foreign Affairs* (1865), Part 1, 186; Wilkinson, *Narrative*, 233.
173	Maffitt commands *Owl*: Emma Maffitt, *Life and Services*, 330, 335, 339.
173	Nine shots fired at *Owl*: *ORN*, Vol. 3, 710–11.
173	780 bales of cotton: Emma Maffitt, *Life and Services*, 346.
173	Mallory writes Maffitt: Emma Maffitt, *Life and Services*, 345.
173	Maffitt buys luxury items: *Maffitt Papers*, University of North Carolina, December 30, 1864.
173	Condition of the *Owl*: Emma Maffitt, *Life and Services*, 351.
174	Connolly on Rawson speech: Connolly, *Irishman in Dixie*, 16.
174	Prioleau on Connolly: *Trenholm Records*, Prioleau to Lafitte, December 12, 1864.
174	*Owl* in Galveston: Forrest, *Odyssey in Gray*, 302; *Galveston Daily News*, April 26, 1865; Maffitt Papers, invoice for duties paid May 5, 1865.
174	*Imogene* in Galveston: Carlin, *Captain James Carlin*, 173.
175	*Ajax*: Hoole, *Four Years*, 108–116; *Despatches*, March 13, 1865; April 8, 1865.
176	*Colonel Lamb*: R. Thomas Campbell, ed. *Voices of the Confederate Navy: Articles, Letters, Reports, and Reminiscences* (Jefferson, NC: McFarland, 2007), 295; Joseph McKenna, *British Ships in the Confederate Navy* (Jefferson, NC: McFarland, 2009), 241.
176	*Booubolina* explodes: *Illustrated London News*, December 14, 1867.
176	Locke to Havana: *Despatches*, Roll 12, June 3, 1865.
176	Locke dies in ship wreck: *Washington Post*, July 16, 1890.
176	Locke in Adderley office: *Treaty of Washington*, Vol. 4, 219.
176	John Braine: *CCGB*, General Appendix, 350.
178	G. T. Watson: *NG*, February 16, 1865; February 25, 1865.
178	Walker in Nassau: Georgianna Walker, *Private Journal*, 120.
178	Prioleau tells Lafitte to work until Charleston unavailable: *Trenholm Records*, February 10, 1865.
178	*Imogene*: Rawson, *Report on the Bahamas*, 53.
178	A. J. Adderley back in Nassau: *NG*, March 15, 1865.
178	C. J. Lightbourne: *NG*, February 4, 1865.
179	Sarah Flagg: *Despatches*, March 1, 1865; March 2, 1865; June 21, 1865; July 17, 1865; August 19, 1865.
180	Wilkinson describes Nassau: Wilkinson, *Narrative*, 246–247.
180	Legislature message: *NG*, February 4, 1865.
180	Rawson speech: *NG*, May 3, 1865.
180	"Others acquired a taste . . .": George Lester, "Nassau and the Blockade Runners," *Confederate Veteran* 22, no. 12, (1914), 572.
180	Lafitte's books and Adderley auctions: *NG*, April 29, 1865.
181	*Stonewall*: *Despatches*, Roll 12, May 10, 1865; *NG*, June 3, 1865.
181	Sidney Root in Nassau: Sidney Root, *Memorandum of My Life*, Atlanta Historical Center (1893); Sidney Root, *Exotic Leaves* (London: William Freeman, 1865)
182	Last week of May departures: *NG*, June 3, 1865.
182	Welsman to Prioleau: *Trenholm Records*, Reel 1, May 31, 1865.
182	Kirkpatrick on Adderleys: *Despatches*, Roll 12, July 17, 1865.
182	Kirkpatricks says Adderley in England: *Despatches*, Roll 12, July 17, 1865.
182	Royal Victoria up for auction: *NG*, July 1, 1865.

Chapter 14: Like a Town Sacked and Burned by the Enemy

183 Our trade has collapsed: Neely, *Great Bahamas Hurricane*, 178.
183 Hurricane losses: Neely, *Great Bahamas Hurricane*, Chapter 9.
184 American consulate minor damage: *Despatches*, Roll 12, October 15, 1866.
184 Sacked and burned: Neely, *Great Bahamas Hurricane*, 129.
184 *Salvador* seized: "The Queen v. James Carlin," *Law Journal Reports* 39 (1870), 33–37.
184 Whiting's paper: *The Historical Magazine, and Notes and Queries Concerning the Antiquities, History, and Biography of America* 8, no. 5 (1864), 190.
186 Hawley funeral: *NYT*, November 14, 1884.
187 Howell death: *New York Herald*, January 6, 1873.
187 Sargent death: Sargent, *Epes Sargent of Gloucester and his Descendants*, 291.
187 Darling death: Obituary from Ann Morley Carmel.
188 Nesbitt later life: 1870 US Federal Census 1870, John M. Trainor, "Asendency of Charles Nesbitt," *Journal of Bahamas Historical Society* 3 (1981), 8.
188 Rahming later life and death: *Brooklyn Daily Eagle*, September 30, 1895; *NYT*, April 19, 1879; *New York Evening Express*, November 12, 1867; personal communication, Ann Morley Carmel.
188 Eneas later years: *New York Sun*, March 3, 1877; *New York Herald*, July 28, 1880; *New York Sun* December 1, 1881, and March 3, 1877; *Brooklyn Daily Eagle*, March 4, 1877.
188 Maffitt later years: Emma Maffitt, *Life and Services*, Chapters 25–30.
188 Passailaigue still settling with Importing and Exporting Company: *William C. Bee Records*, SCHS, April 28, 1866. Kirkpatrick and Adderley property: *Records Concerning Confederate Property in Nassau*, NA.
188 Kirkpatrick recommends Passailaigue: *The Papers of Ulysses S. Grant*, Mississippi State University, Thomas Kirkpatrick to Hamilton Fish, September 3, 1869; *Despatches*, Roll 13, Kirkpatrick to Fish November 20, 1869.
190 Trenholm firm makes $20 million: Wise, *South Carolina Encyclopedia*.
190 Waller lawsuits: *Trenholm Papers*, Reel 2.
191 Bulloch on Heyliger: Bulloch, *Secret Service*, Vol. 2, 233.
191 Heyliger later years: England and Wales National Probate Calendar and Free BMD Death Index, 1837–1915; *Confederate Applications for Presidential Pardons*, NA; *New Orleans Times-Picayune*, September 28, 1866; *Will of Lewis Heyliger*, Probate Service UK.
191 Leamington popular with ex-Confederates: David Stevens, *Dancing with the Philistines: The Life and Times of Colonel Caleb Huse* (Ann Arbor: Edwards Brothers Malloy, 2015), 646–649.
192 Mrs. Stanard: Brian Burns, *Curiosities of the Confederate Capital: Untold Richmond Stories of the Spectacular, Tragic and Bizarre* (Mount Pleasant, SC: Arcadia Publishing, 2013), Chapter 15; Elizabeth Fries Ellet, *The Queens of American Society* (New York: Charles Scribner and Company, 1867), 420–421; C. Vann Woodward, ed., *Mary Chestnut's Civil War* (New Haven: Yale University Press, 1981) has many references to Martha Stanard; Thomas Cooper De Leon, *Belles, Beaux and Brains of the 60's* (New York: G. W. Dillingham, 1909), 198–200; Georgiana Walker, *Private Journal*, 76, 86; James Morris Morgan, "The Lost Cause", *Atlantic Monthly* 119, (1917), 501–502.
192 Emile Le Mesnil: *Official Register of LSU New Orleans Grammar School 1859* (New Orleans: Louisiana State University, 1859), 6.

193	Tom Taylor on Lafitte: Taylor, *Running the Blockade*, 26.
193	Lafitte back to Charleston: *Charleston Daily News*, July 22, 1866; *NY Passenger Lists*.
193	Lafitte supports church: *The Catholic Church in the United States of America: Undertaken to Celebrate the Golden Jubilee of His Holiness, Pope Pius X* (New York: Catholic editing Company, 1914), 133.
193	Lafitte letters: Courtesy Robert Lafitte Howells.
193	Lafitte death: *New Orleans Times-Picayune*, May 22, 1887.
193	Bayley on petty commerce: C. J, Bayley Report on the Bahamas for the Years 1860–1864, Bahamas Archives, 10.
194	Weech to England: *NG* ad on January 27, 1865; Robert Weech's daughter (1866) and son (1873) born in London, courtesy Ann Morley Carmel.
194	Adderley and Harris later years: John Gorman, "The Adderley Family in the New World," *Journal of the Bahamas Historical Society* 22 (2000), 31–41.

Sources

Primary Sources

Manuscripts

Atlanta Historical Center

Sidney Root, Memorandum of My Life, 1893

Bahamas Archives

C. J, Bayley Report on the Bahamas for the Years 1860–1864
Colonial Office Files

David M. Rubinstein Rare Book and Manuscript Library, Duke University

Francis Warrington Dawson family papers, 1386–1963

Library of Congress

Confederate States of America Records

Chronicling America
Consular and Other Missions
Diary of Judah P. Benjamin 1861–1864
Extracts from Letterbooks, 1861–1865
Navy Department, 1861–1865, Log of Vessels in Bermuda and Nassau
Robert Wilson Shufeldt Papers, 1836–1910

Merseyside Maritime Museum, Liverpool

The Business Records of Fraser, Trenholm and Company of Liverpool and Charleston, South Carolina 1860–1877

220   Sources

Mississippi State University Libraries

The Papers of Ulysses S. Grant

National Archives

1860 US Federal Census Slave Schedule
Compiled Records Showing Service of Military Units in Confederate Organizations
    Confederate Applications for Presidential Pardons
Confederate Papers Relating to Citizens or Business Firms
Correspondence with Consuls Concerning Blockade Runners
Despatches from US Consular Offices 1789–1906 Rolls 10,11,12, 13 Letters of Application
    during the Administration of Abraham Lincoln and Andrew Johnson 1861–1869
Memoranda book relating to agents and supplies for 1864, Chapter V, Vol. 27 Papers
    Pertaining to Vessels of or Involved With the Confederate States of America.
Records Concerning Confederate Property in Nassau
Records of District Courts of the United States, Admiralty Case Files US Consular Records
    for Nassau 1821–1935, Record Group 84
US Federal Census 1850, 1860, 1870, 1880.

University of Rochester

Thurlow Weed Papers

South Carolina Historical Society

J. D. Aiken letterpress copybook and letters, 1864–1865
William C. Bee and Company Records, 1848–1912
Bull family papers, 1737–ca. 1900
Charles Kuhn Prioleau correspondence, 1860–1865
Theodore D. Wagner papers, 1853–1863
Edward Willis papers, 1854–1906

South Caroliniana Library, University of South Carolina

John B. Lafitte Papers

Wilson Library, University of North Carolina

John Newland Maffitt Papers

Published Primary Sources

Accounts and Papers of the House of Commons 39. London: 1862.
Accounts and Papers of the House of Commons 72. London: Harrison and Sons, 1863.
Bacot, John Thomas Watson. *The Bahamas: A Sketch*. London: Longmans, Green, Reader,
    and Dyer, 1869.

Bernard, Mountague. *A Historical Account of the Neutrality of Great Britain during the American Civil War*. London: Longmans, Green, Reader and Dyer, 1870.
Blun, Henry. *Reminiscences of My Blockade Running*. Savannah: Braid and Hutton, 1910.
Bulloch, James. *The Secret Service of the Confederate States*. 2 volumes. New York: G. P. Putnam's Sons, 1885.
The Counter Case of Great Britain as Laid before the Tribunal. Washington: Government Printing Office, 1872.
Correspondence Concerning Claims against Great Britain. 6 volumes. Washington: Government Printing Office, 1869–1871.
Connolly, Thomas. *An Irishman in Dixie: Thomas Connolly's Diary of the Fall of the Confederacy*, edited by Nelson D. Lankford. Columbia, South Carolina: 1988.
Edge, Frederick Milnes. *The Destruction of the American Carrying Trade, a Letter to Earl Russell*. London: William Ridgway, 1864.
Ellet, Elizabeth Fries. *The Queens of American Society*. New York: Charles Scribner and Company, 1867.
Ford, Frederick, *Census of the City of Charleston, South Carolina for the Year 1861*. Charleston: Evans and Cogswell, 1861.
Forrest, Douglas French. *Odyssey in Gray: A Diary of Confederate Service, 1863–1865*. Edited by William N. Still Jr. Richmond: Virginia State Library, 1979.
Gardner, Charles. *Gardner's New Orleans Directory for 1861*. New Orleans: Charles Garnder, 1861.
Gibbs, Frederick Waymouth. *The Foreign Enlistment Act*, London: William Ridgway, 1863.
Haywood, P. D. *The Cruise of the Alabama*. Boston and New York: Houghton, Mifflin and Co., 1886.
Hobart-Hampden, Augustus C. *Never Caught*. London: John Camden, 1867.
Hunnicutt, James. *The Conspiracy Unveiled: The South Sacrificed*. Philadelphia: J. B. Lippincott, 1863.
Jones, John B. *A Rebel War Clerks Diary at the Confederate States Capital*. 2 volumes. Philadelphia: J. B. Lippincott, 1866.
Kell, John McIntosh. *Recollections of a Naval Life: including the Cruises of the Confederate States Steamers, "Sumter" and "Alabama."* Washington: The Neale Company, 1900.
The Liverpool Commercial List. London: Seyd and Co., 1866.
Mackie, J. Milton. *From Cape Cod to Dixie and the Tropics*. New York: G. P. Putnam, 1864.
New Orleans Annual and Commercial Register of 1846. New Orleans: E. A. Michel and Co., 1846.
Official Register of LSU New Orleans Grammar School 1859. New Orleans: Louisiana State University, 1859.
Official Register of the Officers and Acting Midshipmen of the United States Naval Academy. Washington: William A. Harris, 1859.
Papers Relating to the Foreign Affairs of the United States for 1863, 1864, 1865. Washington: Government Printing Office.
Papers Relating to the Treaty of Washington. Washington: Government Printing Office, 1872.
Porter, David Dixon. *The Naval History of the Civil War*. New York: Sherman Publishing Co., 1886.
Rawson, Rawson W., *Report on the Bahamas for the Year 1864*. London: Eyre and Spottiswoode, 1866.

Reports of Cases in Prize: Argued and Determined in the Circuit and District Courts of the United States for the Southern District of New York, 1861–65, Samuel Blatchford. Washington: Government Printing Office, 1866.
Reports of Committees of the House of Representatives Made during the First Session Thirty-Eight Congress, Report from the Committee on Public Expenditures on the New York Custom House. Washington: Government Printing Office, 1864.
Riddle, Albert Gallatin. *Recollections of War Times.* New York: G. P. Putnam's Sons, 1895.
Roberts, Giselle, ed. *The Correspondence of Sarah Morgan and Francis Warrington Dawson.* Athens: University of Georgia Press, 2004.
Root, Sidney. *Exotic Leaves Collected by a Wanderer.* London: William Freeman, 1865.
Schiebert, Justus. *Seven Months in the Rebel States during the North American War, 1863.* Tuscaloosa: Confederate Publishing Company, 1958.
Semmes, Raphael. *Memoirs of Service Afloat during the War between the States.* Baltimore: Kelly, Piet, and Co., 1869.
Sorrel, G. Moxley. *Recollections of a Confederate Staff Officer.* Washington: The Neale Company, 1905.
Taylor, Thomas E. *Running the Blockade.* London: John Murray, 1896.
Thompson, Robert Means, and Richard Wainwright, eds. *Confidential Correspondence of Gustava Vasa Fox, Assistant Secretary of the Navy, 1861–1865.* 2 volumes. New York: The Naval History Press, 1918.
Walker, Georgianna. *The Private Journal of Georgiana Gholson Walker, 1862–1865, with Selections from the Post-War Years, 1865–1876.* Tuscaloosa: Confederate Publishing, 1963.

Newspapers

Abbeville (South Carolina) Press
Albany Argus
Atlanta Constitution
Bahama Herald
Baltimore Sun
Boston Traveller
Brooklyn Daily Eagle
Canandaigua Daily Messenger
Charleston Daily Courier
Charleston Mercury
Charlotte Western Democrat
Chicago Tribune
The Commercial & Financial Chronicle, Bankers' Gazette, Commercial Times, Railway Monitor, and Insurance Journal, Volume 6, William B. Dana & Company, 1868
Galveston Daily News
Illustrated London News
The Index, London
Nassau Guardian
New Orleans Daily Crescent
New Orleans Times-Picayune
New York Daily Tribune
New York Evening Express

Sources

New York Herald
New York Times
New York Herald
New York Times
New York Tribune
Savannah Republican
New York Sun
Washington Post
Wilmington Journal

Secondary Sources

Articles

Balance, Virginia C. "A New Look at Old Books: The Collection of the Nassau Public Library in the Mid-19th Century," *International Journal of Bahamian Studies* 19 (2013) pp. 31–45.
Byrne, Frank J. "Rebellion and Retail: A Tale of Two Merchants in Confederate Atlanta," Georgia Historical Quarterly 79, no. 1 (1995), pp. 30–56.
Dalleo, Peter. "Montell and Co., the James Power and the Baltimore-Bahamas Packet Trade 1838–1845," *Journal of the Bahamas Historical Society* 30 (2008), 5–14.
Dickinson, Thomas. "Running the Blockade," *The Era Magazine* 13, no. 4 (April 1904), p. 249–254.
Drysdale, Richard. "Blockade-Running from Nassau," *History Today* 27, no. 5 (1977), pp. 332–337.
Elliott, Charles B. "The Doctrine of Continuous Voyages," *American Journal of International Law* 1, no. 1 (Jan. 1907), pp. 61–104.
Ferguson, Emma. "Running the Blockade: A Confederate Reminiscence," *Lippincott's Monthly Magazine* 52 (1893), pp. 493–502.
Fielding, William J. "Everybody in Nassau Has a Dog, and They Bark All Night: Potcakes, a History," *Journal of the Bahamas Historical Society* 28 (2006), pp. 36–43.
Goolsby, J. C. "Crenshaw's Battery, Pegram's Battalion," *Southern Historical Society Papers*, 28, (1900), p. 362.
Gorman, John. "The Adderley Family in the New World," *Journal of the Bahamas Historical Society* 22 (2000), p. 31–43.
Hetherington, Bruce, and Peter Kower, "A Reexamination of Lebergott's Paradox About Blockade Running during the American Civil War," *Journal of Economic History* 69, no. 2, (2009), 528–532.
The Historical Magazine, and Notes and Queries Concerning the Antiquities, History, and Biography of America 8, no. 5 (1864), p. 190.
Hunt, Carleton. "Fifty Years' Experience in Practice at the Bar," *Report of the Louisiana State Bar Association*, 1908, p. 49.
Hunt's Merchant's Magazine and Commercial Review 45 (1861), p. 517.
Jervey Theodore D. "Charleston during the Civil War," *Annual Report of the American Historical Association*, 1914, pp. 167–176.
Johnson, Ludwell. "Commerce between Northeastern Ports and the Confederacy, 1861–1865," *Journal of American History* 54, no. 1 (1967), pp. 30–42.

Lester, George. "Nassau and the Blockade Runners," *Confederate Veteran* 22, no. 12, (1914), p. 572.
Lofquist, William S. "Identifying the Condemned: Reconstructing and Analyzing the History of Executions in the Bahamas," *International Journal of Bahamian Studies* 16 (2010), pp. 19–34.
M'Lawler, J. R. O'M. "The Bahamas or Lucayos Islands," *Colburn's United Service Magazine and Naval and Military Journal* 14 (May 1861), pp. 96–98.
Maffitt, Emma, "The Confederate Navy," *Confederate Veteran*, 25, no. 6 (1917), p. 264.
Morgan, James Morris. "The Lost Cause," *Atlantic Monthly* 119 (1917), pp. 500–508.
Negus, Samuel. "A Notorious Nest of Offence: Neutrals, Belligerents, and Union Jails in Civil War Blockade Running," *Civil War History* 56, no. 4 (2010), pp. 350–385.
"Otis Kimball and Augustus Arnold v. the Steamship Dispatch and Benjamin Buck, Master," *Western Law Monthly* 4 (1863) 209–213.
Preston, Samuel. "In the Palmy Days of Wrecking," *Frank Leslie's Popular Monthly* 39 (1895), pp. 49–53.
Price, Marcus. "Masters and Pilots Who Tested the Blockade of the Confederate Ports, 1861–1865," *American Neptune* 21, no. 2, (1961), p. 81–106.
"The Queen v. James Carlin," *Law Journal Reports* 39 (1870), pp. 33–37.
Saunders, Gail. "The Blockade Running Era in the Bahamas: Blessing or Curse?" *Journal of the Bahamas Historical Society* 10 (1998), p. 14–18.
"South Carolina's Centennial," *Rural Carolinian* 6, no, 14 (1875), p. 775–776.
Trainor, John M. "The Ascendancy of Charles Rogers Nesbitt, Politician, Civil Servant, and Administrator," *Journal of the Bahamas Historical Society* 3 (1981), p. 3–12.
Valladigham, Edward N. "Piracy or Privateering?" *Pearson's Magazine* 10, no. 1, (1903), p. 82–88.
Williams, Patrice. "Personalities: Stephen Dillet, 1845–1930," *Journal of the Bahamas Historical Society* 7 (1985) pp. 23–24.
"The Yellow Fever Plot." *Medical and Surgical Reporter* 12, no. 35 (1865), pp. 565–567.

Books

Albury, Paul. *The Story of the Bahamas*. New York: St. Martin's Press, 1976.
Baird, Nancy. *Luke Pryor Blackburn: Physician, Governor, Reformer*. Lexington: University Press of Kentucky, 2009.
Barry, Craig L., and David C. Burt. *Suppliers to the Confederacy II: S. Isaac Campbell and Co., London, Peter Tait and Co., Limerick*. Oslo: Stainless Banner Publishing Company, 2014.
Bennett, John. *The London Confederates. The Officials, Clergy, Businessmen and Journalists Who Backed the American South during the Civil War.* Jefferson, NC: McFarland, 2008.
Bernath, Stuart L. *Squall across the Atlantic*. Berkeley: University of California Press, 1970.
Berwanger, Eugene H. *The British Foreign Service and the American Civil War*. Lexington: University Press of Kentucky, 1994.
Bethell, A. Talbot. *The Early Settlers of the Bahamas and Colonists of North America*. Westminster, MD: Heritage Books, 2008.
Briggs, Herbert W. *The Doctrine of Continuous Voyage*. Baltimore: Johns Hopkins Press, 1926.
Bonham, Milledge Louis. *British Consuls in the Confederacy*. New York: Columbia University, 1911.
Bunnell, A. O. *Dansville 1789–1902*. Dansville, NY: Instructor Publishing, 1902.

Burns, Brian. *Curiosities of the Confederate Capital: Untold Richmond Stories of the Spectacular, Tragic and Bizarre*. Mount Pleasant, SC: Arcadia Publishing, 2013.
Byrne, Frank. *Becoming Bourgeois: Merchant Culture in the South, 1820–1865*. Lexington: University Press of Kentucky, 2006.
Campbell, R. Thomas, ed. *Voices of the Confederate Navy: Articles, Letters, Reports, and Reminiscences*. Jefferson, NC: McFarland, 2007.
Carlin, Colin. *Captain James Carlin, Anglo-American Blockade Runner*. Columbia: University of South Carolina Press, 2017.
The Catholic Church in the United States of America: Undertaken to Celebrate the Golden Jubilee of His Holiness, Pope Pius X. New York: Catholic Editing Company, 1914.
Charleston Chamber of Commerce. *A Tribute of Affection and Respect from the Chamber of Commerce, Charleston, S.C., December 20, 1876*. Charleston, 1876.
Cochran, Hamilton. *Blockade Runners of the Confederacy*. Indianapolis: Bobbs-Merrill, 1958.
Cohen, Andrew W. *Contraband*. New York: Norton and Company, 2015.
Cory, Charles. *The Birds of the Bahamas Islands*. Boston: Estes and Lauriat, 1890.
Corthell, Elmer, *The Atlantic & Pacific Ship-Railway Across the Isthmus of Tehauntepec, in Mexico, Considered Commercially, Politically & Constructively*. New York: Bowne and Company, 1886.
Craton, Michael. *A History of the Bahamas*. Waterloo, Ontario: San Salvador Press, 1986.
Crawford, Samuel Wylie. *The History of the Fall of Fort Sumpter*. New York: F. P. Harper, 1896.
Currie, Gilbert E. *The United States Insurance Gazette and Magazine of Useful Knowledge*, Vol. 14, no. 79. New York: Gilbert Currie, 1862.
Davis, Charles S. *Colin J. McRae: Confederate Financial Agent*. Tuscaloosa: Confederate Publishing, 1961.
De Leon, Thomas Cooper. *Belles, Beaux and Brains of the 60's*. New York: G. W. Dillingham, 1909.
Douglas, Robert. *Island Heritage: Architecture of the Bahamas*. Trinidad: Darkstream, 1992.
Drysdale, William. *In Sunny Lands: Out-door Life in Nassau and Cuba*. New York: Harper and Bros., 1881.
Easterby, J. H., ed. *The South Carolina Rice Plantation as Revealed in the Papers of Robert F. W. Allston*. Columbia: University of South Carolina Press, 1945.
Goodwin, Doris Kearns. *Team of Rivals*. New York: Simon and Schuster, 2005.
Gordon, Ann. D. ed. *The Selected Papers of Elizabeth Cady Stanton and Susan B. Anthony. Volume 1*. New Brunswick, NJ: Rutgers University Press, 1997.
Hawley, Elias S. *The Hawley Record*. Buffalo: E. H. Hutchinson and Company, 1890.
Hay, David and Joan. *The Last of the Confederate Privateers*. Edinburgh: P. Harris, 1977.
Hershkowitz, Leo. *Tweed's New York: Another Look*, Garden City, NY: Anchor Press/Doubleday, 1978.
Hoole, William Stanley. *Four Years in the Confederate Navy*. Athens: University of Georgia Press, 2012.
Hussey, John. *Cruisers, Cotton and Confederates*. Merseyside: Countyvise, 2009.
Ives, Charles. *The Isles of Summer or Nassau and the Bahamas*. New Haven: Charles Ives, 1880.
Johnson, Howard, *Bahamas from Slavery to Servitude, 1783–1933*. Gainesville: University Press of Florida, 1997.
Johnson, James Weldon. *Along This Way: The Autobiography of James Weldon Johnson*. Boulder, CO: De Capo Press, 2000.

Johnson, Whittington. *Post-Emancipation Race Relations in the Bahamas*. Gainesville: University Press of Florida, 2006.

Karson, Lawrence. *American Smuggling as White Collar Crime*. New York: Routledge, 2014.

Larabee, Ann. *The Dynamite Fiend: The Chilling Tale of a Confederate Spy, Con Artist, and Mass Murderer*. New York: Palgrave, 2005.

Lightbourn, Ronald G., *Reminiscing II: Photographs of Old Nassau*. Nassau: Ron Lightbourn, 2005.

Lonn, Ella. *Foreigners in the Confederacy*. Chapel Hill: University of North Carolina Press, 1940.

Lonn, Ella. *Salt as a Factor in the Confederacy*. Washington: The Neale Company, 1933.

Maffitt, Emma Martin. *The Life and Services of John Newland Maffitt*. Washington: The Neale Company, 1906.

Mahin, Dean B. *This Blessed Place of Freedom: Europeans in Civil War America*. Washington: Brassey's, Inc, 2002.

Marquis, Greg. *In Armageddon's Shadow: The Civil War and Canada's Maritime Provinces*. Montreal: McGill-Queen's University Press, 2000.

McKenna, Joseph. *British Ships in the Confederate Navy*. Jefferson, NC: McFarland, 2009.

Mehrlander, Andrea. *The Germans of Charleston, Richmond and New Orleans during the Civil War Period, 1850–1870: A Study and Research Compendium*. Berlin, New York: De Gruyter, 2011.

Milby, E. Burton. *The Siege of Charleston*. Columbia: University of South Carolina Press, 1982.

Mitchell, Margaret. *Gone with the Wind*. New York: Macmillan, 1936.

Neely, Wayne. *The Great Bahamas Hurricane of 1866*. Bloomington: IUniverse, Inc, 2011.

Nepveux, Ethel. *George Alfred Trenholm and the Company That Went to War 1861–1865*. Charleston: Ethel Nepveux, 1994.

Nepveux, Ethel. *George A. Trenholm: Financial Genius of the Confederacy*. Charleston: Ethel Nepveux, 1998.

Northcroft, G. J. H. *Sketches of Summerland, Giving Some Account of Nassau and the Bahama Islands*. Nassau: Nassau Guardian, 1900.

Owsley, Frank Lawrence. *King Cotton Diplomacy*. Chicago: University of Chicago, 1931.

Powles, Louis Diston. *The Land of the Pink Pearl*. Boston: Estes and Lauriat, 1890.

Reports of Cases Decided in the Vice-Admiralty Court of New Brunswick from 1879–1891: With an Introduction on Admiralty Jurisdiction. Saint John: J. and A. McMillan, 1894.

Robinson, William Morrison. *The Confederate Privateers*. New Haven: Yale University Press, 1928.

Saunders, Gail. *Race and Class in the Colonial Bahamas, 1880–1960*. Gainesville: University Press of Florida, 2016.

Saunders, Gail, and Michael Craton. *Islanders in the Stream, Vol. 1 and 2*. Athens: University of Georgia Press, 1999 and 2000.

Sargent, Emma. *Epes Sargent of Gloucester and His Descendants*. Houghton Mifflin, 1923.

Scarborough, William. *Masters of the Big House: Elite Slaveholders of the Mid-Nineteenth-Century South*. Baton Rouge: Louisiana State University Press. 2006.

Scharf, John Thomas. *History of Baltimore City and County, from the Earliest Period to the Present Day*. Philadelphia: L. H. Everts, 1881.

Scharf, John Thomas. *History of the Confederate Navy from Its Organization to the Surrender of Its Last Vessel*. New York: Rogers and Sherwood, 1887.

Sebrell II, Thomas E. *Persuading John Bull: Union and Confederate Propaganda in Britain, 1860–65*. Lanham, MD: Lexington Books, 2014.

Sehlinger, Peter J. *Kentucky's Last Cavalier: General William Preston, 1816–1887*. Lexington: University Press of Kentucky, 2004.

Sheehy, Barry. *Montreal: City of Secrets*. Montreal: Baraka Books, 2017.

Shingleton, Royce. *High Seas Confederate: The Life and Times of John Newland Maffitt*. Columbia: University of South Carolina Press, 1994.

Smith, Henry Bascom. *Between the Lines: Secret Service Stories Told Fifty Years After*. New York: Booz Brothers, 1911.

Spencer, Warren F. *The Confederate Navy in Europe*. Tuscaloosa: University of Alabama Press, 1997.

Stark, James H. *Stark's History and Guide to The Bahama Islands*. Boston: James H. Stark, 1891.

Stevens, David. *Dancing with the Philistines: The Life and Times of Colonel Caleb Huse*. Ann Arbor: Edwards Brothers Malloy, 2015.

Tinker, Keith. *The Bahamas in American History*. Bloomington, IN: Xlibris, 2011.

Todd, Richard Cecil. *Confederate Finance*. Athens: University of Georgia Press, 1954.

Vandiver, Frank E., ed. *Confederate Blockade Running through Bermuda, 1861–1865; Letters and Cargo Manifests*. Austin: University of Texas Press, 1947.

Vanider, Frank E. *Ploughshares into Swords: Josiah Gorgas and Confederate Ordnance*. Austin: University of Texas Press, 1952.

War of the Rebellion: The Official Records of the Union and Confederate Armies. Washington: Government Printing Office, 1880–1901.

War of the Rebellion: The Official Records of the Union and Confederate Navies. Washington: Government Printing Office, 1896.

Wilkinson, John. *The Narrative of a Blockade Runner*. New York: Sheldon and Company, 1877.

Wilson, Frank I. *Sketches of Nassau*. Raleigh: The Standard, 1864.

Wilson, Harold S. *Confederate Industry*. Jackson: University Press of Mississippi. 2002.

Winks, Robin. W. *The Civil War Years: Canada and the United States*. Baltimore: The Johns Hopkins Press, 1998.

Wise, Stephen, *Lifeline of the Confederacy: Blockade Running during the Civil War*. Columbia: University of South Carolina Press, 1991.

Woodward, C. Vann, ed. *Mary Chestnut's Civil War*. New Haven: Yale University Press, 1981.

Wright, James Martin. *History of the Bahama Islands, with a Special Study of the Abolition of Slavery in the Colony*. New York: Macmillan, 1905.

Theses and Dissertations

Blume, Kenneth John. "The Mid-Atlantic Arena: The United States, the Confederacy, and the British West Indies, 1861–1865." PhD dissertation, SUNY Binghampton, 1984.

Edwards, Frank Tousley. "The American Consular Service in the Bahamas during the American Civil War." PhD dissertation, Catholic University, 1968.

Peters, Thelma Peterson. "The Bahamas and Blockade-Running during the American Civil War." Master's thesis, Duke University, 1939.

Tinker, Keith. "Nassau and Blockade Running, 1860–1865," Master's thesis, Florida Atlantic University, 1982.

Watts. Gordon P. "Phantoms of Anglo-Confederate Commerce: An Historical and Archaeological Investigation of American Civil War Blockade-Running between Bermuda and Wilmington, N. Carolina." PhD dissertation, University of St. Andrews, 1997.

Wise, Stephen R. "Lifeline of the Confederacy: Blockade Running during the American Civil War." PhD dissertation, University of South Carolina, 1983.

Websites

Wise, Stephen R. South Carolina Encyclopedia. "Blockade Running" http://www.scencyclopedia.org/sce/entries/blockade-running/, Access Date July 8, 2018

Civil War Talk. "Notable Blockade Runner Captains." https://civilwartalk.com/threads/notable-blockade-runner-captains.78616/page-2 Access Date August 4, 2018.

Frajola. "Civil War Blockade of the Southern Coasts" http://www.rfrajola.com/NAB/NABpart3.pdf. Accessed July 10, 2018.

Blue Curry. "Repair Work." http://www.bluecurry.com/12.2.curry.pdf?id=9253218 July 11, 2018

Fold 3. "Confederate Applications for Presidential Pardons."

Ancestry.

"US City Directories, 1822–1995."

"England and Wales National Probate Calendar and Free BMD Death Index, 1837–1915."

"US Naturalization Records 1840–1957."

"Massachusetts Marriage Records 1840–1915."

"Slave Registers of former British Colonial Dependencies, 1813–1834."

"US Passport Applications, 1795–1925."

"Passenger Lists of Vessels Arriving at New York, New York, 1820–1897."

Index

Abaco, 36, 38, 61, 99–100, 102, 145
Abrams, Julian, 133, 150, 162
Adams, Charles, 12, 27, 175, 177
Adderley, Abraham, 48, 163
Adderley, Augustus John, xiii, 91; background, 49, 52; in England, 178, 181, 193–94; joins Henry Adderley and Co., 62; in New York, 62, 142; ship ownership, 98, 114, 135; as sportsman, 63, 116; temper, 63
Adderley, Edwin, 61
Adderley, Henry, xi, xiii, 27, 41, 55, 60–62, 71, 73, 76, 77, 78, 102, 116, 124, 136, 137, 150, 161, 167, 168, 170, 171, 176, 178–79, 190; auctions Heyliger and Lafitte furniture, 181; background, 37, 48–49; Bibles for Confederate soldiers, 116; and *China*, 89–90; and coal, 60, 82, 84, 87, 158; and Darling, 51–52, 187; in England, 93, 108, 181–82; and *Gladiator*, 62, 73–74; and Heyliger, 72, 74, 80, 95; and Lafitte, 72, 91; later life, 189, 193–94; and Montell, 25–26, 87, 148; and *Oreto*, 80–81, 84–86, 92, 97–98; pre-war business connections, 24–27, 52, 62, 138; residence, 163; in Scotland, 153; and *Time*, 87–88; and Trenholm, 25, 61, 70; and wealth, 83, 91, 117, 132, 145, 147, 163–64, 184; and Whiting, 24, 66, 86, 102
Adderley, Mary Ann Perpall, 11, 48
Adderley, Nehemiah, 48
Albury, William Daniel, 50, 52, 150
Alfred, Prince of Saxe-Coburg and Gotha, 3, 27–28, 35, 40, 76
Allen, Charles, 82

Anderson, George Campbell, xiv, 60, 68; attorney for Adderleys, 63, 85; background, 47; Confederate sympathies, 47, 63; at Heyliger and Laffite party, 92; later years, 188; and Maffitt, 177; Nassau Races, 116; and *Oreto*, 84–86, 91, 97; on Whiting, 118; Whiting's opinion of, 103
Anderson, Robert, 10, 12, 17
Archibald, Edward, 21
Arnold, Augustus, 66, 95, 129–30

Bahama Herald, 27, 46, 67, 71, 76–77, 91, 95–96, 99, 101, 106–7, 112, 116, 141
Baldwin, John, 26, 27, 30
Baltimore, 24–25, 48, 104, 143, 188
Barney, Hiram, 88–91, 145–47
Barnum, P. T., 95
Bartow, John A., 24–25, 87, 179
Bayley, Charles John, xiv, 25, 78, 90, 99, 103, 106, 114, 126–27, 135–37, 150, 167, 193–94; background, 44–45; Confederate sympathies, 47, 126; and Hawley, 121; and Heyliger, 104; later years, 187–88; and Maffitt, 113; and *Oreto*, 81, 84–87, 97, 100; personality, 172; and police, 151; speech to legislature and recall to England, 119–20, 153; trip to England, 47, 54–55, 76
Beach, John, 90–91, 102, 132, 179
Beaufort, 12, 72, 88, 100, 115, 117, 143
Bee, William C., xiv, 132
Begbie, Thomas Sterling, 131–32
Benjamin, Judah, xiv; and Braine, 139; and Heyliger, 28–29, 31–32, 60, 68, 73–75, 82, 104, 106, 114–15, 122, 140, 158, 167–68;

229

and Maffitt, 69, 75; as secretary of state, 82; as secretary of war, 30; and Trenholm, 61–62, 69
Benjamin, Lewis, 141–42, 146–49
Bermuda, 37, 82, 91, 95, 97, 139, 141, 161, 178, 191; and blockade running, 52, 144, 162; and coal, 83; and Confederate ships, 23–24, 166–67, 173, 175; and yellow fever, 136, 159–60
Bird, Captain George Edward, 24, 31–32, 73–74
Bisbie, D. T., 32
Black, Charles, 28
Blackburn, Luke, 160
Bogert, George Clark, 133, 150, 162
Boston, 23, 25, 29, 35, 65–66, 70, 79, 131, 143, 176, 187
Bourne, John, xv, 82–83
Boyd, Samuel, 162
Bradford, Samuel Dexter, 102
Braine, John Clibbon, 137–39
Bravo, David, 28
British Queen, 94–95, 110–11, 117, 118, 129, 134; arrives from England, 78; involvement in blockade running, 142; issues in New York, 88–89
Buck, Benjamin, 95
Bulloch, James, xv, 14–15, 23–24, 79–80, 83, 92, 190–91
Burnside, Bruce L., 124, 168
Butler, William G., 101–2, 110

Carlin, James, 127, 165, 174, 184
Caufield, Charles, 100
Chambers, George, 132, 179
Charleston, xiv, 9–11, 13–14, 17, 30–31, 36, 48, 64–65, 70–72, 74, 87, 97, 101, 107, 118, 137, 140, 149, 162, 174, 176, 186, 190, 193; and blockade running, 22–23, 25–26, 28, 31–32, 52, 61, 69, 73, 75–77, 82–83, 90–91, 104–5, 115, 117, 120, 124, 126–27, 132–33, 135, 139, 143–44, 148, 158, 164–65, 167, 169–70, 173, 178–79
Chase, Salmon, 88–90, 144
Clements, Nehemiah, xv, 26, 160
coal, 24, 70, 81, 95, 113–14, 129, 138, 148, 175; accumulations in Nassau, 31–41, 59–60, 82, 84, 158, 167, 181; importance to blockade runners, 12, 52, 59; issues for US ships in Nassau, 59–61, 103, 105, 138, 150, 172; from New York, 87–88, 90–91, 142; in Whiting's boat, 101, 110
Collie, Alexander, 108, 123, 132, 161
Connolly, Thomas, 4, 174
Corsica, 134, 153, 157, 167, 172, 180–82; capacity, 78, 134, 171; involvement in blockade running, 140–42; problems with Nassau harbor, 134
Coxetter, Louis, 106, 127
Crenshaw, James, 108, 132, 181
Crenshaw, Lewis, 108
Crenshaw, William, 108, 122–23, 132
CSS Alabama, 13, 15, 79, 92, 105–6, 121, 125, 165, 167, 186
CSS Florida. See *Oreto* (*CSS Florida*)
Cunard, Edward, 89
Cunard, Samuel, 35, 88

Darling, Timothy, xiv, 19–20, 48, 50, 65, 94, 135, 187; background, 50–52; later life, 187; implicates Wolf brothers and de Jongh, 145–47; residence, 41, 163; and Royal Victoria, 39, 116, 171; support of Union cause, 51–52, 187; and US consuls, 52, 102, 157
Davis, Jefferson, xiv, 21–22, 98, 111, 172, 182; and Braine, 139; and Heyliger, 29, 130; and Lafitte, 193; and Martha Stanard, 192; and privateering, 13–14; and Root, 90; and Sterrett, 4
Dawson, Frank, 72, 80, 193
Dillett, Stephen, 38, 44, 46, 63, 117, 145
Doctrine of continuous voyage, 53–54
Doty, Lockwood L., 112
Dudley, Thomas, 11, 80
Duguid, James Allen, 80–81, 84–86, 96–97
Dumaresq, John D'Auvergne, 47, 134, 139, 167, 175, 184, 188

Edwards, Pierrepont, 88
Eleuthera, 37–38, 89, 124
Elliott, Charles B., 54
Ells, Thomas B., 64
Eneas, Antonio, 50

Eneas, George, 50
Eneas, Joseph, xiv, 50, 122, 146–49, 186, 188
Erlanger bond, 123, 131

Farrington, Daniel Shepherd, 50, 89, 122
Ferguson, James, 106–8, 122–23, 140, 153, 179, 190
Floyd, Richard S., 71, 73, 101
Florida, 10–11, 36–37, 48, 54, 68–69, 76, 100, 104–5, 139, 158, 184–86; Key West, 32, 54, 61, 100, 103, 115, 145, 172
Forrest, Douglas French, 71–73, 124, 180
Fort Sumter, 10–12, 16–17, 70, 87, 101
Fourgeaud, Mary Virginia, xiii, 71, 80, 83, 180, 193

Galveston, 51, 165, 174–76, 178
Gansevoort, Guert, 97–98, 102
George, John Saffery, 50, 52, 89, 91, 115, 136, 150, 163, 170, 178, 183
Georgia, 10–11, 15, 69, 71, 90–91, 107, 153, 162, 188
Gladiator, 24, 28, 31–32, 59–62, 68–69, 73–76, 82, 94
Grinnell, Moses, xiv, 16, 18, 97, 112–13, 117, 122

Haiti, 37, 44, 137
Halifax, 24, 26, 52, 138, 145–46, 152, 178; and Confederate ships, 162, 166–67, 174–76; increased blockade running activity, 159–60
Hancock, E. C., 133, 162
Harris, George David, xiv, 63, 74; and *Ajax*, 175; background, 49, 52, 62; and blockade running, 91; and Henry Adderley, 62, 93; and Kirkpatrick, 179, 182; later life, 181, 193–94; and *Oreto*, 84–85, 92, 96; residence, 72, 181; and *Stonewall*, 181; and US consular office, 135, 151, 157–58; warehouse, 163
Hart, Benjamin Woolley, xiv, 94–95, 99, 108–9, 123, 190
Havana, 23, 86, 89, 92, 174–77, 181, 191; and blockade running, 52, 144, 162, 178; and Braine, 138–39; and coal, 82; and Cunard ships, 35, 77–78, 89, 134, 172, 180;

and Heyliger, 29–31, 60; and *Oreto*, 85, 92, 101, 113–14
Hawley, Seth Cotton, xiii, 157, 185; accepts consular position, 112–13; and blockade running, 114, 120–22, 126–27; departs Nassau, 125–26, 151; efforts to improve intelligence system, 119, 121–22, 126, 161; later life, 186; and State Department, 80; and Thompson, 126, 151
Haymann, Sylvain, 115–16, 150
Helm, Charles, xv, 30–31, 100, 138–39, 175
Heyliger, Lewis, xiii, 75–76, 85, 96, 109, 122, 130, 134, 159, 165, 166, 168, 170, 175, 178–79, 181, 189–90; and Adderley, 60, 74, 95, 163; appointed depositary, 123–24; arrival in Nassau, 28, 30; background, 28–29; and British officials, 60, 68, 104–5, 114, 167–68; and coal, 82–83; description, 31, 71, 118–19; duties, 140; and *Gladiator*, 31–32, 68, 73–75; and Hart, 94–95; and *Herald*, 82–83, 97; and Laffite, 69, 71, 95, 106–8, 114, 121, 149, 161, 170, 172; later life, 191–92; leaves Nassau, 180; letters to newspapers, 81–82, 125; and Maffitt, 68–69, 75, 92, 113; New Orleans friends in Nassau, 72, 131, 133, 162, 174; and *Oreto*, 80–81, 91, 97; residence, 72; social status in Nassau, 116, 118–19, 161; and Waller, 106, 152–53; and yellow fever, 158
Hickley, Henry, 85–86, 96–97
Hobart-Hampden, Augustus Charles, 127–29
Hoffnung, Abraham, 141–42, 146–47, 149
Hog Island, 39, 60, 68, 82, 121, 134–35, 158, 184, 194
Holmes, Abraham Turton, 50, 89, 150
Hotze, Henry, 73
Howell, John Sands, xiii, 96, 125, 149, 161; background, 66–67; and dry dock, 108, 135, 144, 149, 157, 194; and Kirkpatrick, 157–59; later life, 187; and letter to Lincoln, 113; and *Oreto*, 97; provides information to US consuls, 161; and Royal Victoria, 66, 92, 137, 150, 171; and Whiting, 66, 102, 118
Huse, Caleb, xv, 14–15, 24, 94–95, 106, 108, 122–23

Isaac, Henry, 94–95, 99
Isaac, Samuel, 94

Jackson, Charles, xiii, 22, 150; and Adderley, 63; background, 19; and Hawley, 121–22, 125; later life, 187; and Locke, 137, 176; and Kirkpatrick, 161; at Royal Victoria Hotel, 19, 73, 108; and Thompson, 126, 157; and Whiting, 21, 63–66, 87, 111, 113
Jervey, Lewis Simons, 132, 150, 162, 179, 190
Johnson, Alexander, 50, 91, 98–99, 117, 136, 149–50, 178–79
Johnson, George, 150, 161, 171, 182
Johnson, Samuel Otis, 50, 89, 150
Jones, Edward, 84–86, 96–97, 101
Jorss, Henry, 91

Kane, Elisha, 16–17, 87, 186
Karnak, 20, 26, 31, 38–40, 54, 66, 74, 76–78; and blockade running, 88–89, 142; capacity, 134; first voyage to Nassau, 35; wreck and salvage, 77–78, 95, 129
Keith, Alexander, 160
Kemp, Charles Henry Edward, 50, 150
Kenner, Duncan, 29
Kimball, Otis, 66, 95, 129–30
Kirkpatrick, Anna, 157, 159
Kirkpatrick, Thomas, xiii, 162, 164, 171–72, 175, 181, 185; accepts consular position, 152; background, 151; on blockade running, 165, 169, 177; death of wife, 159; and Harris, 157, 179; and Henry Adderley, 181–82; and Howell, 158; later life, 187–88; and *Mary*, 167; in Nassau, 157; and Passailaigue, 189; and Rawson, 177; salary, 160; and spies, 161, 171, 179; and Thompson, 157
Klingender, Melchior, 10
Knowles, Michael C., 50, 89, 150
Kursheedt, Gershom, 28, 94

Lafitte, Edward, xiv, 9–10, 69, 107, 193
Lafitte, Euphrosine, xiii, 71–73, 108, 174, 180, 193
Lafitte, John Baptiste, xi, xiii, 10, 72, 75, 85, 87, 90–91, 108, 131, 147, 162, 168, 174, 178, 180, 181; and *Alliance*, 70; arrival in Nassau, 71; background, 69–70; description, 70, 71, 193; donates books, 180; family, 71, 101, 113, 124; and *Gladiator*, 73–74; and Heyliger, 71, 82, 92, 95, 106–8, 114, 121, 125, 149, 161, 163, 168, 170, 172; and *Karnak*, 77; later life, 192–93; wealth, 161, 193
Lasere, Emile, 29
Lathrop, Francis, 87
Lawton, Alexander, 140, 152
Lee, Robert E.: battles, 93, 96, 104, 109, 127; and Ferguson, 106; and Lafitte, 193; and Maffitt, 69; and Stanard, 192; and supplies, 169; surrenders, 175–76, 178
Lees, John Campbell, 47, 63, 67, 86, 92, 96–98, 153
Le Messurier, Frederick, 77, 134, 181
Lightbourne, Cornelius, 111, 178
Lincoln, Abraham, 14, 16, 101, 125; assassination, 176; and blockade, 11, 13; and Chase, 90; 1860 election, 9; issues Emancipation Proclamation, 110; letters to, 101–2, 113, 118; and Mason and Slidell incident, 23
Liverpool, 22–23, 31, 60, 70, 74–76, 80, 82, 87, 93, 108, 129, 139, 145, 166–67, 174–76, 188–89; and Beach and Root, 90–91; importance as port, 10, 35, 115, 132, 159, 162; and *Oreto*, 80–81, 84; and Trenholm, 9–10, 12, 14, 71, 79, 107, 165, 182, 190
Locke, Vernon Guyon, 137–38, 176
Lockwood, Robert, 31, 102, 127
Lockwood, Thomas, 17, 22, 30–32, 63–64, 68, 74, 127, 162, 175–76
London, 46, 49, 54, 68, 89, 96, 131, 166, 176, 188–89, 193; and *Gladiator*, 24, 28; postwar, 191, 194; source of merchandise for Nassau, 88; supplies policeman to Nassau, 170
Low, Andrew, 23, 79–80, 112
Low, John, 23, 79–81, 83, 93, 96–97, 112, 174–75
Lowe, Matthew, 121
Lyons, Richard, xv, 88, 90, 140

Maffitt, Florie, 83, 101
Maffitt, John, xiii, 81, 92, 139, 175–76; background, 69; and blockade running, 69, 75–76, 80–81; description of by Semmes, 92; later life, 188–89; nearly arrested, 177; and *Oreto*, 83–86, 98–101, 113–14, 127, 166; and *Owl*, 139, 165, 173–74; pranks against Whiting, 77; and Sterrett, 3–4, 133; and yellow fever, 99–100, 166
Mahoney, Cornelius, 107, 132
Mallory, Stephen, xv, 23, 30, 79, 85, 97, 139, 173–75, 180
Marshall, Edward W., 91
Mason, James, 22–23, 62, 72, 89, 105
Matamoras, 52, 143, 159, 172, 178
McKillop, H. F., 84–86
McKinstry, James, 103
McRae, Colin, 123, 131, 139, 152, 190
Meadows, John Gray, 49, 89, 181
Memminger, Christopher, 30, 123
Mends, James, 111
Menendez, Manuel, 50
Menendez, Ramon Antonio, xiv, 49, 50, 115, 179
Merritt, Isaac, 15–16, 19–20, 61, 66, 111
Milne, Alexander, 86, 114
Minturn, Robert Bowne, Jr., 117–18
Mobile, 69, 85, 101, 113, 143–44
Montell, Francis T., xiv, 24–26, 87, 148–49, 161, 179, 188
Montreal, 79, 141, 160
Moore, Thomas Kingsbury, 50, 159
Moore, Thomas Overton, 29, 31
Morphy, Paul, 72
Moseley, Edwin, 46, 124
Mueller, Charles Gustav, 132, 150, 179, 190
Murray, Robert, 157–58, 161
Murray-Aynsley, Charles, 128–29
Myers, Abraham, 123, 140

Nassau: after war, 6, 183–86, 188–89, 194; as blockade running hub, 26–28, 31, 54, 62, 75, 78, 81–82, 88, 90–92, 104, 106–8, 127–28, 134, 139, 144, 150, 159, 162, 164–65, 169, 179–80; and Confederate sympathies, 21, 23, 46, 60, 72, 77, 89, 96, 98, 104, 106, 109–11, 113, 162; and crime, 5, 46, 64, 96, 116–17, 151; history and description, 35–43; improvements, 5, 47, 96, 115, 120, 135, 151, 180, 185
Nassau Guardian, 46, 51–52, 81, 96, 124–25, 140, 151, 159, 163, 172, 187
Nesbitt, Charles Rogers, xiv, 27–28, 35, 187, 194; background, 46–47; fills in for Bayley, 153, 167; and Heyliger, 104; and Kirkpatrick, 167, 177; later life, 188; and *Oreto*, 84; and Whiting, 21, 32, 59–60, 87, 103
New Orleans, 20, 25, 28–29, 31, 48, 51, 72, 75, 88, 94, 116–17, 131, 133, 143, 162, 174, 191–93
New Providence, 3, 99, 106, 108, 131, 148; channels for blockade runners, 61; geography and history, 35–39, 68; after hurricane, 184; schools, 45
New York custom house, 89, 104, 140–50, 158
New York Times, 10, 19, 48, 51, 53, 61, 68, 74, 78, 98, 120, 136, 171
North, Frederick, 91

Oreto (*CSS Florida*): 1862 arrival in Nassau, 80–81, 174; 1863 arrival in Nassau, 114, 177; becomes *CSS Florida*, 100; construction of, 15, 80; in Cuba, 100–101; and Maffitt, 83, 127, 166, 177; in Mobile, 101, 113; moved to Cochrane's Anchorage, 81, 84; outfitted at Green Cay, 99–100; towed back to Nassau, 85; trial of, 47, 86, 91–93, 95–98, 168; and Whiting, 94, 97, 113

Palermo, 80, 84
Paris, 13, 50, 96, 152
Parker, John. *See* Vernon Locke
Passailaigue, Charles Sidney, xiii, 14, 73, 179, 189–90
Perpall, Charles Robert, xi, 49, 84–85, 91, 134, 137, 150
Philadelphia, 13, 24, 26, 48, 59, 104, 111, 143
Prioleau, Charles, xv, 15, 21, 166, 176, 182, 190; British citizenship, 10, 90; cannon

as gift to South Carolina, 11; on Connolly, 174; and *Gladiator*, 24; and Lafitte, 70–71, 107, 168, 178; organizes bazaar, 165; and Trenholm, 9–10, 12
privateering, 13–14, 37, 73, 84–85, 137–38, 175, 177

Rahming, John, xiv, 21, 50, 87, 91, 94, 103, 135, 146, 148–50, 186, 188
Randolph, George, 82, 95–97, 108–9
Rawson, Rawson W., xiv, 47, 167, 172, 174–75, 177, 180, 183
Renouard, Gustave, 49–50, 137, 150
Richmond, 4, 14–15, 26, 51, 79, 96, 106–9, 124, 130, 132, 134, 138, 159, 191–92
Risley, David, 143
Rogers, Woodes, 37
Root, Henry, 161, 179
Root, Sydney, 90–91, 102, 132, 179
Royal Victoria Hotel, 5, 19–20, 41, 43, 71, 87, 118, 164, 185, 194; built, 39; closes, 185; description, 39–40, 67, 116; employees, 96, 149, 171; and Howell, 66, 108, 135, 157, 161, 187; and Johnson, 150, 182; and residents, 72–73, 75, 81, 83, 91–92, 102, 108, 113, 127, 129–31, 137, 147, 170–71; and sanitation, 116, 135, 152; and yellow fever, 99
Russell, John, xv, 13, 27, 81, 88–90, 175–77

Saint John, 24, 26, 68, 70, 136–38; and coal, 82; as false destination, 60–62, 68, 84–85, 133, 135, 145
salt, 37, 115, 116, 137
Sargent, Epes Dixwell, xiii, 125, 161, 189; background, 19–20; and dry dock, 108, 135; later life, 187; and Lincoln letter, 113; proposes wrecker as a spy ship, 122; testifies in New York, 149–50; and yellow fever, 20, 100
Sands, Charles Tyldesley Rhodes, 50
Saunders, Henry Rowland, xi, xiv, 26, 49, 50, 62, 66, 82, 89, 115, 143, 150
Saunders, John Henry, 64–65
Saunders, Pembroke, 49, 82, 115, 142–43, 150
Saunders and Son, 49, 60, 76, 91, 108, 136, 149, 163–64, 178–79

Savannah, 22–25, 38, 48, 52, 76, 79, 104, 190
Sawyer, Robert Henry, xi, xiv, 25–26, 48–50, 52, 62–63, 115, 163
Sawyer and Menendez, 163; and blockade running, 76, 89, 91, 108, 114, 149–50, 178–79; and coal, 60; and *Corsica*, 134; and mail, 145; new warehouse, 136
Scotland, 80, 114, 120, 153, 171, 174
Seddon, James, xv, 108, 123, 152
Semmes, Raphael, 15, 92–93, 99, 105
Senac, Felix, 73
Senac, Ruby, 73
Seward, William, xv, 30, 113, 114, 161; assassination attempt, 176; and British, 27, 88, 90, 114; and Hawley, 112, 120, 125–26, 186; and Kirkpatrick, 151–52, 157–58, 161, 167, 169, 171, 175–77, 181–82; and Lafitte, 70, 74; and *Oreto*, 84, 98; and Whiting, 24, 26, 64–66, 86–87, 89, 94, 101–3, 110–11, 115, 117–19
Sharp, Thomas, 152–53, 164
Simpson, Myer M., 133, 162
Slidell, John, 22–23, 29, 62, 72, 80, 89, 105, 131
Soulé, Pierre, 29, 72, 133, 192
Stanard, Martha, 192
Stanton, Henry, 146
Sterrett, William Boyd, xiii, 4–5, 133, 174, 190
Stockman, William, xiv, 26
Stribling, Christian, 99

Tappan, Jeremiah, 16, 18, 65, 113, 126
Taylor, Tom, 36, 129–31, 158, 160–61, 169, 193
Thompson, Thomas B., 46, 67, 76, 91, 95–96
Thompson, William Charles, xiii, 126–27, 135, 145–46, 149, 151–52, 157, 185
Toombs, Robert, 30
Trenholm, Alfred, 71, 124
Trenholm, George, xi, xiii, xiv, xv, 10, 15, 23, 30, 55, 60, 71, 90, 94–95, 124, 161, 174, 192; background, 9; and blockade running, 12, 21–22, 24, 28, 61–62, 68–69, 75, 82–83, 109, 127, 134, 140, 143, 165–68, 176, 182; as Confederate secretary of the treasury, 15, 180, 190; later life, 190, 193; and Mason and Slidell, 22; offers financial services to Confederacy, 14; residence, 70

Tuomey, John, 10, 17, 162
Turtle, John Josiah, 50, 89, 91, 98, 150, 188

Varree, John, 111
Vincent, Daniel B., 70
Vizetelly, Frank, 131

Wagner, Theodore, xiv, 9, 12, 30, 71, 132, 161, 190
Walker, Leroy, 29
Walker, Norman, xv, 159–60, 178, 191
Waller, Richard, xiii, 106–7, 123, 134, 136, 140, 152, 164, 180, 190–91
Washington, DC, 5, 77, 79, 96, 103, 112, 119, 143, 160
Watson, Lewis Grant, 132
Webb, Yorick, 85
Weech, Robert William Henry, 49, 52, 89, 115, 136, 150, 170, 194
Weech, William James, 49–50, 115, 150
Welles, Gideon, 12, 60, 64, 105, 120, 122, 125–26, 150
Welsman, James, 9, 14, 182, 190
Whetton, William, 112
Whitley, Fletcher, 27, 47, 60, 84, 134
Whiting, Samuel, xiii, 19, 22, 24–25, 26, 68, 74–75, 90–92, 100, 112, 121, 135, 152, 157, 158, 161; accused of being a traitor, 101–2; and *Adirondack*, 102–3; arrival in Nassau, 20; background, 16–17; and British officials, 32, 59, 81, 84–86, 100, 103, 111, 115; and coal, 59–61, 103, 148; drinking problems, 18, 64–65, 111, 118, 185; final days in Nassau, 117–19; financial issues, 66, 94, 102, 104, 112–13; and Fort Sumter, 10, 16; and hostile environment, 20–21, 26, 65–66, 72, 86–87, 89, 95, 97, 110; and Jackson, 19, 63, 65–66, 87; later life, 186; lectures, 17, 67, 186; and Lockwood, 17, 64; and Nassau merchants, 62; and *Oreto*, 81, 84, 91, 94, 96–99, 113–14; pranks, 77, 86; resignation, 111; testimonial in support of, 66; wife, 66, 110–11; and Wilkes, 105–6
Wibray, James, 28
Wier, Benjamin, xv, 26, 138, 145, 160

Wigg, George, 131
Wilkes, Charles, 23, 72, 105–6, 114, 117, 120–22, 124–27, 164
Wilkinson, John, 163, 166, 172, 179
Wilmington, 4, 36, 80, 83, 100, 130, 133, 136, 173–76, 189; and blockade running, 20–21, 23, 25–26, 52, 69, 76, 81, 104–5, 114–15, 117, 120, 126–28, 131, 133, 135, 139, 141, 143–44, 148, 158–59, 162, 164–66, 169–70, 173
Wolf, Aaron, xiv, 141–42, 145–47, 149–50, 160, 178–79, 190
Wolf, George Garcia, 140–41, 144–47, 149–50
Wright, William, xv, 26, 61

Yellow Fever, 20, 36, 130, 134, 136, 166, 173; 1862 epidemic, 99–100, 103–4, 110, 121, 127; 1864 epidemic, 158–60, 174

BAHAMAS OVERVIEW AND KE

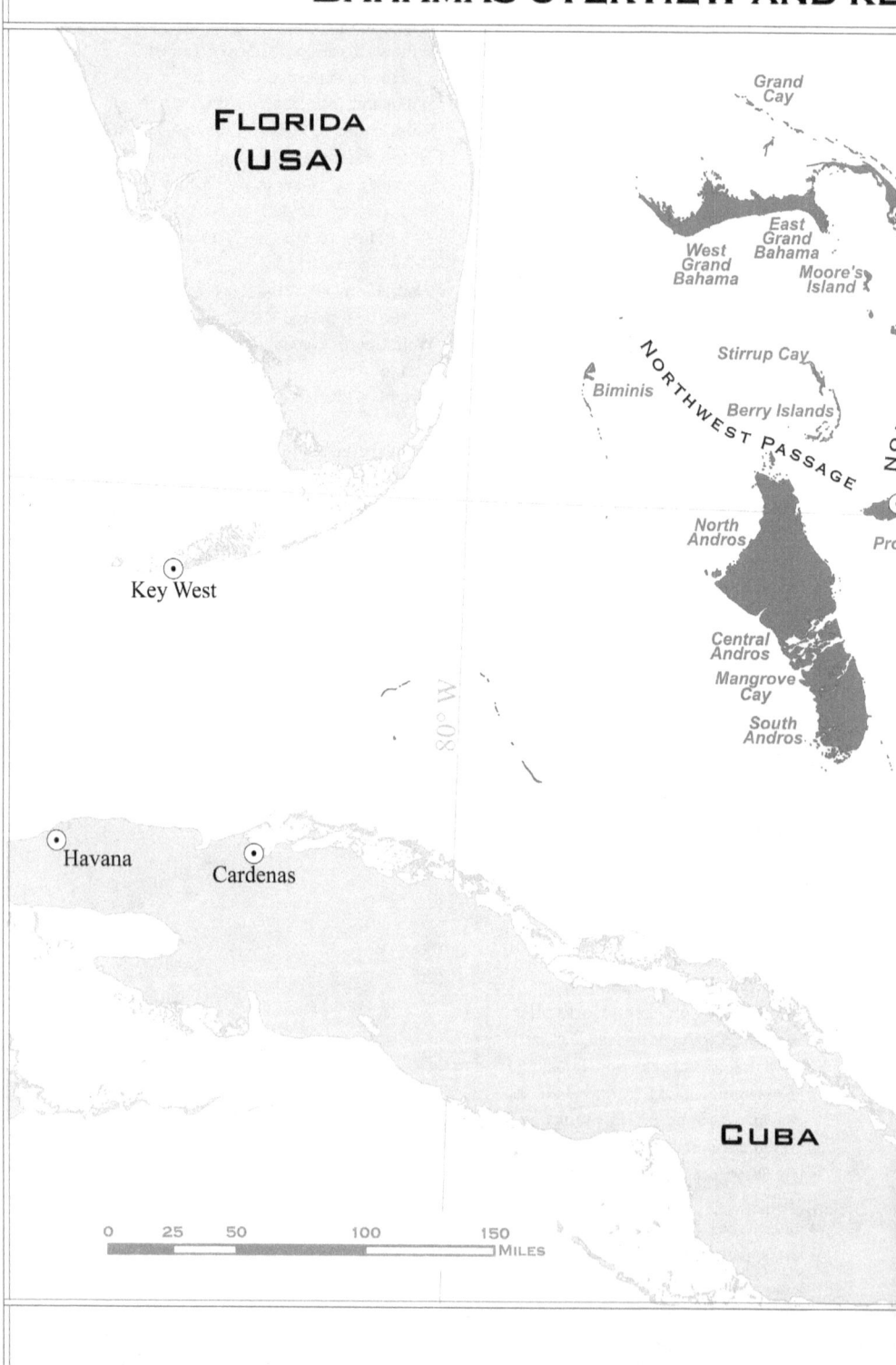

PASSAGES DEPARTING NASSAU

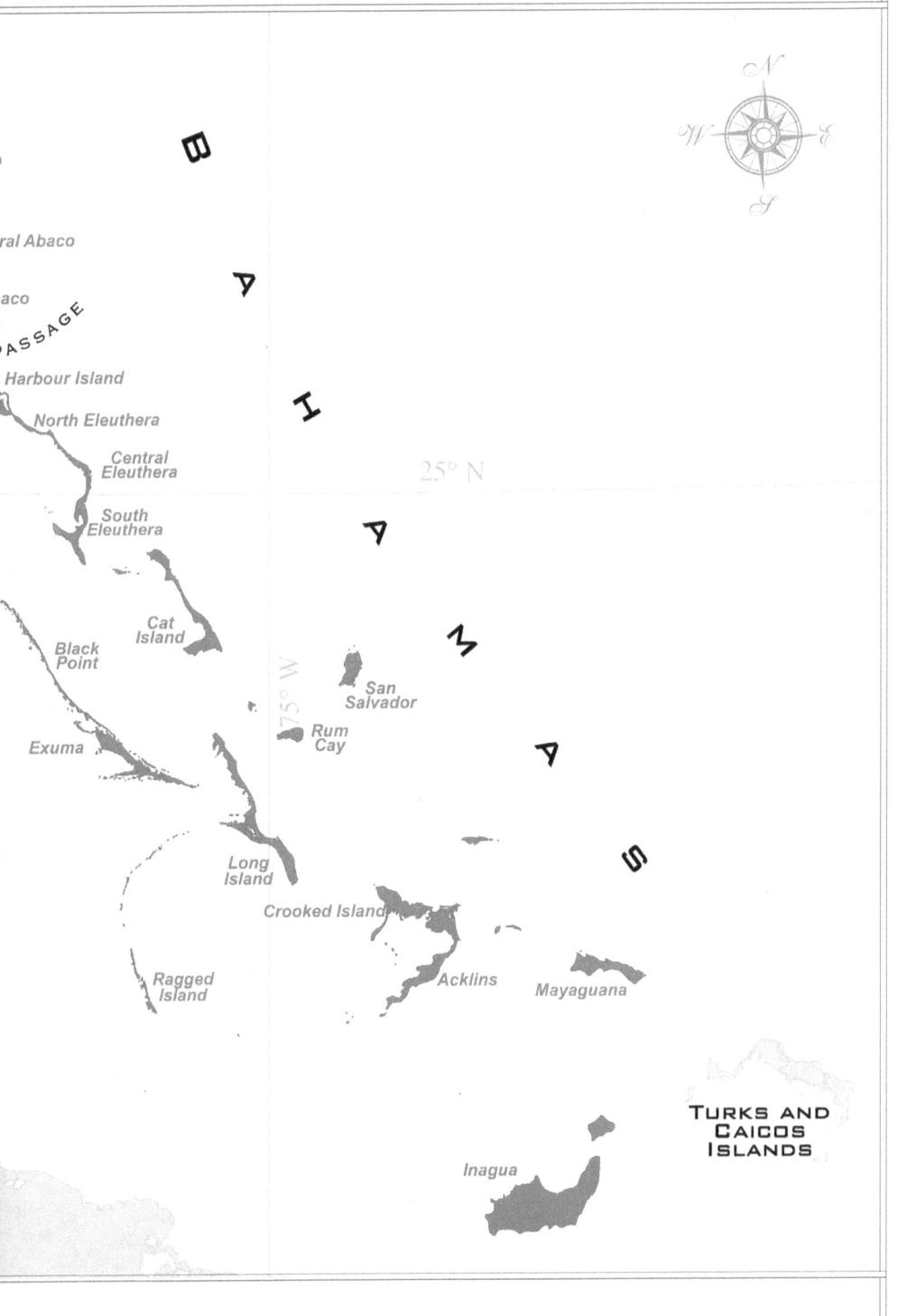

About the Author

Credit William Reach

Charles D. Ross is professor of physics at Longwood University. He has written three other books devoted to the Civil War and has appeared on The History Channel, PBS, and National Geographic Channel. He lives with his wife Julie in Farmville, Virginia.

www.ingramcontent.com/pod-product-compliance
Lightning Source LLC
Chambersburg PA
CBHW030614230426
43661CB00053B/1987